WRITING AND REWRITING THE HOLOCAUST

Jewish Literature and Culture

Series Editor, Alvin Rosenfeld

WRITING AND REWRITING THE HOLOCAUST

Narrative and the Consequences of Interpretation

JAMES E. YOUNG

INDIANA UNIVERSITY PRESS
Bloomington and Indianapolis

First Midland Book Edition 1990

*Publication of this work has been supported in part
by a grant from the Abraham and Rebecca Stein Faculty
Publications Fund of New York University, Department of English.*

Manufactured in the United States of America

Library of Congress Cataloging-in-Publication Data

Young, James Edward.
Writing and rewriting the Holocaust.

Bibliography: p.
Includes index.
1. Holocaust, Jewish (1939–1945)—Historiography.
2. Holocaust, Jewish (1939–1945)—Personal narratives—
History and criticism.   3. Holocaust, Jewish (1939–1945),
in literature.   I. Title.
D810.J4Y58   1988   940.53'15'039240072   87-35791
ISBN 0–253–36716–6
ISBN 0–253–20613–8 (pbk.)

2 3 4 5 6   94 93 92 91 90

CONTENTS

Preface

This study began when I realized that none of us coming to the Holocaust afterwards can know these events outside the ways they are passed down to us. In attempting over several years to learn all there was to know of the annihilation of European Jewry during World War II, I found that my knowledge and understanding of events were dependent on their representations by victims in diaries, by survivors in memoirs, by historians and philosophers in their investigative works, and even by our communities in contemporary Jewish liturgy and days of remembrance. On devoting myself to the study of this era, therefore, I gave myself as well to the study of its representations. The twin aims of my study and teaching of Holocaust narrative have necessarily become both a deep knowledge of events and an awareness of how this knowledge is gained.

Unfortunately, the sheer horror at the core of the Holocaust has often swamped other, more important historical and literary questions. The pathos and outrage that move so many students to study this period and others to avoid it altogether become for some the object of Holocaust inquiry. For these students of Holocaust writing, critical inquiry too often begins and ends with how the horror of mass murder is represented, or how the terror of such suffering is grasped. The present study does not inquire into the thematic representation of bloody horror, but into the narrative representation of events themselves. Rather than concentrating on the numbing shock evoked by the calculated murder of a people, this study asks precisely how historical memory, understanding, and meaning are constructed in Holocaust narrative.

At Yad Vashem Memorial Authority in Jerusalem, lecturers to student groups, tourists, and soldiers introduce their presentations through a similar method. In beginning our study of the Holocaust, they announce, we start by looking at: how the Germans understood the Jews in their midst, and how this understanding led to their massacre of innocents. This is followed with an equally—perhaps more—important look at how the Jews then understood their own predicament and the Germans' intentions—and how this understanding led to particular Jewish responses. In my own teaching at both Yad Vashem and American universities, I ask these questions as well, and then extend them to ask how we, in the next generation, now understand the entire matrix of events. For as the killers' and victims' grasp of events influenced their actions, I find that our own understanding and remembrance of events now lead directly to our responses to the world around us. In fact, it was precisely this self-inquiry on my part into how I live in and respond to the world after the Holocaust that inspired—and has since become the guiding reason for—this study.

The impossible questions that drove me long ago away from the song of Keats's nightingale to the Holocaust survivor's whisper have moved many other scholars before me to the study of this literature. Inasmuch as these writers have begun the critical dialogue I am attempting to sustain, I am humbly indebted to all of them. In particular, this present work owes a vast debt to the writings of Alvin Rosenfeld, Lawrence Langer, David Roskies, Alan Mintz—and especially Sidra Ezrahi, whose work brought me to Israel and whose compassionate counsel nourished me there, both as part of her family and as part of the larger—more volatile—family that is *Am Yisra'el.* Two other teachers have also contributed to this study in ways they may never fully fathom: Thomas A. Vogler, who brought me back to literature through his belief that writing and what I had to say about it can make a difference in this world; and Murray Baumgarten, who brought me into the fold of critically thinking Jews.

Several dear friends and colleagues who read parts of this manuscript and shared their learning with me will also find their imprint in these pages. It would have been impossible to persevere without crucial advice and encouragement from Paul Mann, Susan Shapiro, Robert McMahon, Geoffrey Hartman, Anita Norich, and Saul Friedländer. Less visible in these pages, but no less present in the inner life that has borne them are: Benni and Tali Bar-Yosef, Peter Brod, Toman and Libuše Brod, Daša Najbrtova, Wiebke Suhrbier, Clive and Fran Sinclair, Dan and Elly Wolf, and Rabbi Alfred Wolf.

I also owe a great debt of gratitude to the Dorot Foundation in the person of Joy Ungerleider-Mayerson for endowing the Dorot Teaching Fellowship at New York University, under which most of this book was written. In allowing my teaching and writing in Jewish literature to nourish each other in equal measure, the chair of the English department at New York University, John Maynard, and the associate vice-president for Academic Affairs, Leslie Berlowitz, also deserve special praise for administering the Dorot Fellowship so graciously. Other institutions and people have also given of themselves generously over the course of this writing. I am grateful to the University of California and its regents for their fellowships; to the YIVO Institute in New York for access to its human and archival resources; to the Institute of International Education and the Israel Government for their generous grant; to the Institute of Contemporary Jewry and its director, Yehuda Bauer, for the Alexander Silberman Fellowship at the Hebrew University in Jerusalem; to the National Endowment for the Humanities for the Summer Stipend; to Elly Dlin and Shalmi Bar-Mor in the Education office at Yad Vashem Memorial Authority in Jerusalem for the opportunity to teach and learn there; to Joanne Rudof and Sandra Rosenstock at the Video Archive for Holocaust Testimonies at Yale University for their expert assistance; and to T. Carmi and Limor Raviv for checking my Hebrew translations.

It is finally to my family that I owe the least articulable but most profound thanks: to my mother and father, brother and sister for their encouragement, love, and patience along every step of what has at times been as difficult a path to comprehend as it has been to traverse; to my grandparents, who were the first to teach me that the love of ideas and of life are really one and the same calling; and to my wife, Lori J. Friedman, whose love gives new reason for my life's work, even as it has added several months more to my writing time. It is to these special people in my life—and others unnamed here—that I remain forever indebted. But it is to the coming generations that I hope to repay this debt, and it is to them that I dedicate this study.

Acknowledgments

Parts of this study have appeared previously in different form. I would like to thank the editors of the following journals and collected volumes for permission to reprint portions of articles: Geoffrey Hartman, ed., *Bitburg in Moral and Political Perspective* (Bloomington: Indiana University Press, 1986); *Clio: A Journal of Literature, History and the Philosophy of History*; *Contemporary Literature*; *Dimensions: A Journal of Holocaust Studies*; *Jewish Chronicle*; *Midstream*; *Modern Judaism*; *New Literary History*; *Partisan Review*; *Philological Quarterly*; *PMLA*; *Studies in Contemporary Jewry* (New York: Oxford University Press, 1986 and 1987), vols. III and IV; and *University of Hartford Studies in Literature: A Journal of Interdisciplinary Criticism*.

For her exquisite photographs of memorials in Poland, I am grateful to Monika Krajewska; and for providing me with stills from *Shoah* and from video testimony taping sessions at Yale, I thank Sarah Talbot of New Yorker Films and the Yale University Office of Public Information, respectively.

WRITING AND REWRITING
THE HOLOCAUST

Introduction

Narrative and the Consequences of Interpretation

> Human beings do not live in the objective world alone, nor alone in the world of social activity as ordinarily understood but are very much at the mercy of the particular language which has become the medium of expression for their society. It is quite an illusion to imagine that one adjusts to reality essentially without the use of language and that language is merely an incidental means of solving specific problems of communication or reflection ... We see and hear and otherwise experience very largely as we do because the language habits of our community predispose certain choices of interpretation.
>
> —Edward Sapir

I. WRITING THE HOLOCAUST

To a great extent, Holocaust studies have always been interdisciplinary: historical inquiry provokes political and sociological questions, while philosophical and religious inquiry inevitably entail larger literary issues. With the rise of contemporary literary and historical theory, scholars of the Holocaust have come increasingly to recognize that interpretations of both the texts and events of the Holocaust are intertwined. For both events and their representations are ultimately beholden to the forms, language, and critical methodology through which they are grasped. Religious meaning and significance, historical causes and effects, are simultaneously reflected and generated in Holocaust narrative—as well as in the names, periodization, genres, and icons we assign this era. What is remembered of the Holocaust depends on how it is remembered, and how events are remembered depends in turn on the texts now giving them form.

Instead of isolating events from their representations, this approach recognizes that literary and historical truths of the Holocaust may not be entirely separable. That is, the truths of the Holocaust—both the factual and the interpretive—can no longer be said to lie beyond our understanding, but must now be seen to inhere in the ways we understand, interpret, and write its history. Indeed, since the facts of the Holocaust eventually obtain only in their narrative and cultural reconstructions, the interrelated problems of literary and historical interpretation might now be seen as conjoining in the study of "literary historiography." This is not to question the ultimate veracity in any given account, but it is to propose a search for the truth in the interpretation instrinsic to all versions of the Holocaust: both that interpretation which the writer consciously effects and that which his narrative necessarily accomplishes for him.

In some ways, the critical impulse to assert simultaneously both historical events and the shapes they take in writing predates by hundreds of years the contemporary obsession with the "sign." We might consider as one critical model the tactful manner in which the sixteenth-century Jewish historiographer Azariah de' Rossi formulated a similar inquiry in his collection of antiquarian essays, *Me'or Einayim*. In turning to the historical significance of conflicting talmudic tracts on the massacre of Alexandrian Jewry, Azariah finds, not surprisingly, that in three different versions, the chief murderer was three different people:

> Our eyes behold three different passages concerning it, for the Jerusalem Talmud has stated that the evil murderer was the emperor Trajan . . . and the Babylonian Talmud in tractate *Sukkah* said it was Alexander of Macedon, while in tractate *Gittin* it changed its opinion to write that it was Hadrian. And if we have now begun to investigate the [historical] truth of these matters, that is not because of the thing in itself, for what was—was [mai de-havah havah], but only because we are concerned that the words of our sages in relating well-known events should not appear to contradict one another. . . .
>
> At any rate, even were we to admit that some stories reached the ears of the sages with some distortion, and that this is how they related them to us, that in no way diminishes their stature. . . . And even though this chapter consists mostly of inconsequential investigations, for it will be said "what was— was, and there is in it no relevance to law or observance," still, the refined soul yearns to know the truth of everything.[1]

The "truth of everything" here includes something more than previously authoritative facts that happen to contradict one another. As a critical historian, Azariah was not disputing the essential facts, but only questioning the retelling of such facts: "what was—was," he reminds us. How "what was" is told, however, remembered and shaped by legends and laws, becomes the aim of the critical historian, even when it means baring apparent contradictions. As Yerushalmi tells us, this kind of historiography led to Azariah's being banned and branded as a heretic in many of the most traditional quarters, which was not necessarily due to Azariah's questioning of these texts' authority or legitimacy. Rather, in Yerushalmi's words, "The essential innovation in Azariah's approach lay in his attempt to evaluate rabbinic legends, not within the framework of philosophy or Kabbalah, each a source of truth for its partisans, but by the use of profane history, which few, if any, would accept as a truth by which the words of the sages might be judged" (p. 72). That is, the effrontery to tradition lay in looking at written history as a record of events *and* legends, thereby seeming to denigrate both the historicity of such texts and the legends out of which such texts were constructed.

While previous studies of Holocaust literature have begun to raise some of these hermeneutical issues, there has also been an unmistakable resistance to overly theoretical readings of this literature. Much of this opposition is well founded and stems from the fear that too much attention to critical method or to the literary construction of texts threatens to supplant not only the literature but the horrible events at the heart of our inquiry. That is, if Holocaust narrative is nothing but a system of signs merely referring to other signs, then where are the events themselves? To concentrate on the poetics of a witness's testimony, for example, over the substance of testimony seems to risk displacing the events under discussion altogether. By seeming to emphasize the ways we know the Holocaust to the apparent exclusion of the realities themselves, critics threaten to make the mere form of study their content as well. Instead of drawing closer to events, in this view, critics would impose an even greater distance between readers and events. Other potential and equally unacceptable consequences of an unlimited deconstruction of the Holocaust include the hypothetical possibility that events and texts never existed outside each other and that all meanings of events created in different representations are only relative.

Because we are now dependent on mediating texts for our knowledge, however, does not make these texts alone the object of our study, or make the meanings generated in these mediated versions less valuable. For the significance and meaning of events created in these texts often reflect the kind of understanding of events by victims at the time; and as these "mere" interpretations led to their responses, the interpreted versions of the Holocaust in its texts now lead us to our actions in the world in light of the Holocaust. That is, by sustaining the notion of these interpretations' agency in events, the contemporary critic can assert both the historicity of events and the crucial role interpretation played in the events themselves. This is not to deny the historical facts of the Holocaust outside of their narrative framing, but only to emphasize the difficulty of interpreting, expressing, and acting on these facts outside of the ways we frame them.

Applied carelessly, however, contemporary theory and its often all-consuming vocabulary can obscure as much as it seeks to illuminate in this literature. In fact, one of its major liabilities has been a relative inaccessibility to those outside its methodological code, which has limited its practical applications to other than critical texts. This has been a special shame since many of its pioneers (e.g., Barthes, Lévi-Strauss, even Susan Sontag) had initially enjoined this approach not to mystify but to clarify the workings of current culture, history, and literature and their inevitable interpenetration. This is why particular aspects of deconstruction and semiotic analysis—specifically those diverting attention from historical realities—are carefully constrained here. But other qualities of critical analysis encouraged in contemporary inquiry, such as sensitivity to hermeneutical activity within the production of texts, hold much value in this study. For these aspects seem ideal for understanding more deeply the cause and effect relationship—the reciprocal exchange—between events and their interpretations as they unfolded, as well as the ways Holocaust narrative reflects, creates, and leads us toward particular meanings in events afterwards.

One may indeed wonder, after Robert Alter, whether the "larger social and cultural purposes of scholarship are better served by pondering the literary refractions of mass murder or by undertaking . . . a critical biography of Sholem Aleichem."[2] But by suggesting that these two academic pursuits are mutually exclusive somehow, we overlook the ways in which "the literary refractions of mass murder" and Sholem Aleichem's view of the universe may, in fact, have everything to do with each other. As should become clear, in fact, the purely literary and the purely historical worlds were never really pure of each other, but were often all too tragically interdependent.[3] Contrary to those who see the world and its representations operating independently of one another, "life" and "life-in-writing"—catastrophe and our responses to it—have always interpenetrated; in this way, literature remembers past destructions even as it shapes our practical responses to current crisis.

For, as Hayden White has suggested, "contemporary critical theory permits us to believe more confidently than ever before that 'poetizing' is not an activity that hovers over, transcends, or otherwise remains alienated from life or reality, but represents a mode of praxis which serves as the immediate base of all cultural activity. . . ."[4] If we recognize this "poetizing" activity also as one of the bases of worldly praxis, then the issue here becomes not just "the facts" of the Holocaust, but also their "poetic"—i.e., narrative—configuration, and how particular representations may have guided writers in both their interpretations of events and their worldly responses to them. As becomes painfully clear, it was not "the facts" in and of themselves that determined actions taken by the victims of the Holocaust—or by the killers themselves; but it was the structural, mythological, and figurative apprehension of these facts that led to action taken on their behalf.

The case for a critical literary historiography of the Holocaust is thus justified neither by finding new meanings in the Holocaust, nor by rendering ingenious interpretations of its texts, but rather by considering the possible *consequences* of interpretation—for both the victims at the time and for the survivors in their understanding of a post-Holocaust world. The critical aim of such a reading must therefore never be merely to deconstruct Holocaust narrative into so many columns of inert myths, grammars, and figures. Instead of engaging in a sterile pursuit of deep mythological, religious, and linguistic structures constituting only the literary texts of the Holocaust, the aim here is to explore both the plurality of meanings in the Holocaust these texts generate *and* the actions that issue from these meanings outside of the texts. Rather than merely deconstructing this narrative or its criticism, or de-historicizing it altogether, I attempt here to re-historicize it by looking beyond interpretation to its consequences in history.

Until now the historians' concern with Holocaust narrative has often been to unravel its myths and tropes in order to excavate the "historical actuality" of events. While literary scholars have also attempted to penetrate narrative for its underlying facts, they have tended more often to focus on the narrative strategies by which writers represent the Holocaust. In addition, like many of the traditional exegetes before them, some critics have viewed themselves as much the guardians of these texts as their interpreters. In this view, the critical task has included protecting—even privileging— texts like the Holy Scriptures and survivors' testimony from "heretical" readings that undermine these texts' authority. As a consequence, even the most insightful and theoretically informed Holocaust literary scholars have often preferred to excavate previously unknown works, collecting them into literary histories, where they can be subjected to either historical or new critical analysis. The aim here, however, is to understand the manner in which historical actuality and the forms in which it is delivered to us may be intertwined: it is to know what happened in how it is represented.

This is to suggest that the events of the Holocaust are not only shaped *post factum* in their narration, but that they were initially determined as they unfolded by the schematic ways in which they were apprehended, expressed, and then acted upon. In this way, what might once have been considered merely a matter of cultural, religious, or national perspective of the Holocaust assumes the force of agency in these events: world views may have both generated the catastrophe and narrated it afterward. Thus perceived, history never unfolds independently of the ways we have understood it; and in the case of the Holocaust, the interpretation and structural organization of historical events as they occurred may ultimately have determined the horrific course they eventually took.

This is to move beyond the question of whether or not literary and historical accounts of the Holocaust are "perspective ridden" to understand how various literary forms, cultural and religious traditions, and precedent experiences have indeed shaped the Holocaust. In this way, the critical reader can begin to assess the manner in which these "versions of the Holocaust" may have determined both the historical responses taken on their behalf—actions comprising the ultimate index to the kind of knowledge we possess—and the understanding subsequent generations infer from these versions. If pursued with care and tact, a sensitivity to these issues might add significantly to our understanding of both the Holocaust as it happened and of its history-as-it-is-written in literature.

II. INTERPRETING HOLOCAUST NARRATIVE

In his review of the first full-length study of Holocaust literature, Edouard Roditi admonished its author, Irving Halperin, for ignoring what he called the "philosophical-religious and cultural-sociological backgrounds that might have helped him to distinguish clearly the various influences which have determined the different attitudes and reactions of the witnesses whose writings he analyzed: Primo Levi's liberal-positivist Italian middle-class background, Viktor Frankl's academic and typically German philo-sophical idealism, Elie Wiesel's Hassidism modified later by post-war French existentialism, Chaim Kaplan's Jewish enlightenment, etc. . . . "[5] While Roditi was probably aware of the theoretical implications of this criticism, neither he nor those who immediately followed extended this particular critique. Instead, Roditi enunciated the general attitude Holocaust literary criticism was to assume over the next decade when he declared that it is actually the "steadfastly objective eyewitness observations" of diarists like Kaplan, Herman Kruk, Zelig Kalmanovitsh, and Mary Berg that are so valuable to us. That is, Roditi suggests that it is not the manner in which witnesses have apprehended and related experiences, but the "steadfastly objective" quality of their writing that constitutes its value. The "various influences" that may indeed have determined the different witnesses' re-actions were thus subordinated early on to the very facts these influences ultimately shaped.

This distinction between the hard facts of the Holocaust and the per-ceived softness in their literary reconstruction has also been enforced by historians, who remain especially wary of the potential displacement of hard history by its novelistic versions. Toward the end of his study of "Jewish history and Jewish memory," for example, Yerushalmi observes that "The Holocaust has already engendered more historical research than any single event in Jewish history, but I have no doubt whatever that its image is being shaped, not at the historian's anvil, but in the novelist's crucible" (p. 98). While it is true that the "image of the Holocaust" is indeed being shaped in fictional narrative, we might ask what the difference is between the "his-torian's anvil" and the "novelist's crucible." Is it really that between iron-hard history and the concoctions of the novelist's imagination? Are his-torical tracts of the Holocaust less mediated by imagination, less troped and figured, or ultimately less interpretive than the fictions of the Holo-caust? In what way do historians fictionalize and novelists historicize? What are the differences between the kinds of Holocaust knowledge each nar-rative form brings us?

It may be true, as Yerushalmi suggests, that "even where the Jews do not reject history out of hand, they are not prepared to confront it directly, but seem to await a new, metahistorical myth, for which the novel provides at least a modern temporary surrogate" (p. 98). But it is no less true that the old "metahistorical myths" also inform—even constitute—all that is now regarded as Jewish historiography. For it may not be a matter of whether or not we are merely prepared to confront—and thereby record—history directly, without the "metahistorical myths" that frame our discourse, but whether or not we can record history without these myths. Just as it was never the task of ancient scribes and rabbis to preserve the specific historical details of catastrophe so much as it was to preserve the traditional paradigms by which events were to be understood and interpreted, contemporary narrators of the Holocaust find that all they can preserve now are also the metahistorical myths by which they have known history.[6] Hard history and memory of specific events may always be subordinate to the meaning of such history, its interpretation within the tradition, and the shape of traditional paradigms after such history.

In fact, hermeneutic distinctions between histories and fictions of the Holocaust are blurred further still when we recall that contemporary forms of historical narration have in themselves derived partly from the form of the English novel as it had developed by the nineteenth century.[7] So even though an eminent Holocaust historian like Yehuda Bauer would warn against searching only for what he considers to be the "metaphysical comprehension" of the Holocaust engendered by imaginative writers, preferring instead more concrete questions—such as "What were the bases of Jew-hatred? Who were the murderers? When was the mass murder planned and how? Was there a way of rescue? What were the effects of the Holocaust on the Jewish people, in Israel, and in the Diaspora?"[8]—he may be overlooking both the metaphysical sources of these questions and the metaphysical assumptions underlying any narrative formulation of their answers. Bauer fears that if these questions are not faced, imaginative works by Katzenelson, Wiesel, Kovner, and Sachs cannot be intelligible or meaningful: "Without a return to the . . . arduous task of actually knowing something about the Holocaust, the symbolic descriptions that occupy, quite legitimately, the center of the literary stage in Holocaust literature, become just another escape route for the superficial" (p. 46). Without keeping in mind the more subtly symbolic nature of historical discourse itself, however, we also risk a certain uncritical complacency, in which we privilege one kind of knowledge about the Holocaust over another, when we might only be comparing one kind of knowledge with another. For "knowing" something about the Holocaust may have everything to do with the inescapably literary character of historical knowledge.[9]

In anticipation of possible objections to this narratological approach to history based on the legitimate fears that fictional discourse might then usurp the "history of the Holocaust" altogether, it may be appropriate to reiterate here the explicitly ontological distinctions between historical events and fictional events that Hayden White has recalled in the face of similar objections. "*[H]istorical events* differ from *fictional events* in the ways that it has been conventional to characterize their differences since Aristotle," White has written. For, as he continues,

> Historians are concerned with events which can be assigned to specific time-space locations, events which are (or were) in principle observable or perceivable, whereas imaginative writers—poets, novelists, playwrights—are con-

cerned with both these kinds of events and imagined, hypothetical, or invented ones. The nature of the kinds of events with which historians and imaginative writers are concerned is not the issue. What should interest us in the discussion of "the literature of fact" or, as I have chosen to call it, "the fictions of factual representation," is the extent to which the discourse of the historian and that of the imaginative writer overlap, resemble, or correspond with each other. Although historians and writers of fiction may be interested in different kinds of events, both the forms of their respective discourses and their aims in writing are often the same.[10]

Indeed, as White has also shown, the opposition of history to fiction is in itself a relatively new idea, arising with positivist notions of "scientific objectivity." "Prior to the French Revolution," White tells us, "historiography was conventionally regarded as a literary art. More specifically, it was regarded as a branch of rhetoric and its 'fictive' nature generally recognized" (p. 123). It was also understood, White continues, that "many kinds of truth, even in history, could be presented to the reader only by means of fictional techniques of representation" (p. 123). That is, it was clear then in ways that have since been obscured that the poet's truth has never really acceded in authority to that of the historian so much as the historian's truth has always been "poetic." Historical truths of the Holocaust might no longer be equated with the putative facts as such, but in White's words, they might now be equated *"with a combination of fact and the conceptual matrix within which [the fact has been] located in the discourse*. The imagination no less than the reason ha[s] to be engaged in any adequate representation of the truth; and this mean[s] that the techniques of fictionmaking [are] as necessary to the composition of a historical discourse as erudition might be" (p. 123, emphasis added).

As troubling as the implications of this insight might be for literary testimony, its impact has been felt—and thus addressed—most keenly by historical theorists, who recognized immediately its consequences for "objectivity" in historical narrative. Essays by White, Barthes, and others suggest that historians have traditionally attempted to make the same leap of faith between event and its displacing sign as the poet in his "willing suspension of disbelief."[11] For the classical historian, they say, the double bind has always been the automatic subterfuge of historical facts by his written medium. "It is a problem," White has written, "because insofar as the historian's discourse is conceived to *have a style*, it is also conceived to *be literary*. But insofar as a historian's discourse is literary, it seems to be rhetorical, which is anathema for those who wish to claim the status of objective representation for historical discourse."[12]

One of the consequences of this realization has been an almost obsessive tendency by writers of both historical and now documentary discourse to rid their narrative of all signs of style in order to distinguish between factual and fictional works. Though, as White reminds us, even "this effort was, of course, a rhetorical move in its own right, the kind of rhetorical move Valesio calls the 'rhetoric of anti-rhetoric' " (p. 122). In this view, even so-called style-less modes of writing—such as "new journalism" or "new factuality"—become styles in themselves. An author's "new factuality" accomplishes not so much the unmediated rendition of facts as it does a "rhetoric of fact." The aim in such a style is not to write unmediated facts, but to convince the reader that such facts, now of a particular color and cast, have been established.

In what has become a classic statement on the significance of narrative that purports not to create significance in its representation, Roland Barthes suggests that the literary critic pay special attention to writing in which

> the author seeks to stand aside from his own discourse by systematically omitting any direct allusion to the originator of the text: the history seems to write itself. This approach is very widely used, since it fits the so-called "objective" mode of historical discourse, in which the historian never appears himself. What really happens is that the author discards the human persona but replaces it by an "objective" one; the authorial subject is as evident as ever, but it has become an objective subject. This is what Fustel de Coulanges revealingly and rather naïvely calls the "chastity of history."[13]

And as he goes on to remark, this narrative style has not only served the historians but has been of particular value to the novelists—especially the realists—who have incorporated it as part of their fiction:

> At the level of discourse, objectivity, or the absence of any clues to the narrator, turns out to be a particular form of fiction, the result of what might be called the referential illusion, where the historian tries to give the impression that the referent is speaking for itself. This illusion is not confined to historical discourse: novelists galore, in the days of realism, considered themselves "objective" because they had suppressed all traces of the *I* in their text. (P. 149)

As we find in the cases of Holocaust literary testimony and documentary fiction, however, the reasons for an author's self-effacement vary significantly. At times, it may only be an attempt by survivors to make credible otherwise incredible events; other writers seek deliberately to naturalize particular historical interpretations of events. But ultimately all writers of objective or factual narrative assert at least two kinds of significance: that in the way they represent events and that in a style that represents itself as style-less. Barthes concludes here:

> Elimination of meaning from "objective" discourse only produces a new meaning; confirming once again that the absence of an element in a system is just as significant as its presence. This new significance extends to the whole discourse, and in the last analysis constitutes what distinguishes historical discourse from all others; it is reality, but surreptitiously changed into shamefaced mean-

ing: historical discourse does not follow reality, it only signifies it; it asserts at every moment: *this happened*, but the meaning conveyed is only that someone is making that assertion. (P. 154)

Thus, the Holocaust writer faces an especially painful quandary: on the one hand, the survivor-scribe would write both himself and his experiences into existence after the fact, giving them both expression and textual actuality; but on the other hand, in order to make his testimony seem true, he would simultaneously efface himself from his text.

Insofar as any written work is born of a specific moment in time, it might be regarded quite naturally as a fragment or artifact of the particular age that produced it. In this figurative sense, most literary responses to the Holocaust might also be considered as "documents" of the dark age that produced them. Unlike other historically based literature, however, the writing from and about the Holocaust has not been called upon merely to represent or stand for the epoch whence it has derived, which would be to sustain the figurative (i.e., metonymical) character of its "literary documentation." But rather, writers and readers of Holocaust narrative have long insisted that it literally deliver documentary evidence of specific events, that it come not to stand for the destruction, or merely point toward it, but that it be received as testimonial proof of the events it embodies. For the compelling reasons I shall explore in Part I, the figurative reference to literary works as "documents of an age" has hardened for the Holocaust diarists and memoirists into the literal—if unachievable—aim of their writing.

Rather than coming to Holocaust narrative for indisputably "factual" testimony, therefore, the critical reader might now turn to the manner in which these "facts" have been understood and reconstructed in narrative: as a guide both to the kinds of understanding the victims brought to their experiences and to the kinds of actions they took on behalf of this understanding. At issue here are neither "the facts" of the Holocaust nor their deconstruction in a critical reading of "documentary narrative." Nor is the aim here merely to apply current principles of narrativity and historical discourse to Holocaust narrative. The purpose of this particular inquiry is rather to explore the implications and consequences of these principles for our understanding of the Holocaust as it is represented in "narrative testimony."

Instead of damaging the credibility of these works, this critical approach might affirm the truth of interpretation and understanding that attends every narrative of the Holocaust. Far from transcending or displacing the events of the Holocaust, the governing mythoi of these writers are actually central to their experiences. For the "poetics" of literary testimony not only framed the writers' experiences as they unfolded, shaping both their understanding and responses; but the language, tropes, and selected details of their texts ultimately shape our understanding of events afterwards. The actions we take in the current world in light of the Holocaust are necessarily predicated on our understanding of the Holocaust, as it has been passed down to us in the victims' and survivors' literary testimony.

The role of the critic here is not to sort "fact" from fiction in Holocaust literary testimony, but to sustain an awareness of both the need for unmediated facts in this literature and the simultaneous incapacity in narrative to document these facts. Once we understand the literary and phenomenological origins of this overwhelming impulse in Holocaust writers to deliver evidence of events, we can accept this need even as we look beyond it. In the alternative hermeneutics of Holocaust literary testimony that follows, I attempt to shift critical emphasis away from the diaries' and memoirs' claim to documentary evidence, to their more tenable function as historical exegesis. In the process, I hope also to redefine and to limit the critical conception of "documentary narrative" at large, relieving it of ends necessarily beyond its reach.

I.

Interpreting
Literary Testimony

ONE

On Rereading Holocaust Diaries and Memoirs

There are no facts in themselves. For a fact to exist, we must first introduce meaning.

—Friedrich Nietzsche

... a 'fact' must be regarded as 'an event under description.'

—Hayden White

Yet, I swear I saw all this with my own eyes.

—Chaim A. Kaplan

INTRODUCTION

Violent events and massive human suffering of the kind exemplified in wars and massacres, revolutions and counterrevolutions, plagues and earthquakes seem always to have stimulated an outpouring of what might be called "factually insistent" narrative. In fact, as Yosef Hayim Yerushalmi reminds us, the rabbis used to refer generically to written histories of the Gentile nations as *sifrey milchamot* (books of wars).[1] Which is not to deny that wars and cataclysms have evoked more than their share of Jewish historical writing as well: most agree that the resurgence of Jewish historiography in the sixteenth century was generated specifically by the mass expulsion of Jews from the Iberian peninsula the century before (pp. 58–59). And as Jewish historical writing was revived by one disaster, it has been sustained by too many others: hence, the veritable explosion of Jewish historiography in the aftermath of the Holocaust.

It is almost as if violent events—perceived as aberrations or ruptures in the cultural continuum—demand their retelling, their narration, back into traditions and structures they would otherwise defy. For upon entering narrative, violent events necessarily reenter the continuum, are totalized by it, and thus seem to lose their "violent" quality. Inasmuch as violence is "resolved" in narrative, the violent event seems also to lose its particularity—i.e., its facthood—once it is written. In an ironic way, the violent event can exist as such (and thus as an inspiration to factual narrative, it seems) only as long as it appears to stand outside of the continuum, where it remains apparently unmediated, unframed, and unassimilated. For once written, events assume the mantle of coherence that narrative necessarily imposes on them, and the trauma of their unassimilability is relieved.

At the same time, however, there seems also to be a parallel and contradictory impulse on the part of writers to preserve in narrative the very *dis*continuity that lends events their violent character, the same discontinuity that is so effectively neutralized by its narrative rendering. The eyewitness scribe, in particular, has aspired both to represent the sense of discontinuity and disorientation in catastrophic events and to preserve his personal link to events—all in a medium that necessarily "orients" the reader, creates continuity in events, and supplants his authority as witness. As a result, the more violently wrenched from a continuum a catastrophe is perceived to be, the more desperate—and frustrated—the writer's attempts become to represent its events as discontinuous.

Until recently, however, it was generally assumed that the nature either of violence in general or of the Holocaust in particular determined whether or not its events were available to realistic literary representation. In an early discussion of catastrophic fact in literature, Frederick Hoffman recognized both the attempts at a factual style and the limitations for fact in any such "style" at all.[2] "In an extremely literal sense," Hoffman wrote, "a 'factual style' is one that excludes as much as is linguistically possible . . . ," adding that the basic problem of the "literature of violence is to find an adequate means of recording fact independently of structural subterfuges" (p. 159). Inasmuch as "violence tends to destroy structures, to isolate experiences, to force them away from containing forms," Hoffman concluded that it is primarily *violent* events that fall outside factual representation (p. 159).

On the other hand, Terrence Des Pres has suggested that the experiences Holocaust survivors describe are so horrible that they actually resist the fictionalizing that, he acknowledged, informs most remembering.[3] Though Des Pres was attempting here to emphasize both the extremity of these experiences and the veracity of the survivors' testimony by framing the issue this way, he also implied that in their enormity, these experiences somehow force themselves directly into language as unvitiated facts, without being mediated or shaped by structures of mind, culture, and narrative that ultimately lend this testimony its voice. Like many readers, Des Pres seems to suggest that the literal facts of the Holocaust are both the primary aim and achievement of a survivor's testimony.

In a more widely shared view, Saul Friedländer echoes the sentiments of many other critics when he suggests that, beginning with the First World War and culminating in Auschwitz, reality itself became so extreme as to outstrip language's capacity to represent it altogether.[4] In the face of Holocaust realities, writes Friedländer, literary realism has necessarily given way to unabashedly archetypal and mythological representations: "During our period both the capitalist jungle and the Stalinist hell have produced literary characters of formidable verisimilitude. We can recognize the Herzogs, the Portnoys, and all the Babbitts of the world; the universe of the GPU prisons, of *The First Circle* and the Gulag, has given us its Denisovitch as well as its Matriona. But the terrain of the most extreme upheaval of our time [i.e., the Holocaust], which remains a fixed point in the imagination of our epoch, provides us with only shadows or myths."[5]

But by referring as he does to "the Herzogs, the Portnoys, and all the Babbitts in the world," Friedländer tacitly recognizes that even the most "realistic" characters in literature are also "types"—i.e., constructs—that owe their shapes as much to antecedent myths and figures of the imagination as they do to objects in the world. The point is that neither violence per se nor the sheer extremity of the Holocaust "killed" realism as a viable or appropriate literary response to these events. But rather, in Robert Scholes's words, "It is because reality [itself] cannot be recorded that realism is dead. All writing, all composition, is construction. We do not imitate the world, we construct versions of it. There is no mimesis, only *poeisis*. No recording. Only construction."[6]

Instead of highlighting this critical insight, the Holocaust has compelled writers to assume the role of witnesses to criminal events, actually rehabilitating the mimetic impulse in these writers rather than burying it altogether. Holocaust writers and critics have assumed that the more realistic a representation, the more adequate it becomes as testimonial evidence of outrageous events. And as witness became the aim of this writing, "documentary realism" has become the style by which to persuade readers of a work's testamentary character. For the survivor's witness to be credible, it must seem natural and unconstructed.

As with the graphic artists of this period, particularly the expressionists and other vehement antirealists, the closer writers came to the ghettos and death camps, the more likely they were to redefine their aesthetic mission as one of testifying to the crimes against them and their people.[7] In the minds of victimized writers and artists, if concrete action was to be taken in response to these atrocities, concrete evidence needed to be delivered to the world in as many forms as possible. In fact, as Des Pres reminds us, for diarists like Emmanuel Ringelblum, Zelig Kalmanovitsh, Mary Berg, and so many others, bearing witness was less a "literary" act and more a "biological necessity" (p. 31); for some like Chaim Kaplan it was even a "national obligation."[8] So acute was the fear that their experiences would remain, in Himmler's horrifying words, "a never-to-be-written page in history," that "literary testimony" became for many victims the sole reason to survive. When survival and the need to bear witness become one and the same longing, this desperate urge to testify in narrative cannot be underestimated.

In light of the profound inquiry into the nature of historiography and the essential literariness of "historical facts" by theorists like Barthes and White, however, this somewhat literal approach to positive testimony in literature becomes increasingly problematic to sustain. For in addition to eliminating the myth of a "natural language"—in which the object in the world and its sign are perceived as one—the doctrine of the arbitrariness of signs also disposes of any evidentiary function language might be called upon to serve; no matter what the intent, or how legitimate the motivation, the narrative documentarist attempting to bring forth a worldly object through its sign succeeds only in transmitting the sign itself. In fact, once we acknowledge the structural incapacity in narrative to document anything beyond its own activity as construction, it may even be critically irresponsible to insist that Holocaust narrative actually establish the documentary evidence to which it aspires. For by emphasizing the putative documentary function of Holocaust narrative over its valuable interpretive achievement, the critic might even be leaving this narrative vulnerable to undeserved—and ultimately irrevelant—criticism regarding historical points of fact in the event of conflicting "testimonies."

In an essay on the essential literariness of historical narrative, Lionel Gossman addresses the conflict this notion poses for positivist historians. "Despite decades of demonstrations by philosophers and historians themselves that history is a construct," Gossman writes, "the belief that it is an immediate representation of reality, and the historians' own complicity with this belief, have remained remarkably vigorous. Indeed, the tenacity of the belief itself is something that requires explanation."[9] Just as tenacious among Holocaust writers and historians, this belief in narrative's direct representation of events will be explored here with an eye toward understanding it. For without first addressing the issue of a text's seemingly literal meaning as evidence, we cannot move on to a fuller understanding of the production of meaning in literary testimony, or ultimately to the kinds of actions that issue from this meaning.

I. LITERARY ORIGINS OF TESTIMONY

In both Torah and Talmud the injunction to relate one's witness of an iniquity is taken by the rabbis as explicitly commanded: "And he is a witness whether he has seen or known of it; if he does not utter it, then he shall bear his iniquity" (Lev. 5:1). As a traditional definition of witness, this obligation becomes significant in both of its parts: not only is a witness described as someone who both knows and sees an event, but, as elaborated in Talmud (Sanhedrin 30a), once an unjust event is known, it must by law be reported. And if one can become a witness merely by knowing of an event, then implicit in the testimonial act seems to be the possibility for making more witnesses by informing others of events. Inasmuch as the idea of witness is so intricately tied into the legal process of establishing evidence in order to achieve justice, it seems possible that these biblical and legal obligations to bear witness play some traditional role in the Holocaust victims' conceptions of themselves and their roles as witnesses.

In this context, we might consider also the etymological histories of terms like "witness," "testimony," and "document"—all of which figure at some level the narrative activity of Holocaust diarists and memoirists. One of the first references to witness in Torah is the figurative witness imputed to a pile of stones erected by Jacob and Laban to symbolize their agreement (Gen. 31:44–49). Possibly in order to distinguish between this material kind of witness and that later ascribed to scripture itself, the only Aramaic words in the entire Torah—*Yegar-sahadutha* (stone-heap of witness)—are used instead of the Hebrew *edut* (or as translated by Jacob, *Gal-ed*). In Laban's words, "This mound (*gal*) is a witness (*ed*) between you and me this day" (Gen. 31:48).

In its English past, "testimony" derives from the Latin for "witness" (*testis*), while "witness" in turn derives from both the abstract concept of becoming conscious of (or to know) something and literally seeing a thing. To testify is literally "to make witness"—an etymological reminder that as witness and testimony are made, so is knowledge. In addition to establishing evidence, the term "document" retains echoes of both its Latin origin *documentum*—a lesson—and its French root *docere*—to teach. As a result, documenting an event suggests both establishing it as fact and teaching about it. The very figures of witness, testimony, and documentary thus point respectively to having seen events, having been part of events, finding significance in events, and then teaching about and finding meaning through the transmission of events. By keeping both the legal and etymological histories of these terms in mind, we retain the multidimensional character of witness as it is figured in Holocaust survivors' literary testimony.

In his study of "responses to catastrophe in modern Jewish culture," David Roskies confirms after Yerushalmi that even though catastrophic events have generated an enormous amount of Jewish historiography, the specific "facts" of destruction were never really the aim of early Jewish historical writing: "What was remembered and recorded was not the factual data but the meaning of the desecration."[10] For as Roskies makes clear throughout his study, the details of destruction have always been figured in the stock of traditional paradigms available to the scribes. Because the rabbis thus passed down not the particulars of history but rather the larger interpretive patterns by which history was to be understood, Roskies correctly warns against the uncritical preoccupation of many contemporary readers with the strict chronology and historical setting of biblical events.

But when he extends this argument in his discussion of Chaim Nachman Bialik's poetry to suggest that "The will to bear particular witness had to be cultivated," and that it is not "an innate faculty of humankind, Jewish or otherwise" (p. 135), Roskies may be overlooking the other ways in which scripture itself is figured rhetorically as a "literature of testimony." For in many ways, the need both to imbue narrative with the full weight and authority of its objects and to invoke "witness" as the basis of this authority may be as old as the Book itself.

In moving from the legendary realm of Genesis to the historical world of Exodus, for example, the biblical scribes seemed to devote considerable effort to reinforcing the testamentary—i.e., eyewitness—authority of their narrative. Indeed, even though the Pentateuch invokes the highest possible authority for its "truth" (what better author than God, or more faithful scribe than Moses?), we find in the text repeated attempts to establish an eyewitness link between events and their scriptural representations. In Exod. 25:16, scripture itself is referred to as *edut*—which literally means witness, testimony, or evidence, and which is also the origin of the modern Hebrew term for "written document" (*edut bichtav*). In addition to describing the decalogue as "testimony," the scribes have also sought to reinforce the historical authority of otherwise incredible events in the narrative of Exodus by emphasizing the quality of witness within the text itself. After God parts the Sea of Reeds, for example, it is written: "Thus the Lord saved Israel that day out of the hand of the Egyptians; and Israel *saw* (*va'yireh*) the dead Egyptians upon the seashore. And Israel *saw* the great work which the Lord did upon the Egyptians, and the people feared the Lord; and they *believed* the Lord, and in His servant Moses" (Exod. 14:30–31). As the basis for God's covenantal authority derives from what he has done in history, the source of scripture's authority derives from its essence as witness—as *edut*— to God's deeds. Because the people *saw* the great work of the Lord, Israel believed the Lord; and because they were witness to the work of the Lord, their words would now carry the testamentary authority necessary to document the reality of what they saw.

The startling implication here is that the divine source of the scriptures seemed inadequate in the scribes' eyes as a basis for "authority" and needed to be supplemented by a further testamentary authority constructed within the text. Faced with the implicit arbitrariness of their narrative—which may have been perceived to undercut the divine authority they had been entrusted to transmit—the scribes of the Pentateuch seem already to have been experimenting with rhetorical and literary strategies for reinforcing their text's historical authority. As is true for subsequent documentary narrative, the operative trope and principle of "holy scripture" here is thus its explicitly eyewitness character as *edut*. The Book of Exodus emerges not only as a paradigm for the myths of exile, freedom, and return, but also as a textual prototype for subsequent "documentary narrative"—the quintessential *sifrut ha'edut* or "literature of testimony." In weighing the various motives for literary testimony in Holocaust writing, we might take into account the ultimate conceptual paradigm in Jewish literature for scripture itself.

In light of this divine precedent, it may not be surprising that the great majority of Holocaust scribes locating themselves within the Jewish literary tradition have adopted "testimony" as their personal task. It is surprising and even ironic, however, that Elie Wiesel would then overlook what amounts to a long tradition of literary testimony to proclaim that "If the Greeks invented tragedy, the Romans the epistle, and Renaissance the sonnet, our generation invented a new literature, that of testimony."[11] For as he later notes, he is consciously writing from within the Jewish tradition, adopting quite naturally the aims and methods of the *sofer* (scribe), whose task it has been, in Wiesel's words, neither to comment nor to interpret, but "to transcribe what was heard and *seen*—a difficult task that allowed for no mistakes. The talmud tells how the brilliant scribe Rabbi Meir was told by his master, Rabbi Ishmael: "Be careful. Should you omit or add one single word, you may destroy the world.' This was an exaggeration, of course, but it proves the point about the scribe's being the instrument of the events he recorded."[12]

As "an instrument of events," the scribe is in this view a neutral medium through which events would write themselves. And as part of the events he records, the scribe seems to endow his testimony with an ontological authority that verifies both the authenticity and—by extension—the facticity of his record. Like *edut*, the literary testimony of the Holocaust thus seems to accrue an ontologically privileged status, similar to that of earlier "testament." Indeed, by invoking the ancient texts as their sources of figuration, not only do Holocaust scribes seem to bring sacred scriptural figures into the present, but these same figures tend also to sanctify the current texts, to confer on them as privileged a status as the holy texts on which they are modeled. By referring to the reports of Holocaust survivors as the "stories of a new Bible," for example, Primo Levi confirms the widely held conceit that this writing is as *kadosh* (holy) as its prototype.[13] This privileging of the survivors' testament, however, also seems to extend the rabbinical dialectic between "holy scripture" and its exegesis to the study of Holocaust narrative, which creates an initial—if arbitrary—dichotomy between the survivors' testimony and its interpretation. Yet by acceding to such a rigid division between testimony and interpretation, not only do we overlook the fundamental ways in which biblical narrative itself is constructed and even self-interpreting, but we ignore the ways in which Holocaust literary testimony is also constructed and interpretive.[14]

Two examples of this tendency to separate testimony and interpretation come to mind here, one from the overall movement of Elie Wiesel's immense corpus, and one from the manner in which Terrence Des Pres has organized his own study of "life in the death camps." Of Wiesel's many works, only *Night* would "testify" to his experiences; his succeeding novels and commentaries seem mostly to recall the memories of his experiences in order to find, create, and often to question their religious and historical significance. As a memoir, *Night* would first establish the events as "facts," which then become the objects both of his later interpretive fictions (described by others as midrash) and of his own philosophical probing.[15]

This tendency to establish a referential core of Holocaust testimony, onto which commentary is then appended, is even more pronounced in the textual configuration of Des Pres's *The Survivor: An Anatomy of Life in the Death Camps*. In what amounts to an extended literary-critical essay on several survivors' testimony, Des Pres gives narrative voice to hundreds of otherwise unrecorded accounts even as he explicates these same accounts, abstracting from them what he considers to be appropriate motifs for their understanding. He thus encodes the testimony of these survivors and then decodes it in a single text, explicitly invoking it as pure and undiluted experience. By distilling the survivors' testimony into its blackest essence, indenting it and setting it off in heavy black type around which he weaves his own astute commentary, Des Pres (who is not Jewish) even seems to recall the textual configuration of the Talmud itself. All of which lends not only a certain scriptural authority to his witnesses' accounts but a ritual authority as well to his own exegesis of the survivors' "testament."

On the one hand, even as a privileged text, the survivors' testament demands interpretation by the critical exegetes, which in the tradition serves to "complete" the text by finding meaning in the events it relates. But on the other hand, this separation also implies that only the exegete, and not the scribe, is making meaning in the text, that in itself the text is a pure and normative rendering of events. In this view, the maker of the text is not the scribe so much as the event itself (recall Wiesel's definition of the *sofer* as "instrument of events"), which neglects the meaning created in the narrative act. One result of this enforced distinction between "sacred" testimony and its critical exegesis is a fundamental confusion between a text's authenticity and its authority as "fact." That is, by imputing to an ontologically *authentic* text an indisputably authoritative factuality, the reader confuses the kinds of privilege a survivor's testimony necessarily demands. For even though a survivor's testimony is "privileged" insofar as it is authentic, the factuality of his literary testimony is *not* necessarily so privileged.[16]

II. THE DISPLACEMENT OF TESTIMONY

In response to the "unwriting" of the Holocaust by the pseudohistorical revisionist Arthur Butz and his so-called Institute for Historical Review,[17] Elie Wiesel finds that fiction may be inadequate in its treatment of the Holocaust, insofar as it fails to establish the facts.[18] Implicit in this remark, however, is the assumption that witnesses' testimony does establish evidence of the facts. Yet as he recognizes elsewhere, the problem may be less a matter of literary form than it is a matter of language itself. Words, says one of Wiesel's characters, "destroy what they aim to describe, they alter what they try to emphasize. By enveloping the truth, they end up taking its place."[19] Instead of finding their reification in literary testimony, the facts are displaced by it altogether. In addition to the phenomenological and cultural assumptions underlying the very nature of writing, part of this tenacious need for the real on the part of Holocaust diarists and memoirists may also derive from their anxieties of displacement of events by their own texts.

Like the biblical scribes, Holocaust survivors suspect that if events are perceived after the fact as coming to exist only in their literary testimony, then their experiences might also be perceived as having never existed outside of their narrative. For diarists and memoirists attempting to document events, the possibility that they are somehow supplanting events—or even creating new ones—in their writing becomes nearly unbearable. As the "pseudorevisionists" of the Holocaust have demonstrated by exploiting the ever-palpable dichotomy between words and events, if one can write the Holocaust, and even rewrite the Holocaust, then perhaps one can also *un*write the Holocaust. For the writer who may have survived solely in order to testify to real experiences, this negation of the real in narrative—and not just its displacement—drives him further to insist on the absolute facticity of his literary testimony.

Though both fiction and nonfiction writers of the Holocaust may share in this need to achieve a convincing factual authority in their respective narratives, the sources of their need vary significantly. For even though ghetto-diarists, survivor-memoirists, and docu-novelists all seem to fear that the essential rhetoricity of their medium inadvertently fictionalizes the events themselves, the diarists and memoirists also fear that the empirical link between their experiences and their narrative is lost in literary construction. As moved as the novelists may be to imbue their fiction with documentary authority, the dilemma this displacement poses for diarists and memoirists attempting to retain—not just create—a testimonial authority is inordinately acute. It thus seems all the more perverse that the survivor-scribe's experience with words becomes in itself an object lesson in the arbitrariness of signs and the ways narrative tends to usurp the events it would represent.

As a witness to the crimes against self, family, and people, the diarist's and memoirist's desire to testify is a sympathetic one. If to witness events is to participate in them, even to become a walking trace of them, then to testify would seem to affirm for the writer just this intimate link with experience. But if the function of literary testimony then becomes to establish facts or evidence, it grows apparent first of all to the writer that he may be demanding of narrative an impossible task. For the diarists and memoirists intuit that in asking literature to establish the facts of the Holocaust—or evidence of events—they are demanding not just that words signify experiences, but that they become—like the writers themselves—*traces* of their experiences. Their impossible task is then to show somehow that their words are material fragments of experiences, that the current existence of their narrative is causal proof that its objects also existed in historical time.

Though there may be nothing in the text to discriminate between autobiographical and fictional narratives, as Philippe Lejeune has made clear, the reader of diaries and memoirs does enter into what Lejeune calls an "autobiographical pact" with the writer.[20] It is not a question of actual fact that separates autobiography from fiction, in Lejeune's view, but a question of the right to claim experiences as one's own: the right to invoke the empirical bond that has indeed existed between a writer and events in his narrative. For even as we acknowledge that, like "documentary fiction," narratives of the diarists and memorists are constructed, we must also insist on maintaining the ontological differences between them. It is to recognize the difference between narrative that fabricates its authenticity as part of its fiction and that which attempts to salvage, however tenuously, an authentic empirical connection between text, writer, and experience.

As becomes all too clear to the writer, however, he is often the only one to recognize this "right." Unlike the novelist who may not have been there, Holocaust diarists and memoirists may feel no need to manufacture this link between their words and experiences, which are palpably united in themselves. Especially for the diarist who reported events as they played themselves out before his eyes, the words he inscribed on a page seemed to be living traces of his life at that moment: his eyes, his engraving hand, and the ink on paper all appeared to be materially linked in the writing act itself. But it is just this perception of words being bodily linked to events that constitutes both the source of these words' evidentiary authority for the writer and the point at which they lose this same authority for the reader. For inasmuch as the diarists and memoirists see themselves as traces of experiences, and their words as extensions of themselves, the link between words and events seems quite literally *self*-evident: that which has touched the writer's hand would now touch the reader. Whether the diarists and memoirists write these events from memory or at the very moment they occur, words and events remain linked by the inscribing hand, a literal part of both the experience and the record of it.

But for the reader with only words on a page, the authority for this link is absent. The words in a translated and reproduced Holocaust diary are no longer traces of the crime, as they were for the writer who inscribed them; what was evidence for the writer at the moment he wrote is now, after it leaves his hand, only a detached and free-floating sign, at the mercy of all who would read and misread it. Evidence of the witness's experiences seems to have been supplanted—not delivered—by his text. Once he withdraws from his words, the writer has in effect also withdrawn the word's evidentiary authority, the only link it ever had to its object in the world. The writer's absence thus becomes the absence of authority for the word itself, making it nothing more than a signifier that gestures back toward the writer and his experiences, but that is now only a gesture, a fugitive report.

For Holocaust survivors who may have lived solely to bear witness and who believed they could bring the *realia* of their experiences forward in time through their words, the perception that their experiences now seem to dematerialize beneath the point of a pen becomes nearly unbearable.

The possibility that, once committed to paper, a witness's testimony could be perceived as a fabrication of reality and not the trace of it he had intended, would seem to mock a witness's very *raison d'être*. And to compound the dilemma, the more insistently a survivor-scribe attempts to establish the "lost link" between his text and his experiences in the text, the more he inadvertently emphasizes his role as maker of the text, which ironically— and more perversely still—further undermines the sense of unmediated fact the writer had attempted to establish. Both the writer's perceived absence from the text and his efforts to relink himself to it thus seem to thwart—and thereby inflame still further—the testimonial impulse.

III. GENERIC FORM AND THE STRUCTURES OF TESTIMONY

Because the diarists wrote from within the whirlwind, the degree of authority in their accounts is perceived by readers to be stronger than that of the texts shaped through hindsight. Operating on the same phenomenological basis as print journalism, in which the perceived temporal proximity of a text to events reinforces the sense of its facticity, diaries can be far more convincing of their factual veracity than more retrospective accounts.[21] Like photographs, which represent themselves as metonymical remnants of their objects, the diary accrues the weight and authority of reality itself. But while the exigencies of time and memory may weigh heavily on the factuality of a given report, they are in other ways no less mediational than the linguistic, cultural, and religious patterns of mind and expression that frame a writer's narrative moment by moment, during or after the Holocaust. For even the diarists themselves—once they enter immediate experience into the tropes and structures of narrative—necessarily convert experience into an organized, often ritualized, memory of experience.

In addition to the narrative mediation of a writer's language, generic properties of the diary also organize and structure literary witness in particular ways. That events are broken into hourly, daily, or weekly increments, into discrete entries event by event, or chronicled place by place already creates particular strictures on the kind of witness the diarist makes. The diarists who participated in Ringelblum's communal *Oneg Shabbat* archive were motivated to record events far different from those reported in a more personal record, like Mary Berg's diary. These distinctions do not make one witness's account less accurate than another's; but the reasons for which diarists wrote and the focus of their witness inescapably regulate, and at times restrict, the diarist's record. In the end, these formal and generic constraints contribute as much to the meaning and significance of these diaries as do the figures and selection of details in the diaries themselves.

In his essay on "Autobiography and Historical Consciousness," Karl J.

Weintraub considers the structuring factors inherent in the diarist's activity: "The diurnal entries of the diarist are governed by the very fact that a day has its end. Even if in the maturing diarist a sense of selection begins to be guided by the growing awareness of what this person values and does not value, the journal entry is the completed precipitate of each day. It has its very value in being the reflection of but a brief moment; it attributes prime significance to the segments of life."[22] Whether the diarist of the ghetto is diurnal or nocturnal, whether he writes weekly or monthly, or only at any available chance, depending on the chaotic forces around him, the whole of the diary is organized around factors which in themselves contribute toward meaning. Depending upon the availablity of paper, writing instruments, candles, all the details that amount to life in hiding or under siege, events enter the diaries in particular ways, through allusion only, or at times not at all. And ultimately, just because events were not recorded in the diaries does not mean they did not happen.

In fact, what was excluded from the diaries of ghetto writers like Kruk, Kalmanovitsh, Ringelblum, and Kaplan assumes a critical importance in itself. Even though they may have been writing their journals explicitly for posterity's sake, the ghetto diarists remained ever aware that these works might be discovered prematurely. Thus, they not only refrained from discussing too openly their plans for resistance but occasionally addressed the potentially hostile captors of their diaries through circumlocutions or misleading names and details. In these cases, the diarists were forced to choose between disclosure for history's sake and nondisclosure for their own sake. If the only way to guarantee a particular mission's success seemed to be to ignore it in a daily journal, then the omission was sealed. Though intimately involved in planning the Warsaw Ghetto uprising, for example, Ringelblum thus refrained from any mention of it in his diary. Unlike the memoirists, the diarists necessarily considered both the sources they were creating for subsequent histories of their time and the consequences their writing might have for the events they were recording. This dimension of the diarists' sense of their works' consequences needs to be fully acknowledged as an essential part of the Holocaust diaries' phenomenology.[23]

In addition to time and place, the diarists' very language, traditions, and world view played crucial roles in the making of their literary witness. It may always be difficult to distinguish between the archetypal patterns the ghetto diarist has brought to events, those he perceived in or inferred from them, and those that exist in his narrative. As raw as they may have been at the moment, the ghetto and camp experiences were immediately refined and organized by witnesses within the terms of their *Weltanschauungen*. Hasidic Jews, Bundists, Labor Zionists, Revisionists, and even Jewish converts to Catholicism may have shared the "same" fate. But each victim "saw"—i.e., understood *and* witnessed—his predicament differently, depending on his own historical past, religious paradigms, and ideological explanations.

Hashomer hatsa'ir, the young guard of the Zionist left wing, may have perceived events at the time no more "accurately"—or "factually"—than did the Hasidic Jews in the East or the more fully assimilated Jews in the West. But in grasping their circumstances in terms of the Zionist scenario— which included both the most dire of warnings and specific plans of action (e.g., resistance and immigration to the Yishuv in Palestine)—the "young guard" responded much differently from their non-Zionist brethren in both narrative and in deed. Both Zionists and non-Zionists may have responded appropriately according to their respective ideologies, but of the many responses, some proved also to be more appropriate to survival.

In choosing to write in Hebrew over Yiddish, the ghetto scribes Kaplan and Kalmanovitsh may not have deliberately chosen every specific allusion and figure in their Hebrew over those in Ringelblum's Yiddish, but they did locate events within different linguistic realms all the same. For even as both languages share many of the same myths and tropes, their written traditions and the kinds of significance each accords events are often quite disparate. Where Hebrew tends to locate events in the sanctified linguistic sphere of scripture, rabbinical disputation, and covenant,[24] Yiddish (as the daily language and in many literal ways the *mama-loshen*, or *mother* tongue) often brought into sharper relief the details of daily life and its hardships. Community, politics, and organization had a vocabulary in Yiddish not developed at that time in Hebrew. Conversely, questions of theodicy, covenant, scriptural antecedent, and even the interpretation of events "as text" had a lexicon in Hebrew they did not have in Yiddish. Though it may have been possible to discuss most things in both languages, each one also predisposed certain choices of interpretation and perception for the diarists, as well as the selection of details and issues entered into the diary on a given day.

In a slightly different context, it is worth comparing the language, themes, preoccupations, and conclusions of the two best-known Holocaust diaries of "young people," *Young Moshe's Diary* and *The Diary of a Young Girl*. Both Moshe Flinker and Anne Frank were Dutch-reared, teen-aged diarists in hiding, who eventually perished in the camps. But where Moshe was reared in a religious home, a Zionist, and wrote his diary in Hebrew, Anne was assimilated, non-Zionist, and wrote in Dutch. Alternately jaded and optimistic, Anne's diary reflects both the darkness around her and her own compulsion to be—and therefore, it seems, to *see*—good. "It's really a wonder that I haven't dropped all my ideals," Anne writes two weeks before her capture,

because they seem so absurd and impossible to carry out. Yet I keep them, because in spite of everything I still believe that people are really good at heart. I simply can't build up my hopes on a foundation consisting of confusion, misery, and death. I see the world gradually being turned into a wilderness, I hear the ever appraoching thunder, which will destroy us too, I can feel the sufferings of millions and yet, if I look up into the heavens, I think that it will all come right, that this cruelty too will end, and that peace and tranquility will return again.[25]

In the stage version, the sunnier parts of this entry are spoken by Anne to Peter, after which she implores him to "look at the sky. Isn't it lovely?"[26] Even though she felt the suffering of millions, in the context of her assimilated world view, it seems to have been as an extremely sensitive and intelligent member of the human community, and not as one who identified herself as part of a collective Jewish tragedy.

In contrast, Moshe Flinker identified with practically all of Jewish history and politics from the start of his diary: as a self-conscious Zionist who writes in Hebrew, he is both ideologically and linguistically part of his people. Following his afternoon prayers on the last day of his diary, Moshe writes, "The sky is covered with bloody clouds, and I am frightened when I see it. . . . 'Where do these clouds come from?' . . . everything is clear to me. . . . They come from the seas of blood . . . brought about by the millions of Jews who have been captured and who knows where they are? 'We are the bleeding clouds. . . . We are witnesses; we were sent by our people to show you their troubles. . . . ' "[27] Though both of these young diarists met the same end, they grasped their circumstances in radically different ways. Where Anne might have seen beauty and hope in a fiery sunset, Moshe "saw" only apocalypse. The "vision" of events in these diaries depended on the languages, figures, and even religious training that ultimately framed these testimonies.

Where the diaries were intended to record contemporaneous responses and to be used possibly as evidence against the killers in subsequent trials, reports by the first eyewitnesses like Auschwitz escapees Rudolf Vrba and Alfred Wetzler were intended specifically to generate responses to contemporary events, to move the allies and potential victims to action. Like the diarists, these escaped eyewitnesses perceived themselves as fragments from ongoing events; unlike the diarists, they felt capable of stopping these same events by relating them. As Vrba and Wetzler discovered, however, the unquestionable authenticity of their reports ultimately mattered less than their audience's response to this testimony. Intended primarily to inform the Allies and Jewish councils in Europe of the Nazis' plan at Auschwitz to begin the extermination of Hungarian Jews, this report ran up against a wall of bureaucracy and incredulity that finally neutralized its initial reason for coming into being.[28]

In fact, one of the shared characteristics of diaries and the first eyewitness reports from Poland (technically "memoirs") is precisely the awareness that these words might affect the outcome of events under description. The aim of a press release issued by the American Representation of the General

Jewish Workers' Union of Poland in 1943 is expressly to move American Jewish groups and Allied governments to action against the killings already under way. Before detailing the mass killings he has seen in Warsaw and Belzec, an anonymous speaker establishes himself both as an eyewitness and as a man with a mission: "In August, 1942, I was in the ghetto of Warsaw and at the end of September, in the City of Belzec where the Nazis are carrying out their horrible mass slaughter of Jews."[29] He describes how he has already related these events to diplomatic representatives in Great Britain, who listened sympathetically before telling him that in view of his horrible experiences, it was his "overwrought imagination that was painting macabre pictures and that all [he] related could not be true. . . . We are only too well aware that in the free and civilized world outside, it is not possible to believe all that is happening to us. Let the Jewish people, then do something that will force the other world to believe us . . . " (p. 1). Written by an underground activist to other presumed activists in the American labor movement, this report is based on the premise that written testimony leads to action. Unlike memoirs written after events, these first reports tend to be more self-reflexive and aware of their words' immediate impact on readers. In this way, they are not calls for reflection or contemplation of the events' meaning (even as they suggested meaning) so much as they are demands for immediate action and justice.

Holocaust historians and archivists have long recognized that the problems complicating their readings of memoirs transcend merely taxonomic or generic issues. From the outset of their study of Holocaust memoirs, researchers have raised questions regarding both the use and the nature of eyewitness memoirs. If memoirs were to be used as evidence, what kind of evidence will it be, and to what end will it be used? In expressly addressing the "Problems Confronting 'Yad Washem' in Its Work of Research," historian Benzion Dinur attempted to delineate both the duties of the newly established memorial authority in Jerusalem and the methodology by which "evidence" of the catastrophe and resistance would be both preserved and presented. "From every point of view," Dinur acknowledges, "memoirs and reminiscences of persons who witnessed and experienced the horrors of the European catastrophe, watched it develop, or took part actively in the fight against their Nazi oppressors, either in regular military formations or in the partisan bands, as underground resistance fighters or in the Ghetto revolts, or in any other form, are of major importance."[30]

But the kind of importance remains an open question. In many cases, how the memoirs were to be interpreted determined their very inclusion in the canon of eyewitness accounts. On the one hand, since the aim of Yad Vashem is to document both the catastrophe *and* the resistance, the significance of a particular memoir as evidence of either catastrophe or resistance will necessarily determine its inclusion in the canon of eyewitness. On the other hand, Dinur recognizes at the outset that those who participated are alone in a position to provide unique insight into the unfolding of events, their inner workings. By definition, in fact, those who survived to tell their witness also have a particular grasp of survival and all that led to it—including resistance, faith, hope, and luck. For the Israeli historian, in particular, testimony from one who survived is likely to be considered testimony from one who also resisted; the heroic aspect of these stories is almost intrinsic in their very existence.

In the rest of his preface to research at Yad Vashem, Dinur thus shows a strong theoretical grasp of the problems presented for the evidence seeker in memoirs told after the fact:

> These memoirs must be treated in the same way as any other testimony and must, of course, be properly examined. The plain and unvarnished character of the narration and the presence of the narrator on the spot at the time constitute in themselves no guarantee of the authenticity of such memoirs. The reason need not be any desire to "amend" or to "improve" upon actual events for any ulterior purpose. It is difficult for the individual to liberate himself from his own personality. He has a propensity to see the past and his own past experiences, from the vantage point of the present. In such evidence every effort must be made to establish all the facts relating to the narrator, his location and status during the period of the catastrophe, and his subsequent career. (Pp. 19–20)

That is, to modify an axiom regarding the historian, every effort might be made to know the memoirist before knowing the memoir. The figures he brings to his memoir may have much more to do with his current occupation than with the events under his pen. By personality here, Dinur means much more than personality: he refers as well to all aspects of the teller's disposition, to the structures of mind and language that necessarily mediate between the person and events.

In this context, we note that unlike the diarist, the survivor-memoirist begins his testimony with full knowledge of the end, which inevitably contextualizes early experiences in terms of later ones. In recalling details of an early deportation, for example, the survivor cannot suddenly ignore its destination; early actions become much more ominous in retrospect, and the perceived innocence of early deportations at the time is lost. Early details of a testimony assume significance afterwards—and often even figures of representation—they could not have had for victims caught in events. In contrast to a diarist like Chaim Kaplan, who sent out a few pages of his diary at a time and so didn't have a chance to change or correct details of his vision, leaving all contradictions intact, the survivor necessarily unifies his vision in the knowledge of its outcome. By keeping in mind the *post factum* element of these testimonies, we remain aware of both the understanding of events created in their telling and the early understanding of events necessarily lost in their telling after the fact.

Again, as Weintraub argues, in addition to the order a memoirist's narrative imposes on events, the sense of the present and its attending kinds of knowledge also order the past:

> The fact once in the making cannot be seen together with the fact in its result. By this superimposition of the completed fact, the fact in the making acquires a meaning it did not possess before. The meaning of the past is intelligible and meaningful in terms of the present understanding; it is thus with all historical understanding. . . . History and autobiography derive their value from rendering significant portions of the past as interpreted past; for both the incoherent realia of life have been sorted out and those selected have been assigned their fitting place in a fuller pattern of meaning. (Pp. 826–27)

In concluding that "We must keep in mind that one of the requisite qualities for writing reminiscences is that of recreating the 'climate' existing at the time and thereby to reconstruct the past . . . [and that] this quality indeed has determined the importance of reminiscences for historical research," Dinur warns that unmediated testimony or evidence cannot be the aim here. If by climate, he refers only to ambience or emotional milieu, then he is right to warn that it will never be recovered precisely as it was. But if he means by climate the peculiar environmental details and factors impinging on every witness's testimony, shaping details, bringing some into relief and shadowing others, then "climate" will indeed be the aim of literary investigation into the memoirs. For it is not the details that can be brought back to life, but only the understanding of them—that is, the epistemological climate in which they existed at the time.

Charged with preserving, ordering, and collating masses of eyewitness testimony, the historians at Yad Vashem have also remained scrupulously aware of the potential rhetorical uses and abuses of memoir, as well. They know only too well that what was used as legal evidence in war-crimes trials at Nuremberg and Frankfurt, for example, becomes historical source material for some and rhetorical source material for others. In a methodological treatise on the Holocaust historian's use of eyewitness reports, K. Y. Ball-Kaduri even suggests that the primary importance of testimony may only be to add "life and blood to otherwise dry facts known from other sources."[31] That is, by rhetorically animating accounts of events seemingly devoid of human spirit, the quality of eyewitness seems to reconnect a witness's narrative to its human source, thereby reuniting the word with its speaker. The written word is thus infused with the authority of its speaker and, by extension, it is relinked to its object in the world. As we see in subsequent chapters, both fiction and nonfiction of the Holocaust rely heavily upon just this rhetorical aspect of testimony in order to authenticate particular versions of events.

These considerations are not meant to threaten the integrity of the diarist but should change our own focus as readers from the events underlying the diarist's narrative to the explanations and knowledge created in it. The survivor's testimony is important to us in many more ways than merely establishing times and places, names and dates. In looking for the story of events, we need to look at how each story is being told and then being used afterward. For as immediate as the witnesses were to events, their literary testimonies are not altogether *un*mediated: in this light, our aim is to attend to the process itself of testimony, to the literal making of witness in these diaries and memoirs.

IV. THE CONSEQUENCES OF INTERPRETIVE TESTIMONY

That the ghetto or death-camp scribes (of whom there were so few survivors) actually experienced and witnessed the workings of such death and destruction need never be questioned. But that the course of events, their causes and effects, and their meanings are normatively true in a particular diary because the narrator was there is problematic, especially if it diverts attention from the multiplicity of meaning and significance that comes with disparate accounts. The critical aim here is not to discern the truest of five different versions of, say, the Warsaw Ghetto uprising, thereby dismissing four of them for their deviation from the "most" authoritative. More important are the ways that different witnesses understood their roles in the revolt and how these understandings may have determined their actions. Whatever "fictions" emerge in the survivors' accounts are not deviations from the "truth" but are part of the truth in any particular version. The fictiveness in testimony does not involve disputes about facts, but the inevitable variance in perceiving and representing these facts, witness by witness, language by language, culture by culture.

Given these considerations, it becomes less tenable than ever to insist that the body of literature written *in* the Holocaust is more factually veracious—or even more authentic—than that written by survivors after the events. Even though David Roskies is willing to include what he calls "survival literature" (i.e., works written after events) in the Holocaust literary canon, for example, he still distinguishes it from what he terms "real Holocaust literature" (i.e., literature written from within events).[32] More extreme is Yechiel Szeintuch's definition of Holocaust literature, which, Roskies has noted, "would exclude from the authentic canon anything restored from memory even a week after liberation and certainly anything re-edited after the war."[33] As an ontological or literary-historical distinction, the temporal difference between literature written in the ghettos and camps and that written about them may be useful in determining the kinds of transformations and structuring of events endemic to all writing, but not in deciding the degree of transformation. We might investigate how time and place combine with other structurally mediating factors like language and political orientation, for example, to shape the representations of these experiences by different writers. But where the writing from within the whirlwind may be ontologically privileged insofar as it is empirically linked to events, it is not thereby more "real" or "authentic" if these terms denote factual veracity.

Indeed, the horrible irony is that, as nearly all the diarists and many of the survivors remind us, their insights, interpretations, and eyewitness descriptions may even be less reliable in a "factual sense" because of their proximity to events. The philosopher Emil Fackenheim has observed, for example, that it was not until several years after his internment at Sachsenhausen that he began to understand what had happened there. For as he could only recognize later, "When the eye-witness is caught in a scheme of things systematically calculated to deceive him, subsequent reflection is necessary if truth is to be given to his testimony."[34] He realizes that what little coherence and order his experiences may have had at the time were largely manufactured by the Nazis themselves: not to bring understanding or further facts to light, of course, but rather to deceive the inmates and obscure the Germans' actual intentions. As authentic as the prisoner's perceptions were at the time, even these eyewitness accounts were necessarily determined by the ways the Nazis had orchestrated camp and ghetto realities. One of the most frustrating and agonizing insights of all for the eyewitness narrators was the realization that as victims in the ghettos and camps, they were at the mercy of their persecutors in *all* ways—even in their attempts to testify against them.

In his Warsaw ghetto diary, Chaim Kaplan frequently bemoaned the preponderance of rumors in the ghetto, finally vowing not to write anything he had not seen with his own eyes.[35] But even as he valiantly attempted to separate fact from rumor, invoking "eyewitness" as his working criterion, he recognized the extent to which they were often two sides of the same reality. For as the Germans understood so well, by encouraging rumors of atrocities on the one hand and then attributing them to Allied and Jewish propaganda on the other, they were able simultaneously to manipulate both the flow of information about reality and the meaning of such "realities," even as they sustained the disorientation and confusion these realities wrought upon the victims. As Kaplan reported what he saw, he was thus plagued by the profound suspicion that, as in the case of overheard rumors, what "he saw"—and hence "understood"—was also choreographed by the Nazis.

Among numerous examples of this master-structuring of events for the benefit of "eyewitnesses," of course, was the model camp at Theresienstadt, where the cafe façades and even ersatz coffee and cake were provided for inmates being filmed by the Nazis for the Red Cross. But other, more painful, instances of this illusion of reality involve the meaning of even the most genuine of events and activities, such as the amazing level of cultural activity in the Jewish ghettos right up to the moment of their liquidation. It turns out, for example, that while the diarists were faithfully recording the "spiritual resistance" in the ghettos and their assertion of civilized humanity in the face of the Nazis' dehumanizing policies, the Nazis themselves were busy "allowing" such activity, even encouraging it, as a means of preempting anything other than spiritual resistance.

So, even as Ringelblum and Kaplan independently reported the victims' continuing devotion to scholarship, religious study, and culture in the Warsaw ghetto, other "documentarists" saw these realities in completely different ways. In a letter to his superiors in the *Generalgouvernment*, the German Kommissar of the Warsaw ghetto wrote that in his "view," the principle that

> has turned out most advantageously was to allow the Jews maximum freedom to regulate their own affairs inside the district. The entire communal administration lies in their hands. . . . When deficiencies occur, the Jews direct their resentment against the Jewish administrations and not against the German supervisors. Added to that is the widest freedom accorded to the Jews until now in so-called cultural activities. They have theatres, variety shows, coffee houses, etc. The Jews have opened public schools and to a considerable extent developed the trade school system.
>
> All of these measures have produced a certain reassurance which is necessary if their economic capacity is to be exploited for our purposes.[36]

Even as the Jewish victims affirmed life and humanity in this activity, the Nazis saw themselves—not the Jews—as the true architects of this activity; the Nazis thereby naturalized and normalized conditions in the ghetto in order to destroy its inhabitants all the more completely. That learning and scholarship somehow flourished under these conditions, writers still published, and the theatre and symphonies continued to play, is indisputable. But it was the meaning and significance accorded these activities by both killers and victims that ultimately functioned as agents in the perpetration of these atrocities. Real events were thus both "authored" and "authorized" by the various interpretations and understanding that sustained them.

From the diaries we infer how the writers saw themselves, how they grasped their condition in particular figures, and how this grasp led to particular actions. In the case of Czerniakow, for example, one figure in particular reveals several kinds of knowledge to us now—even as it may have determined the diarist's own understanding of himself: "Many people hold a grudge against me for organizing play activity for the children, for arranging festive openings of playgrounds, for the music, etc. I am reminded of a film: a ship is sinking and the captain, to raise the spirits of the passengers, orders the orchestra to play a jazz piece. I had made up my mind to emulate the captain" (pp. 376–77). Though even his role as captain of a sinking ship could not be sustained, this passage simultaneously suggests Czerniakow's private despair and his awareness that his role was therefore not actually to save his "passengers" but only to make their last moments seem as normal as possible.

To a more limited extent, even Czerniakow's suicide becomes less un-expected given this and other figures by which he both represented and seemed to grasp himself, particularly that of the saint and martyr. In his reflections on Czerniakow's diary, Nachman Blumental thus finds that the diarist "began to develop the ideal of the passive martyr, the 'saint,' who accepts pain and suffering in order to redeem and emancipate others . . . a sort of 'Anhelli' . . . who by his suffering purifies the Polish people of its sins and brings about its redemption."[37] Though sainthood and martyrdom may not have been conscious ideals toward which Czerniakow actively as-pired in his ghetto life, as Blumental suggests, as figures of self-under-standing they may nevertheless have provided a framework in which to ground both his condition and his role in the ghetto. As such, they may have explained his actions to himself even as they eventually contributed to them.

In this light, both the larger traditional paradigms Chaim Kaplan brought to his ghetto diary and the specific figures and tropes in his nar-rative become significant: both for the ways they reflect various biblical resonances available to him in Hebrew and for the manner in which they determined the shape and meaning he gave his experiences. That is, his metaphors were never purely descriptive of events but were also *pre*scriptive of particular interpretations. For example, when he wrote, "I gazed at the Dantean scene of Warsaw, and could not stop thinking: are we really guiltier than any other nation? Have we sinned more than other people?" (p. 210), he seemed to allow a somewhat reflexive analogy to draw its conclusions for him. For even though the metaphor of hell and damnation clearly casts no light on the reasons for the singling out of the Jews for extermination, it does begin to explain why Kaplan would entertain such conclusions, even skeptically. It seems that once the analogy was drawn, its extensions fol-lowed almost unbidden.

When Kaplan reflexively balanced a destruction with a corresponding redemption on an almost daily basis in his diary, it may not have been because every catastrophe in the ghetto actually had its redeeming coun-terpart. But in selecting events for the day's journal entry, Kaplan seemed automatically to grasp his situation in terms of the traditional destruction-redemption dialectic, in which every new destruction in the ghetto was automatically accompanied by good news "from the front":

> And so Hitler's army has encircled a metropolis of two million people with heavy artillery, shut off the water supply, damaged the electricity, and deprived them of all food and provisions. And for ten hours let loose a barrage of fire and brimstone and red-hot iron upon them.

Suddenly, however, a new wind blew among the people of the city. We instinctively felt that a change had taken place for our good. That the next hours would bring salvation was whispered from mouth to mouth, brightening every dark and gloomy face. Various rumors were spread in whispers. From the nearby front many soldiers started to pour into the city and were immediately besieged by civilians waiting for some sort of word.

Suddenly a proclamation swept through the city: Armistice! (P. 38)

There was, of course, no armistice on that or any other day for 500,000 inhabitants of the ghetto. But insofar as destruction and redemption are dialectically linked in the covenantal tradition, the tradition itself seemed to select both the details of the day and the significance the diarist found in them. To some extent, even if no event actually occurred to redeem a particular tragedy, the promise of redemption implicit in the governing mythos nearly always did appear to the victims, which generated hope, which in turn may have helped to sustain survival another day. A paradigm like the destruction-redemption dialectic thus seemed to cut two ways: it shaped experience and perception on an illusory basis but possibly also preserved life (or the will to live) on an equally "illusory" basis. Illusory or not, however, the ways in which such a mythos informed the diarist's understanding of himself, his people, and ghetto life held concrete consequences for both the events and the telling of them as they occurred.

Even though the special authenticity and authority that attend all writing from within events might not confer an indisputable factuality on the victims' diaries, they do lend much greater weight to the significance of the interpretations implicit in these narratives. In this sense, the diaries assume importance far beyond whatever "facts" they could possibly deliver, for the interpretive truths reflected and constructed within these narratives may ultimately have constituted the bases for action taken by the writer and his community: the interpretation of events in the writer's narrative, religious, and linguistic schemata might thus be said to have weaved itself back into the unfolding course of events.

Unlike retrospective interpretations of memoirists and even latter-day historians, the diarists' figures and narrative mythoi functioned as agents in their daily lives. As such, a "poetics" of the diarists' testimony becomes invaluable to readers, both for understanding how narrative generates interpretation and how interpretations of events as they occurred may have influenced the course they ultimately took. In the final analysis, nothing can be more "authentic" than the ways in which the diarists' interpretations of experiences gathered the weight and force of agency in their lives; nothing is more authentic than the consequences for a life that issue from the manner in which this life may have been narrated the previous day. In fact, it might thus be said that the ghetto diarist's interpretation of events—and not the putative factuality of an account—is the authentic truth of his narrative.

V. CONCLUSION

The need for evidence in historical writing has always been paramount, used as it is to illustrate and justify particular renderings and explanations of events. But without understanding the constructed nature of evidence itself, and then separating the need for evidence from its actual rhetorical function as that which both naturalizes and is naturalized by a writer's governing mythos, we forfeit a deeper understanding of the interpenetration between events, narrative, and historical interpretation. That is, when we turn to literary testimony of the Holocaust, we do so for knowledge— not evidence—of events. Instead of looking for evidence of experiences, the reader might concede that narrative testimony documents not the experiences it relates but rather the conceptual presuppositions through which the narrator has apprehended experience. If the diarists' and memoirists' literary testimony is evidence of anything else, it is of the writing act itself. That is, even if narrative cannot document events, or constitute perfect *fact*uality, it can document the *act*uality of writer and text. The writer and his link to events may thus be reified not in the writer's words but in the writing activity that brought words to the page. Narrative strategy, structure, and style all become forms of commentary on the writing act itself, now evident by the text it has produced.

In their actuality after the facts, diaries from the camps and ghettos may indeed be taken as literal artifacts of this era. In some cases, the diaries' physical materiality—as scraps of paper, pieces of wood, or torn handbills— may even lend these texts the evidentiary authority repeated attestations from within the narrative cannot. Through what Peirce might have cited as their indexical relation to the events they signify,[38] diaries such as Ringelblum's, which was stuffed into milk cans in Warsaw, or those buried in food tins next to the crematoria at Auschwitz by the *Sonderkommando*, retain their links to time, place, and events. It might thus be to the diary's actuality—not its factuality—that we turn to satisfy our need for evidence in Holocaust literary testimony.

As insistent as the survivor-memoirist is on establishing evidence of the crimes against him and his people, in the end it might be said that, like the diarist-victim who documented his own activity as diarist, the memoirist documents nothing more persuasively than his own existence after the Holocaust. The survivor's literature thus becomes testimony not so much to the deaths at Auschwitz but to his life after Auschwitz. A survivor's writing after the Holocaust is proof that he has defeated the "final solution"; it is indisputable evidence that he now exists, a notion that no survivor ever takes for granted. "I write to prove that I am," says Mendel Mann, "that I exist, that I too am still on the planet. The world condemned me to die. *I write because, through my books, I bear witness to my existence.*"[39] For Mann, writing is the ultimate assertion of self over experience, a refutation (though not a denial) of experiences that might have consumed him. In so many words, Mendel Mann has said, "I write, therefore I am."

In the cases of diarists and memoirists of the Holocaust, writing not only affirms the writer's existence, but it also ensures their literary existence afterwards. By converting their experiences into written texts, the writers become self-sustaining and self-perpetuating. They become those who write and are written, in Derrida's words.[40] In a phenomenology of literary testimony, this point is crucial: for it is only after the survivor has affirmed his own existence that he can then perceive himself as a witness or trace of the events to which he testifies. In this way, the witness attempts desperately to extend "I write, therefore I am" to "I write, therefore the Holocaust was."

Though the dilemma these writers face when they find that their testimony simultaneously objectifies, transforms, and displaces their experiences has paralyzed the literary impulse in some survivors, others persist in their work. The Holocaust survivor who continues to testify in narrative seems to have intuited the paradoxical knowledge that even though his words are no longer traces of the Holocaust, without his words, the Holocaust takes no form at all. That is, even as he realizes that his words are not in themselves proof of events, he finds that what was no longer takes shape outside of his words. He fears the Derridean suggestion that "things come into existence and lose existence by being named," but he finds solace in the Hegelian corollary that there is "simultaneous sacrifice of existence to the word and consecration of existence by the word" (p. 70).

Even though the literary documentarists of the Holocaust are still apt to call theirs a "literature of testimony," on balance this remains partly an effort to assert and even create a testimonial authority in their texts and partly an attempt to satisfy the phenomenological need in their work for this authority. But as I have tried to show, it cannot be a literal description of this literature's actual function. Having explored the sources of this need for testimonial authority in Holocaust narrative, however, we might accept this impulse even as we look beyond it. Though critics of other documentary literature have begun to focus attention on the issue of narrativity in this genre, most stop short of calling into question the documentary and testimonial demands this literature makes upon itself. But by neglecting a narratological critique of these claims themselves, I believe we fail to highlight the crucial difference between this literature's "rhetoric of fact" and invaluable function as historical exegesis.

As most historical theorists now acknowledge, the legitimacy and value of historical sources cannot rest solely on their factual element, in which case readers would be endlessly troubled by conflicting versions. Instead of disqualifying competing accounts, the critical reader accepts that every Holocaust writer has a "different story" to tell, not because what happened to so many others was intrinsically "different," but because *how* victims and survivors have grasped and related their experiences comprises the actual core of "their story." In this view, it is not a matter of whether one set of facts is more veracious than another, or whether the facts have been transformed in narrative at all. The aim of an inquiry into "literary testimony" is rather to determine *how* writers' experiences have been shaped both in and out of narrative. Once we recognize that the "facts" of history are not distinct from their reflexive interpretation in narrative, and that the "facts" of the Holocaust and their interpretation may even have been fatally interdependent, we are able to look beyond both the facts and the poetics of literary testimony to their consequences.

TWO

From Witness to Legend

Tales of the Holocaust

It was like a page torn from some storybook . . .

—Elie Wiesel

I

Before turning to the rhetorical uses of testimony in Holocaust fiction, we might look briefly at another little-explored literary hybrid of the Holocaust: tales and legends of this time told by survivors. On a narrative continuum between the diaries and the fiction, there is a smaller, less perceptible movement from memoir to legend, where survivors retell actual events parabolically, even didactically, around preexisting cultural axioms. In this chapter, I will look at both those stories told according to legendary or mythic formulae and accounts that have in themselves accrued legendary status. Of these two kinds of tales, Yaffa Eliach's "Hasidic Tales of the Holocaust" exemplify the former, Sara Nomberg-Przytyk's "True Tales from a Grotesque Land" the latter. This line between memoirs and legend has never been entirely distinct, and with so much genuine confusion on the parts of publishers, editors, writers, and readers, it demands a closer look. By tracing this movement between witnesses' testimony and their legends, we can keep intact the greater distinction between "novels of memory" written by survivors and "fictional memoirs" by documentary novelists, whose only claim to eyewitness or victimization is fabricated in their fiction.

In this context, what might have remained a relatively benign oversight in a collection with less than scholarly pretensions assumes problematic proportions in Yaffa Eliach's *Hasidic Tales of the Holocaust*.[1] Where in their first printing these tales are "edited by" Eliach, in later editions Oxford University Press has somewhat indecorously whitened over "edited by" with correction fluid, leaving the relationship between Eliach and these tales ambiguously unstated altogether. The title page on current paperback editions indicates that these stories are now "by" Eliach. Unfortunately, these changes on the title page ultimately reflect too aptly both the author-editor's and the publisher's confusion as to whether Eliach was collecting these tales, thereby anthologizing them, or actually writing them herself.

Normally, one wouldn't harp on an otherwise harmless emendation and risk diverting attention from important contributions a book like this can make to Holocaust understanding. But in light of the issues raised in the preceding section, it becomes increasingly difficult to ignore the manner in which events have been recovered and represented. For we now realize that the primary critical issue at hand often is precisely the manner in which literary and ritual forms of remembrance both reflect the nature of events and determine our current understanding of them. In failing to distinguish the shape her own narrative hand has given Hasidic experiences from that of the original storytellers, Eliach betrays a surprisingly ingenuous approach to what are in effect her own works of fiction, written in a Hasidic mode. Though it seems plausible that Eliach has indeed discovered in the Hasidic tale a new genre of Holocaust literature, as she suggests, she may not have found it so much as created it herself.

In brief, Eliach has committed to writing some eighty-nine Holocaust tales gathered over several years from personal interviews with Hasidic survivors, extractions of interviews by her students, *motzeh shabbat* storytelling sessions, and a handful of written remnants left behind by the late Hasidic community of Europe. "The original interviews were conducted in more than nine languages and in numerous dialects," she tells us, and then she continues with a description of her method:

> When I myself did the interviewing, I have indicated so at the end of the tale, and, depending on whether I tape-recorded it or recalled it from conversation, have written either "Based on my interview with" or "I heard it from, or at the house of . . . " I translated the stories into English, extracting the raw material of the tale from the mass of the interview and rewriting it in consistent literary style so as to give the tales a cohesive form and structure. But in the process of transforming the material from documentation to art, I made a conscious effort to remain as faithful as possible to both the literary genre of the Hasidic tale as well as the individual storyteller and the particular historical event. (Pp. xxiii–iv)

That is, the aim here was primarily to preserve the form of the Hasidic tale itself, along with its particular lessons and truths. In simultaneously attempting to preserve the events as well, however, Eliach can finally transmit them only as they are legendarily reformulated to fit Hasidic principles of righteousness and justice. The initial confusion on the title page is thus aggravated in the author's foreword, for even as she acknowledges several layers of structuring, translating, and conforming to genre, she insists on an untenable historicity in these tales: they are simultaneously history and legend, documentation and art.

As important as it is to link these tales and events, Eliach takes her stories one step further still and attempts to verify events through them. "Once the internal organization of these stories emerged and my work on the book became structured, I felt that yet another element was missing: the transformation of the material from testimony to art was not yet complete without historical verification," she writes, and then elaborates:

> Until that point, I had satisfied only two of my disciplines: Hasidism and Holocaust, but not history. I took the tales through yet another phase, completing a cycle from documentation to art and back to documentation. I examined each tale for its historical accuracy and plausibility: Did such an incident indeed take place on a particular date and location as told by the original storyteller? Whenever possible, I verified the events and the credibility of the tale. (P. xxviii)

As understandable as the impulse may be to locate the source of a particular tale, it remains here more a matter of literary historical curiosity concerning the original setting of a tale than a search for historical veracity. Indeed, if the figure of the mythological *zaddik* (righteous man) is as central to these stories as Eliach suggests, and if, "Unlike the Greek or Christian hero, the zaddik possesses a larger-than-life personality and mystical powers which enable him to transcend the historical reality of his surroundings" (p. xviii), then her insistence on the historical credibility of these tales becomes even more puzzling.

For in fact, many of these stories are clearly legendary, anchored firmly in the rich tradition of Hasidic storytelling, often merely re-emplotted to encompass elements of the Hasidic survivors' horrible experiences. In some cases, these stories become the seeds of new legends, tales that in time will achieve a certain legendary status of their own. Taken for what they are— parables that have been collectively recalled, retold, translated, and then written for the first time—these tales ultimately offer fascinating, even inspirational, insight into the humane Hasidic apprehension of the most inhuman of times. But they are not documents of fact amenable to historical verification and analysis, as their author guilelessly insists in her foreword. Rather, they are necessarily allegorical and parabolic in both mode and intent, affirmations of spirit over fact, the triumph of vision over events. These Hasidic tales of the Holocaust document not the history of the Holocaust, or "the inner spiritual world of the Holocaust victim" in general (as Eliach suggests), but a uniquely Hasidic understanding of events, the sustenance of wisdom and tradition in the face of events that would negate both.

In the first story of this collection, "Hovering above the Pit," it is thus not so important that the huge death pit at Janowska, over which Rabbi Spira of Sluzhov is being forced hopelessly to jump, existed precisely in that form and place as Eliach's extensive footnotes insist, or that the original teller of this story, the rabbi, actually leaped over the pit at all. For we have not come to these tales for documentable miracles; nor has the rabbi told his story merely to transmit an event. More important is the ever-faithful rabbi's explanation as to how he and his freethinking friend have—*baruch ha-shem*—landed safely on the other side:

> "Spira, we are here, we are here, we are alive!" the friend repeated over and over again while warm tears streamed from his eyes. "Spira, for your sake, I am alive; indeed, there must be a God in heaven. Tell me, Rebbe, how did you do it?"
>
> "I was holding on to my ancestral merit. I was holding on to the coattails of my father, and my grandfather and my great-grandfather, of blessed memory," said the rabbi and his eyes searched the black skies above. "Tell me, my friend, how did *you* reach the other side of the pit?"
>
> "I was holding on to you," replied the rabbi's friend. (P. 4)

Thus perhaps has Eliach held tightly to the coattails of her own ancestral merit in bringing these stories back to us from the other side of the abyss. But in so assiduously locating these legends in particular times and places, she forces the reader away from the legendary truths and insights these stories endow events, to something else. And in so doing, she suggests that the wisdom created in these legends is more creditable because it stems from actual—rather than imagined—events.

As charming and gentle as these stories are, they remain in this edition somewhat anomalous, neither wholly Eliach's nor the Hasidic storytellers'. Even the author's own story—that of a little Jewish girl bundled into hiding—buried deep in the pages of others' tales, seems to fall somewhere between the apocryphal and the autobiographical. With this critique in mind, the reader might thus allow these stories their own lives and begin to appreciate the ways in which Eliach is as much a part of these tales as they are now a part of her. In fact, it may not matter that she has retold them so innocently. For as listener, she has only done what the storyteller would always ask both of her and of us: that, once we hear these tales, we make them our own. In this way, the story—not the teller—becomes the last ember of the Holocaust, which in being passed down in print would now survive us all.

I I

In a different kind of collection, Sara Nomberg-Przytyk does not attempt to document her experiences, or anyone else's, so much as she finds truth in events by weaving them into the legendary realm. In *Auschwitz: True Tales from a Grotesque Land*, Nomberg-Przytyk simultaneously relates and creates historical truth in the legends of Auschwitz, which she simultaneously writes and rewrites. By narrating her experiences in Stutthof, Auschwitz, and Ravensbrück through a series of highly polished vignettes, Nomberg-Przy-tyk preserves the sense of broken time and lives that might have been artificially mended in one long story. In the process, she also allows each story to generate its own discrete truth, its own possibilities of meaning, without submerging itself in the sea of so many other experiences. Beautifully written by Nomberg-Przytyk and gracefully translated from the Polish by Roslyn Hirsch, each of these "true tales from a grotesque land" might thus stand on its own, each parabolic of a particular theme, the collected mass of which begins to represent one woman's experience of the Holocaust.[2]

From the beginning, the author's ironic sensibility reflects well the grotesque realities of a world turned upside-down, where expectations and conventions are perverted at every step: where victims are inscribed in the books and ledgers of death (not life), and the women, children, and elderly are the first to be murdered (not saved). In a final twist toward the end of her ordeal, the narrator must even show her tattooed number to get into a freight train going back to Poland. Painfully aware of how the Nazis generated this confusion precisely to disorient the victims and to facilitate the murder process, the teller of these tales begins to doubt even her own judgments. Watching as a young and vibrant mother is selected for the gas, the narrator thinks to herself, "She is really young and pretty. Why did they write her number down?" and then adds insightfully, "I trembled at that logic, as though there were some justification in killing the sick, the elderly, and the unattractive" (p. 29). Self-consciously critical of her own archaic logic, she gently reminds the readers to distrust their automatic moral judgments in the face of such events.

Among these tales, several are variations on now-legendary events at Auschwitz: the young Romeo and Juliet lovers who defy the SS right to the moment of their deaths; the killing of newborn babies by the mothers' barracks-mates; the disarming and shooting of an SS officer by a young woman on her way to the gas; the demolition of one of the crematoria by the *Sonderkommando*. As we discover, however, each telling adds new dimensions both to the events and to our understanding of them and their effect on the prisoners themselves. Each version establishes a different set of moral implications, a different frame of critical reference; each raises new questions and is witness to a different act: of resistance, of rage, of courage, of revenge, or of desperation.

To these apocryphal stories, the author adds several of her own, among them the inspired tale of a young madwoman in "Natasha's Triumph." Many other writers have found in madness a singularly appropriate figure for Auschwitz (recall Wiesel's Mad Moshé and Madame Schächter, for two examples). In Sara's story, Natasha, a reportedly deranged nineteen-year-old from Leningrad, is brought to the infirmary with several other lunatics, where she becomes both prophet and tormentor for Joseph Mengele:

"Hey, you! Doctor! Maybe you can come and see us." It was Natasha calling to Mengele; she was speaking to him in beautiful German, her voice radiant with happiness.

"What are you afraid of, coward, you who can murder women and children? Come here. We will discuss your Hitler's crimes. Maybe you want to discuss Stalingrad, where you are dying like mad dogs. . . .

"You will all die in Russia, the way Napoleon did. You are afraid to come to me. You don't want to listen to the truth, you specialist of the gas chambers." (Pp. 95–96)

Only the mad speak the truth in this universe, only they see through the madness of events to grasp them. In Sara's story, Mengele seems to recognize this and so comes to visit Natasha every day, sitting as if at the foot of a seer, "on the chair with his head hung low on his chest" (p. 96).

As the editors of this collection suggest in their critical afterword, however, the value of these stories lies not in their supposed historical record, or in their artful invitation to historical credulity, but somewhere in between. That is, like other literary narratives of the Holocaust, these tales reflect as much an understanding of events as they do the actual details of history. From her opening tale, "Alienation," through "Erika's Red Triangle," "The Dance of the Rabbis," "Old Women," and "The Road Back," among many others, Nomberg-Przytyk allows her imagination to run freely to encompass both the surrealities and realities of history—and the nightmare blend of the two. For as the editors wisely remind us, even though Sara is at some level a documentarist, "it is as novelist that she heightens the reader's awareness of the complexity of the moral and ethical problems posed by Auschwitz" (p. 172). That is, through the narrative interplay of history and imagination, insights and understanding into events are both generated and disclosed. As becomes clear, in addition to heightening the reader's awareness of the moral complexities of Auschwitz, the author of these stories also directs the reader's understanding of these problems through her selection of details and imagery.

The shapes of these tales are not dependent, however, only on the legendary motifs the teller finds and creates in her experiences; they are due in large measure to the effect her experiences have had on her own self-understanding. For in some instances, it is not only the vagaries of imagination and retellings that screen and select details in these stories, but Sara's own identification as both Jew and socialist may have combined with her anticipated first audience (the Polish authorities) to determine part of the shape these stories took when she wrote them in the 1960s. Though all self-editing, along with selection of details, is a form also of self-censorship, it would be presumptuous to suggest that the narrator here has practiced self-censorship only. But like any writer, neither has Nomberg-Przytyk ignored the expectations of her audience—which was going to be the government censors. Having anticipated her publishers' demands, the writer may have figured some of the most heroic acts in political terms. So even though the women plotting the destruction of the crematoria were Jewish communists, it was as communists alone that they acted in Sara's narrative, not as Jews. The ultimate irony, however, was that even though political prisoners (i.e., socialists and communists) seem to outnumber Jews in Sara's Auschwitz, her Polish editors still found too many Jews in it (this was just after the Six-Day War in 1967) and asked her to expunge reference to them altogether. She refused, and the book was turned down. She eventually emigrated, and the book was deposited at Yad Vashem, whence it was recovered and published.

Writing these tales in Poland as a sequel to her first collection about her political internment as a communist before the war, Nomberg-Przytyk thus strives to balance communist with Jewish prisoners. Though Sara represents in her stories all kinds of victims—e.g., Soviet POW's, Gypsies, and Hasidim—nearly all the activists and rebels in the camp are communists, while the ones who suffer most stoically seem to be Jews. Interned as a political prisoner before the war and then as a Jew during the war, she identified in her victimization as prisoner with both communists and Jews and inevitably blurs the distinction between their respective kinds of victimization. In fact, it is not clear in Sara's narrative whether she was sent to Auschwitz as a political prisoner or as a Jew; and this ambiguity in itself seems to represent Sara's own understanding of her situation as a prisoner. In a strange way, even if Sara was interned as a Jew, she was probably saved from death by her political affiliations, which gained her an unqualified kind of *proteksia* among the camp bureaucrats.

But this is only implicit, for as a former political prisoner, she necessarily knows her Jewish internment in terms of her political internment; and then, at the end, faced with renewed political persecution, she seems to understand it in light of her Jewish persecution. As she had feared for her Jewish life in Auschwitz, on her return to Poland, she feared the Poles would now strangle her as a Red (p. 161). At the end of her tales, she seems to understand her condition as a Red in terms of her persecution as a Jew: a natural reflex perhaps for someone victimized separately for both "crimes." So even though her story begins in a Jewish key, it ends in a Red key, with each figure of victimization now informing the other.

As we see in legendary stories that deviate widely from other versions, whether or not events transpired precisely as the author relates them ultimately matters less than the paradigms by which they have been recovered, even reinvented. Thus, in "Revenge of a Dancer," Nomberg-Przytyk relates the tale of a woman on her way to the gas chamber who shot SS *Unterscharführer* Schillinger. Passed from mouth to mouth, from barracks to barracks in the camp, this incident accrued legendary proportions almost immediately at the time, with every teller adding new significance to it. Like other versions, Nomberg-Przytyk's is told in the first person and invokes an eyewitness within the story itself to relate authoritatively what happened. Even though Nomberg-Przytyk could not have been at Auschwitz during this event (she arrived in January 1944, while the shooting occurred in October 1943), her telling and the truths it relates are both reinforced by the fabricated witness in her text. The point is that by the time Nomberg-

Przytyk arrived at Auschwitz, this legend had assumed a life of its own: Nomberg-Przytyk is not witness to this event, but both teller and witness of a legend born of this event.

Since this "dancer's revenge" was memorable for its exemplary heroism, like other versions, this tale reconstructs the woman in classically heroic and martyrological terms. "In my compartment there were women with children and a young dancer from Paris," the eyewitness tells our story's narrator. "She was an unusually beautiful woman, very pleasant and courteous. She helped the mothers keep the children amused" (p. 108). When ordered to strip naked before leaving the train, the dancer refuses and is approached by an SS guard.

> "Beautiful girl, take off your suit," he said quietly, coming closer and closer to her. Then, all of a sudden, with a rapid movement, she grabbed the pistol out of his holster and shot straight at him. After that, she took three steps backward and shot at the SS men who were running all over the place. She saved the last bullet for herself. She fell to the ground. (p. 109)

Because this is the way heroism "is supposed to be," the antifascist organizer of the group declares, "That's how you're supposed to die"—unbroken, proud, and resisting.

In this respect, Nomberg-Przytyk's "true tale" jibes with accounts of other victims, for whom such an act was turned within minutes into exemplary legend. According to Wieslaw Kielar in his memoir, *Anus Mundi: Five Years in Auschwitz*, "This incident passed on from mouth to mouth and embellished in various ways grew into a legend." And as legend, it was told with a particular legendary quality in mind, which now had its objectification for the prisoners in the camp. Kielar continues here to suggest the consequences of this deed in its legendary form:

> Without doubt this heroic deed by a weak woman, in the face of certain death, gave moral support to every prisoner. We realized all at once that if we dared raise a hand against them, that hand might kill; they were mortal, too.
>
> Because they feared the consequences of this significant deed, the SS men tried to terrorize the camp. . . . Reaction [to the shooting] came swiftly; prisoners staightened up, hope grew once more. A spontaneous, although still weak, campaign of self-defense was born.
>
> On the afternoon of that same day some people lined up in the little woods next to crematorium 4 and took to active resistance. When I heard the sound of vigorous gunfire I ran with Waldeck to our stand in Block 15. Strictly speaking, by the time we got there it was all over. Here and there single shots could be heard. The little woods were strewn with corpses, mainly men. They were still dressed.[3]

In her version of the legend, Nomberg-Przytyk has distilled the same aspects that have made this event legendary in the first place: she writes a legend of resistance and dignity, which uses the event as it has been passed down to her. And as Kielar tells us, the spontaneous turning of this event into legend had immediate consequences in itself. Once recounted, it assumed idealized forms by which other prisoners began to measure themselves.

As the editors Pfefferkorn and Hirsch suggest, however, alternate versions of this episode by Kogon and Bettelheim have also been used "as a cudgel . . . on other prisoners who did not do what the ' . . . dancer' did."[4] In Bettelheim's view, of course, both the woman's resistance and the return to her supposed profession as dancer asserted her humanity in the face of the Nazis' dehumanizing killing process. Though in fact, whether or not she was a dancer at all depends on the teller's view: in some stories she dances alluringly to draw Schillinger near, in order to shoot him. In others, she is merely protecting herself against his leering advances. Whether she danced for a living or not, heroic strategy may have turned the woman into a dancer; once referred to figuratively as "the dancer" (as Filip Müller relates below), her occupation in the camp legend was necessarily determined for her.

In fact, the most detailed account of "the dancer" comes in the memoir of Filip Müller, who was present in the changing room of the gas chamber and watched the entire incident. He describes a beautiful woman who attracted the attention of *SS Unterscharführer* Schillinger and Quackernack as she undressed.

> The woman, as soon as she noticed that the two men were ogling her, launched into what appeared to be a titillating and seductive strip-tease act. She lifted her skirt to allow a glimpse of thigh and suspender. Slowly she undid her stocking and peeled it off her foot. From out of the corner of her eye she carefully observed what was going on round her. The two SS men were fascinated by her performance and paid no attention to anything else. . . .
>
> She had taken off her blouse and was standing in front of her lecherous audience in her brassiere. Then she steadied herself against a concrete pillar with her left arm and bent down, slightly lifting her foot, in order to take off her shoe. What happened next took place with lightning speed: quick as a flash she grabbed her shoe and slammed its high heel violently against Quackernack's forehead. He winced with pain and covered his face with both hands. At this moment the young woman flung herself at him and made a quick grab for his pistol. Then there was a shot. Schillinger cried out and fell to the ground. Seconds later there was a second shot aimed at Quackernack which narrowly missed him.[5]

She then disappeared into the back of the crowded changing room, Müller tells us, whence she shot another SS guard who had come to help Schillinger. At this point, the lights went out and the doors were closed, trapping all—including the members of the *Sonderkommando*—in the dressing room. "There was considerable speculation as to the identity of the woman who had fired the shots," Müller writes, after which she is referred to as "that young dancer" by one of the other victims. This was another kind of "death-dance," however, a variation perhaps of the death tango danced by others on their way to the gas chambers.

As the lesson of this tale varied from Bettelheim to Kogon, Nomberg-Przytyk to Kielar, it was altogether different for the SS and for the *Son-derkommando*—the only actual witnesses to survive the event. According to *Sonderkommando* survivors Filip Müller and Stanislaw Jankowski, and to the editors of *SS Unterscharführer* Pery Broad's "reminiscences,"[6] the principal lesson of this experience was the danger to the SS of prisoners who came to grasp their fate in the gas chambers, who realized they had nothing to lose by resisting at the last moment; it was the danger of letting down one's guard in this operation. After the shooting of Schillinger, according to Müller, all but the *Sonderkommando* were gassed or cut down by machine guns in the changing room. The next day, Müller tells us, "The body of the young dancer was laid out in the dissecting room of crematorium 2.. SS men went there to look at her corpse before its incineration. Perhaps the sight of her was to be a warning as well as an illustration of the dire consequences one moment's lack of vigilance might have for an SS man" (p. 89). The significance of this act for the SS is corroborated in *SS Unter-scharführer* Broad's reminiscences as well. For Broad this incident has little to do with heroism but illustrates instead the Nazis' own reasons for continuing the deception of victims: "It also occurred that whole transports were fully aware of their impending fate. The murderers had to be very careful in such cases. Otherwise they could be shot with their own pistols, as had happened in the case of *SS Unterscharführer* Schillinger" (p. 179).

Depending on the teller of the story, this heroine is either Jewish, French, Italian, Polish, Czech, or American; a dancer or a singer; dressed in a bathing suit or a dress; beautiful or plain looking. Depending on who told the tale and who received it, the incident represented courage, desperation, resistance, justice, or hope; and as it represented these categories for the prisoners, it also inspired the prisoners to act on them. Through the different versions of this legend, we come to learn as much about the mythification of events by different populations within the camp as we do about actual events themselves. The variations in this legend from teller to teller thus bespeak the multiplicity of meaning this legend held for both the victims in Auschwitz and for the rememberers afterward.[7]

The aim in comparing several variant versions of the same event is not to find the truest, or the one that corresponds most closely to the reality, or to undermine the credibility of these witnesses. It is rather to trace the manner in which this act has been grasped by several different survivors, how they have assimilated it to other preexisting legends and to their own understanding of the camp, how it has reinforced particular truths already held, how it was molded to conform to their beliefs, and how it was sustained imaginatively as a kind of inspiration to other victims. For as almost all versions make clear, it seems to have become legend precisely because it served so well as both inspiration to and paradigm of resistance. This is a kind of on-the-scene legend-making in which events are immediately and simultaneously recounted, interpreted, imbued with significance, and then passed down as an implied call to action.

Like Eliach, the editors of Nomberg-Przytyk's collection of tales have perceived the need in such narrative for an accompanying critical commentary to clarify the difficulties readers may have with the oxymoronic term "true tales" of the Holocaust. Unlike Eliach, however, Pfefferkorn and Hirsch have not asked the reader to accept these tales as documents of fact but have preferred to delineate the blurred lines between "truth" in fiction, memory, and imagination. "It is a story about the telling of a story," they write, "in fact about the telling of six million stories, or maybe six million tellings of one story . . . " (p. 163). As sensitive as they are to the literariness of history, however, the editors may still be a little too adamant in their distinction between history and fiction. In weighing realistic against what they term novelistic writing, they observe that a swing to pure imagination is as inadequate as pure realism, "for to cast the camp reality into wholly metaphoric structures would undermine the historicity of events." But as we have found in the diaries and memoirs, the problem may be how to do otherwise in literary narrative.

For even though the sense of historicity is indeed ameliorated in metaphoric language, this is not to say that historical truths and understanding are also compromised. For in fact, these truths are actually generated by metaphoric structures, in narrative, and through the mythoi in which they are necessarily framed. The aim in these "true tales" may not be "to portray a grotesque world and yet make it seem historically true," as the editors suggest (p. 168). For a sense of historical truth can be generated quite as easily to reinforce lies as well as facts. But rather, we might come to these tales precisely to see how the author's metaphoric structures and artful language inevitably created understanding of these events for both the victims *and* the readers. Where historical truth stops and fiction begins becomes a less appropriate issue in this view than how the sense—or rhetoric—of historical truth is used within fiction itself to naturalize a novelist's own construction of events.

THREE

Holocaust Documentary Fiction

Novelist as Eyewitness

Imagination and memory are but one thing, which for divers
considerations hath divers names.

—Thomas Hobbes

There is no fiction or nonfiction as we commonly understand
the distinction: there is only narrative.

—E. L. Doctorow

That is what the survivors are afraid of, the tricks of art.

—Arnold Wesker

I

The impulse in Holocaust writers to insist on a documentary link between
their texts and the events inspiring them has not been limited to diarists
and memoirists: it extends to the novelists and playwrights of the Holocaust
as well. Where the diarists and memoirists have struggled to preserve or
reconstruct the eyewitness authority displaced by their narrative, however,
the "docu-novelists" and "docu-dramatists" of the Holocaust work as hard
at manufacturing their own testimonial authority as part of their fictional
discourse. In many cases, their reasons for reinforcing the factual authority
in narrative are similar: all of these writers seem to fear that the rhetoricity
of their literary medium inadvertently confers a fictiveness onto events
themselves. But in many other cases, the novelists' reasons for fabricating
an eyewitness authority in their fiction stem more from traditional aesthetic
and dramatic than from documentary interests. In addition to exploring
the ways in which documentary authority is constructed within Holocaust
fiction, this chapter will look at how testimony is adopted rhetorically as a
narrative strategy in this fiction.

On the one hand, it is difficult to argue with the spirit of Hana Wirth-
Nesher's suggestion that "While all narratives are imaginative reconstruc-

tions, when it comes to those of mass suffering, we should be particularly vigilant about honoring the line between fact and fiction."[1] On the other hand, it may be just as difficult to delineate this border between fact and fiction in the first place; for as long as facts are presented to us in fictionalizing media and fiction is presented as fact, the categories themselves remain all too fuzzily defined. If there is a line between fact and fiction, it may by necessity be a winding border that tends to bind these two categories as much as it separates them, allowing each side to dissolve occasionally into the other.

In an article about William Styron's *Sophie's Choice*, Arnold Wesker also wants to know both "Where we [are] dealing with fact and where with fiction" and "Why, in this novel more than any other, do I want to know?"[2] Even though she is not referring specifically to Styron's novel, Barbara Foley answers this question in part, in reference to a semifictional character in another of the "docu-novels," Gerald Green's *Holocaust*:

> By claiming for Dorf a status halfway between history and myth . . . and by grafting this hybrid creature onto a fictive tale that purports to encompass the enormity of the Holocaust in a single tale of victimization and villainy—Green at once reduces agony to the status of melodrama and distorts the locus of historical responsibility. *Holocaust* is not a fraudulent work simply because it aspires to make history accessible in a popular format . . . ; it is fraudulent because it both proposes a shallow resolution and catharsis and performs a frivolous reshuffling of historical facts.[3]

That is, the problem with this and other "documentary fictions" of the Holocaust is that by mixing actual events with completely fictional characters, a writer simultaneously relieves himself of an obligation to historical accuracy (invoking poetic license), even as he imbues his fiction with the historical authority of real events. By inviting this ambiguity, the author of documentary fiction would thus move the reader with the pathos created in the rhetoric of historically authentic characters, even as he suggests the possibility that both his events and those in the world are fictional.

Several other questions arise at this point: First, why is the writer of Holocaust fiction so forcefully compelled to assert the factual basis underlying his work? That is, why is it so important for novelists like D. M. Thomas, Jean-François Steiner, Gerald Green, and Anatoli Kuznetsov (among others) to establish an authoritative link between their fictions and the Holocaust experiences they represent? Second, to what extent do such claims to historical authority serve this literature's dramatic interests and to what extent its supposed documentary interests? And how does the perception of authority in the Holocaust novel affect the way readers approach and respond to Holocaust fiction? That is, can Holocaust documentary fiction ever really document events, or will it always fictionalize them?

Having explored already the process of making witness in the diaries and memoirs, we now turn to the ways authentic testimony is incorporated into the fictional text by novelists and used as a figure and literary device in Holocaust fiction. In this context, we will examine the rhetorical trope of eyewitness in Holocaust fiction and some of the narrative methods by which it is generated. For even as many novelists would claim on ethical grounds that they have had no "right" to imagine such suffering and must therefore rely on actual witnesses' voices, I find that these claims may in themselves also be part of their novelistic discourse. Whether a writer is attempting to retain an eyewitness authority in his diary or memoir or to fabricate it altogether in his documentary novel, testimony continues to function as the preeminent rhetorical trope underlying the very possibility of a "documentary narrative."

I I

This question of "documentary authority" in Holocaust fiction was brought into particularly sharp relief in the pages of the *Times Literary Supplement*, when letter writer D. A. Kenrick called readers' attention to the rather pronounced debt D. M. Thomas's novel *The White Hotel* owed to Anatoli Kuznetsov's "document in the form of a novel," *Babi Yar*.[4] As Kenrick and other indignant letter-writers pointed out, Thomas has not merely paraphrased Kuznetsov, but has actually quoted directly from the text of Kuznetsov's work, in what seems to be an attempt to infuse the most violent scenes in his Holocaust fiction with what he perceives to be their "documentary authority." The following are passages from both novels, the first from *Babi Yar*:

It began to grow dark.

Suddenly an open car drove up, carrying a tall, well-knit, elegant officer carrying a riding crop. . . . His [Russian] interpreter stood at his side.

"Who are these?" he asked a *Polizei* through his interpreter. There were about 50 people sitting on the hillock now.

"These are our people [Ukrainians]," replied the *Polizei*. "We weren't sure whether to release them."

"Shoot them! Shoot them right away!" stormed the officer. "If just one of them gets away and spreads the story, not a single Jew will come here tomorrow."

. . . "Get going! Move! Get up!" shouted the *Polizei*. They staggered to their feet as though drunk. It was already late, and this was perhaps why nothing was done to undress this group. Instead, they were led through the passage in the sand wall just as they were.

. . . Coming through the passage, they emerged on the brow of a deep sand quarry with almost sheer walls. All were herded to the left, single file, along a very narrow ledge.

The wall rose on the left, and the quarry fell away on the right. The ledge, evidently cut specially for the executions, was so narrow that the victims instinctively leaned against the sand wall so as not to fall in.

Dina glanced down and grew dizzy. The quarry was fearfully deep. Below lay a sea of bloody bodies. She caught sight of light machine guns strung out on the opposite side of the quarry, and also of German soldiers. They had lit a campfire and seemed to be cooking something.

When the file of victims had occupied the ledge, one of the Germans moved away from the fire, took his place at a machine gun and began shooting.[5]

And then from *The White Hotel*, where Thomas's omniscient narrator describes his heroine's fate at Babi Yar:

> . . . it started to get dark.
>
> Suddenly an open car drew up and in it was a tall, well-built, smartly turned-out officer with a riding crop in his hand. At his side was a Russian prisoner.
>
> "Who are these?" the officer asked the policeman, through the interpreter: pointing to the hillock, where there were about fifty people sitting by this time.
>
> "They are our people, Ukrainians. They were seeing people off; they ought to be let out."
>
> Lisa heard the officer shout: "Shoot the lot at once! If even one of them gets out of here and starts talking in the city, not a single Jew will turn up tomorrow."
>
> . . . "Come on then! Let's go! Get yourselves up!" the policeman shouted. The people stood up as if they were drunk. . . . Maybe because it was already late the Germans did not bother to undress this group, but led them through the gap in their clothes.
>
> . . . They went through the gap and came out into a sand quarry with sides practically overhanging. It was already half dark, and she could not see the quarry properly. One after the other, they were hurried on to the left, along a very narrow ledge.
>
> On their left was the side of the quarry, to the right a deep drop; the ledge had apparently been specially cut out for the purposes of the execution, and it was so narrow that as they went along it people instinctively leaned towards the wall of sandstone, so as not to fall in.
>
> . . . Lisa looked down and her head swam, she seemed so high up. Beneath her was a sea of bodies covered in blood. On the other side of the quarry she could just see the machine guns and a few soldiers. The German soldiers had lit a bonfire and it looked as though they were making coffee on it.
>
> . . . A German finished his coffee and strolled to a machine gun . . . [6]

Kenrick notes that many such resemblances might be found and then follows by alleging not plagiarism but rather a more subtle failing on Thomas's part. "It can be argued," Kenrick writes, "that Mr. Thomas has made moving use of the Babi Yar material. But should the author of a fiction choose as his proper subject events which are not only outside his own experience but also, evidently, beyond his own resources of imaginative re-creation?"

Kenrick neglects to mention, however, that Kuznetsov's own novel was also based upon the verbatim transcription of yet another testimonial source. By relying upon the remembrances of the Babi Yar survivor, Dina Pronicheva, as the basis for his narrative, Kuznetsov may also have been "beyond his own resources of imagination." Because he was not a victim and was too young to remember the surrounding details properly—i.e., with appropriate meaning—he has deferred to an actual survivor's testimony and to the authority it carries. If anything, Thomas and Kuznetsov thus seem to share similar motivations in their narrative technique, both believing that in some areas of their own fiction they have neither the right nor the requisite experience to reimagine such suffering.

In his reply to Kenrick, however, Thomas reminds readers that he had, in fact, declared his indebtedness to *Babi Yar* both in the book's acknowledgments and in many interviews. And then, after noting that since his account of Babi Yar is three times the length of Dina Pronicheva's testimony in Kuznetsov's novel and "equally spare in style," he goes on to offer his own critical interpretation—*qua* justification—of this passage:

> This section is where my heroine, Lisa Erdman, changes from being Lisa an individual to Lisa in history—an anonymous victim. It is this transition, reflected in style as well as content, which has moved and disturbed many readers. From individual self-expression she moves to the common fate. From the infinitely varied world of narrative fiction we move to a world in which fiction is not only severely constrained but irrelevant.
>
> At the outset of Part V, the narrative voice is still largely authorial (though affected by Pronicheva's tone) because there is still room for fiction; Lisa is still a person. But gradually her individuality is taken from her on that road to the ravine; and gradually the only appropriate voice becomes the voice which is like a recording camera: the voice of one who was there. It would have been perfectly easy for me to have avoided the possibility of such attacks as Kenrick's, through some spurious "imaginative re-creation"; but it would have been wrong. The witness's testimony was the truthful voice of the narrative at that point: "It started to get dark," etc. This is how it was—for all the victims. It could not be altered. The time for imagination was before; and, in my novel, after. Imagination, at the point quoted by Kenrick, is exhausted in the effort to take in the unimaginable which happened.[7]

In fact, Thomas even tried to make this point clear in the text of the novel itself, when his narrator explicitly attributes the authority for Lisa's experiences to Dina Pronicheva's testimony. As part of his fictional narrative, the author thus informs the reader that "Dina [Pronicheva] survived to be the only witness, the sole authority for what Lisa [i.e., Thomas's fictional heroine] saw and felt," adding, "Nor can the living ever speak for the dead" (p. 251).

Several issues pertinent to the question of literary testimony and authority emerge in this exchange. In noting that the most stunning passages of *The White Hotel* depend for their power on "the moving use" Thomas has made of the *Babi Yar* material, Kenrick suggests that the order of Thomas's fiction has been less "historical" than aesthetic, intended to excite the emotions and merely to move the reader. Sensitive to this charge and to the implication that he has used an authentic resource merely to heighten the horror in his account in order to exploit it further at the aesthetic level, Thomas answers that it is precisely because he was not there that he must constrain his fiction, that there are some events one has no right to imagine. The only legitimate voice, he implies, is the authentic, genuine voice of one who was there, who is empirically—not imaginatively—linked to these experiences.

At the same time, however, Thomas concedes somewhat ingenuously that he has affected an "equally spare style" because the "only appropriate voice becomes that voice which is like a recording camera: the voice of one who was there." But here he loses track, it seems, of whose voice is whose. For is the "appropriate voice" here that of Dina, the eyewitness, or is it the more figurative "voice" of his eyewitness style? If it is a voice that is like a recording camera, it is a style; if it is the literal voice of a person who was there, it is Dina's. For Thomas, however, this voice is both a style *and* Dina's actual voice, for Thomas has appropriated Dina's voice *as a style*, a rhetorical move by which he would impute to his fiction the authority of testimony without the authenticity of actual testimony.

Seemingly torn between presenting Babi Yar as a fictional construct and simultaneously asserting that Babi Yar was not a fiction, Thomas has thus labored to create the authority of an authentic witness within the realm of his text. To do otherwise, he suggests, "through 'spurious re-creation,' " would be to violate the factual integrity of real events, which are now "unimaginable" (i.e., not to be imagined) because they happened. The supreme irony in all of this, of course, is that by invoking Dina Pronicheva's testimony for his authority, Thomas is actually relying on Kuznetsov's own novelistic reconstruction of her account. Kuznetsov's declarations of his work's explicit factuality notwithstanding, Thomas is ultimately invoking a secondhand rendering of a third party's memory, which had been massively censored in the Russian, then rewritten (i.e., "uncensored") by Kuznetsov on his immigration to the West, and then translated: hardly the stuff of "authentic" or unmediated testimony. The point here is that no matter how strenuously Thomas defends his debt to Kuznetsov, as a fiction writer, even one so beholden to certain horrific facts, he is still a maker of illusions, which in this case become all the more persuasive because he imputes to them a testimonial authority. In fact, by so dutifully acknowledging both his debt to Kuznetsov and Lisa's debt to Dina, thereby establishing an apparent link between his text and a past fact, Thomas may be reinforcing the illusion of factual authority precisely in order to absolve himself of responsibility for making such an illusion.

The further irony here is that Thomas is ultimately at no more ethical risk than Kuznetsov himself; in fact, Kuznetsov has gone to much greater lengths than Thomas to reinforce his own rhetoric of fact. In his preface to *Babi Yar*, Kuznetsov frames all that follows with: "The word 'documentary' in the subtitle of this novel means that I am presenting only authenticated facts and documents and that here you will find not the slightest literary invention—that is, not 'how it might have happened' or 'how it should have been' " (p. xv). He invokes Aristotle's distinction between history and poetry precisely to disclaim all poetic license, to distinguish between poetry and history in order to deny anything but historical quality to his narrative. "The result," he has said in an interview, "is not a novel in the conventional sense, but a photographically accurate picture of actual events."[8] As did Thomas, Kuznetsov would also invoke the most persuasive of all documentary representations—the photograph—as a figure for his narrative.

Though the sense of eyewitness is fabricated here, rather than retained as it is in the diaries and memoirs, this quality of witness in testimony thus functions as the operative trope underpinning the factual authority generated in "documentary literature." In this context, we might note further that Thomas's invocation of the "recording camera" as a stylistic model even has a quite literal, if unintentional, dimension as well. For although he has not acknowledged any other authentic sources, Thomas seems in several instances to have based many of his most "graphic" descriptions not just on Dina Pronicheva's novelized testimony, but also on the witness of several well-known photographs of the Riga massacres of Jews by the *SS Einsatzgruppen*, taken in December 1941 by the SS.[9] In this way, photographs become his surrogate experiences of events, which then function both as his own "eyewitness" memory of events and as the source of further authority in his narrative when the readers' own memory of these images is awakened by Thomas's recollection of them. In effect, however, by recalling in narrative the photographs of the SS, Thomas has ironically depended for his testimonial authority on the *Nazis'* "witness" of their deeds; that is, part of the factual authority in Thomas's "victim-based" narrative may ultimately be deriving not just from the testimony of the victims but from that of the photographs taken by the killers themselves.

As Barthes, Sontag, and many others have demonstrated, however, photographs are as constructed and as mediated as any other kind of representation.[10] In fact, as a figure for documentary narrative, the photograph may even be more appropriate than the documentary writers imagined: for the photograph operates rhetorically on precisely the same assumption at work in documentary narrative. That is, as a seeming trace or fragment of its referent that appeals to the eye for its proof, the photograph is able to invoke the authority of its empirical link to events, which in turn seems to reinforce the sense of its own unmediated factuality. As a metonymical trope of witness, the photograph persuades the viewer of its testimonial and factual authority in ways that are unavailable to narrative. One of the reasons that narrative and photographs are so convincing together is that they seem to represent a combination of pure object and commentary on the object, each seeming to complete the other by reinforcing a sense of contrasting functions.

As Terrence Des Pres distinguished between the survivors' testimony and his own commentary in *The Survivor*, Kuznetsov creates a distinction between authentic documents in his work and his own voice. By including "A Chapter of Documents" and several short sections entitled "The Author's Voice," Kuznetsov attempts to create an intertext, in which a hierarchy of speakers' authority is generated. In another example of this tendency, the prize-winning novel *Efraim's Book* ("part diary, part documentary, part interior history," according to the jacket cover), the author Alfred Andersch incorporates into his text courtroom testimony from the Treblinka and Auschwitz trials in Germany in 1965, even as he suggests that such testimony may be phenomenologically unincorporable:

> . . . But there was no explanation for Auschwitz. *On at least one occasion SS-Man Küttner, known as Kiewe, flung a baby into the air and Franz killed it with two shots.* No one has been able to explain Auschwitz. *We saw an enormous fire and men were throwing things into it. I saw a man who was holding something that moved its head. I said: 'For the love of God, Marusha, he's throwing a live dog into it.' But my companion said: 'That's not a dog, it's a baby.'* I am suspicious of anyone who tries to explain Auschwitz.[11]

By citing the source of these lines in a prefatory note and setting them off in italics within the text itself, Andersch disclaims both authorship and authority for them, and in so doing suggests to the reader that the ontological status of these lines differs fundamentally from that of the surrounding "fictional" text. Because these things actually happened, Andersch (like Thomas and Kuznetsov) would claim not to re-create them imaginatively, thereby keeping "facts" separate from "fiction" and absolving himself of responsibility for imagining—and thereby re-perpetrating somehow—the most violent scenes in his novel.

Where Andersch separates testimony from fiction in order to privilege it over his surrounding fiction, others seem to make the distinction in order to privilege the surrounding text as well. And where Thomas would indicate this distinction in relatively subtle ways (in his speaker's asides and in frontispiece acknowledgments), other novelists assert the difference much more graphically. By separating "documents" from his own narrative in *Babi Yar*, Kuznetsov simultaneously heightens the distinction between re-imagined narrative and authentic documents, even as he allows his narrative to draw its authority from the documents he cites. As do photographs and narrative in photojournalistic media, each kind of representation seems to demand and to fulfill the other, providing either the necessary photographic proof or narrative meaning that comes in captions.

Though Kuznetsov's *Babi Yar* is probably the most celebrated work of Holocaust "documentary fiction" (it was also one of the first to call itself a "documentary novel"), there are dozens of others no less insistent on their documentary authority. Among them, we might note that in the preface to Pierre Julitte's *Block 26: Sabotage at Buchenwald,* Joseph Kessel assures the reader that "nothing of the work derives of fiction, and that everything is true, even so to speak, the commas."[12] But, as we find in so many other "documentary novels," the facts of this revolt are necessarily shaped, edited, and explained by both the writer's and his witnesses' linguistic, cultural, and religious perceptions of them. In this vein, Ezrahi has shown us that even though Jean-François Steiner insists repeatedly on the absolute facticity of his documentary novel based on the revolt at Treblinka, the story he writes is ultimately so couched in biblical language and archetypes as to render all of its participants either Jewish martyrs or heroes—a presentation that conflicts markedly with other accounts of the same revolt.[13] As commentary on the events at Treblinka and as representation of how survivors of the revolt have apprehended their experiences, this novel succeeds. But, as Ezrahi observes, even though "this fiction is grounded in reality, it is sustained more by the spiritual authority of authentic testimony than by accurate documentary" (p. 25). That is, it becomes the illusion of documentary authority generated by authentic eyewitnesses that sustains the putative factuality of these texts and, by extension, the power of this fiction.

In a further twist recalling the cases of Thomas and Kuznetsov, the discrepancies between events as they are represented in Steiner's *Treblinka* and as narrated by Vasili Grossman in his version take on an irony of their own. As Thomas drew upon Kuznetsov, and Kuznetsov upon Pronicheva, Steiner seems to have relied heavily on Vasili Grossman's *L'Enfer de Treblinka* for his witness—even though Grossman himself came to Treblinka as a Soviet journalist after the camp was destroyed. Unlike the other authors, however, Steiner does not make direct attribution to Grossman's work. Instead, he acknowledges that three books on Treblinka exist, one of which (*The Hell of Treblinka*) "is by a war correspondent in the Soviet army who interviewed the first witnesses."[14]

In a related case, Cythia Haft notes that the historian Vidal Nacquet discovered that another novel, *Et la terre sera pure,* by Sylvain Reiner, lifted passages directly from Miklos Nyiszli's *Medecin a Auschwitz* (*Auschwitz: A Doctor's Eye-witness Account*), without making any acknowledgment.[15] In the cases of both Reiner and Steiner, where full acknowledgments of source material were not made, the writers seem to have assumed that these other works retained a witness quality their narrative could not have—but which, even if it went uncited, might still infuse the surrounding text with the authority of witness.

By interweaving into fictional narrative the words of actual witnesses, perhaps written at the time, these novelists would thus create the texture of fact, suffusing the surrounding text with the privilege and authority of witness. At a crucial place near the end of *Treblinka*, Steiner thus goes directly to Yankel Wiernek's memoir, not only trusting the eyewitness to tell the story better but, by seeming to yield to the authority of an actual eyewitness, hoping to incorporate this same authority into his text. As Thomas and Kuznetsov have done, Steiner now distinguishes between his mere reconstruction and an authentic witness's memoir—now quoted verbatim—precisely to lend testimonial authority to his own surrounding narrative. And as so often happens in Holocaust fiction, the interpolation comes at a particularly dramatic moment, partly to heighten the drama and, it seems, to shore up the authoritative integrity of the text at its most vulnerable moment: "Everything seems threatened. Only one man can still save the situation: Wiernik. Let us listen to his testimony" (p. 289). As part of the transition from his words to Wiernek's, Steiner turns to both present tense and first person at this moment and indents the testimony, setting it apart from his own. It is, in fact, first-rate storytelling, precisely because it is purportedly verified now by the witness to events just when we needed his authority most.

The interspersing of authentic witness with less authentic finds its place as a narrative technique in all kinds of Holocaust documentary literature, especially in the memoirs. Even the most authentic memoirs, like Leon W. Wells's *The Death Brigade*, often incorporate the witness of diary: the narrative written within events would now suffuse that written after events with an even more privileged authority. As photographs are used to authenticate and to increase the authority in actual witness accounts like Erich Kulka's *Escape from Auschwitz* or Filip Müller's *Eyewitness Auschwitz*, Leon Wells incorporates fragments of his diary into his own memoir precisely at the moment when the killing process begins.[16]

From invoking the "spiritual authority of authentic testimony," however, it is only a short step to fabricating it altogether within a text, whether it is called "fictional" or "nonfictional." Alvin Rosenfeld has noted in this regard that two other writers—John Hersey and Leon Uris—have, as part of their fictions, actually created their own documentary sources. In the editor's prologue to Hersey's *The Wall*, based on Emmanuel Ringelblum's *Notes from the Warsaw Ghetto*, the author exclaims of his own novel, "What a wonder of documentation!" and then goes on to tell the reader that the narrator, Levinson, "was too scrupulous to imagine *anything*," though Rosenfeld reminds us that the writer has actually had to imagine *everything*.[17] Rosenfeld also suggests that if documentary evidence is the aim, the reader might prefer to turn directly to the "actual historical testimonies we do have." But this is to imply that the primary difference between fabricated and "actual" testimony is a matter of actual documentary evidence—when, in fact, neither may actually be evidence but only the persuasively constructed illusion of evidence. Where the nonfiction account attempts to retrieve its authentic connection to events in order to reinforce its documentary authority, fiction necessarily fabricates its link to events in order to reinforce its documentary authority. The difference between fictional and nonfictional "documentary narratives" of the Holocaust may not be between degrees of actual evidential authority, but between the ontological sources of this sense of authority: one is retrieved and one is constructed wholly within the text as part of the text's fiction. As it was for the diaries and memoirs, the operative trope underpinning the documentary character of Holocaust "documentary fiction" is thus the rhetorical principle of testimony, not its actuality.

I I I

At the end of his study of "literary non-fiction," Ronald Weber concludes that "The first task of the writer of literary non-fiction is always *to convince the reader that his work is adequate as history.*"[18] That is, the aim is not to write factual history but merely to persuade the reader that it is factual. If Holocaust documentary fiction depends upon the concept of testimony as a rhetorical trope only in order to provide an "unusually compelling experience for the reader," however, then these writers' narrative methods remain a matter of style. For documentary narratives are in this view compelling as "reading experience" precisely because they claim to be so much more than mere "reading experience."

In a way, the literary documentarist draws on the same sort of ambiguity between factual and fictional narrative that the novelist has always generated. Indeed, much of the force of novelistic discourse seems to derive precisely from the ambiguity its dual claims of fact and fiction stimulate in the reader, as Lennard Davis has noted in his study on the origins of the English novel. "Novels are framed works (even if they seem unframed)," he writes, "whose attitude toward fact and fiction is constitutively ambivalent."[19] By sustaining, encouraging, and even exacerbating what Davis calls the "constitutive ambivalence" toward fact and fiction, a writer like Daniel Defoe ("the journalist *par excellence* of the early eighteenth century") might therefore exemplify the novelist, at least partly because he claimed disingenuously to be a journalist. Where Cervantes drew attention to the fabulative nature of his work and, indeed, both celebrated and marked the confusion of mind that results from mistaking "real" for imaginary worlds, Defoe seems to have delighted in causing just this confusion of mind in the reader. "The process of reading a Defoean novel," Davis remarks, "is that the reader is asked first to believe that the novel is real, and then to understand that the reality of the novel is bogus. In effect, suspension of disbelief is itself suspended" (p. 23).

There is a sense in which part of novelistic discourse becomes not only a matter of "factual fiction," but really an attempt to generate fictional facts. When Defoe "places himself outside of the novel—into the prestructure— by the gesture of authorial disavowal," as Davis observes (p. 17), we might note further that this act remains only a gesture, a sleight of authorial hand by which he would appear to be outside of the narrative he has actually created. Contrary to Davis's contention that these writers are somehow "forced into the position of claiming to be the editor to some found document" (p. 35), we need to recognize this claim as part of the overall fiction of the writer's work. And just as earlier novelists dissembled, veiling their authorial presence to create the illusion of the text's autonomy, contemporary documentary novelists now conflate their narratives with rhetorically factual materials like photographs, newspaper articles, and eyewitness testimony in order to lend them a certain factual authority.

As fundamental to the nature of the novel as this ambiguity might be, however, without keeping in mind the distinction between the novelist's claims to fact and the actual fabulative character of his narrative, the reader risks a certain phenomenological beguilement at the hands of the novelist—and now at the hands of the "documentary novelist"—and not collusion with the novelist, as Davis suggests. By allowing himself to be moved to the willing suspension of disbelief by the documentary novel's contrived historical authority, the reader risks becoming ensnared in the all-encompassing fiction of the discourse itself, mistaking the historical *force* of this discourse for the historical facts it purports to document.

That the reader responds to a work differently when he believes that it is "true" and has actually happened than he does when he believes the work is only "fiction" is a principal part of a documentary fiction's phenomenology; as such, the emotional experience of such an illusion becomes the aim of the writer. If the stimulation of emotional response is the "unique power" in realistic fiction and the "creation of such feelings in the reader [is] the fiction's highest achievement" (p. 16), as Thomas Wolfe might have it, then to read documentary fiction for its factual content would be to mistake the writer's literary means (i.e., apparent factuality) for the ends to which they are employed (i.e., emotional response). Like Weber, Wolfe acknowledges that the greatest advantage of this hybrid narrative is the *sense* that what it represents was real, not that it was real. In this literature, the facts (such as they are) thus remain subordinate to the effect they have on the reader.

In the case of Holocaust documentary narrative, this "rhetoric of fact" is invoked toward a number of different ends; and among them, it seems, is also an emotional response to the "sense of the real," a reinforcement of a work's supposed factuality, and the establishment of the authentic link between writer, text, and events. The purpose for documentary authority in the works of writers like Thomas, Kuznetsov, Steiner, and Andersch thus begins to assume critical importance. If this "rhetoric of fact" is intended to provide an unusually compelling reading experience, merely to move the reader, then Adorno's objections to "Holocaust art" retain a certain validity. For in this case, the authors would indeed be wringing pleasure from the naked pain of the victims. If, on the other hand, these works only want to refrain from conferring an essential fictionality on actual historical events, then we might take into account both the legitimate impulse to document events *and* the manner in which "real past events" are inevitably fictionalized by any narrative that gives them form. Insofar as it works to authenticate—and thereby naturalize—its particular interpretation of events, documentary narrative might even be considered an expressly ideological mode of discourse in both its means and its ends—a proposition that is explored at length in the next section on documentary drama, ideology, and the rhetoric of fact.

FOUR

Documentary Theater, Ideology, and the Rhetoric of Fact

> Documentary Theatre presents facts for examination. . . . In such a theatre, objectivity is likely to be merely a concept used by a ruling group to justify its actions.
>
> —Peter Weiss

> There is not much to argue about here: the means must be asked what the end is.
>
> —Bertolt Brecht

> The perspective of socialist realism is, of course, the struggle for socialism.
>
> —Georg Lukács

I

Until now, Peter Weiss's documentary drama about Auschwitz—*The Investigation*—has been both celebrated and condemned for largely the same reason: its unabashedly political character. Though Andreas Huyssen describes *The Investigation* on the one hand as "perhaps the best drama on the Holocaust" for its power to engage its viewers, he is also quick to warn readers of the play's major flaw:

> The problem is political. *The Investigation* stipulates an unmediated causal nexus between capitalism and Auschwitz. The extermination of the Jews is presented and interpreted as an extreme form of capitalist exploitation. . . . Weiss never attempts to deal with the history and specificity of anti-Semitism in Germany. By blaming Krupp and IG Farben, Weiss subsumes the death of six million Jews to a universal Marxist critique of capitalism.[1]

As limited as its political interpretation of Auschwitz is, *The Investigation* succeeded nevertheless as political theater precisely because of its explicit suggestion that its audience go beyond conventional representations of

Auschwitz to the "facts," and then beyond the facts to their purported origins. Embraced by many in Germany for making an ideological—as opposed to emotional—critique of Auschwitz and the Frankfurt trials, Weiss is rejected by many others for having made the wrong kind of ideological critique.

"Whether German documentary dramatists are committed to a political party [may well be] a moot point," as Jack Zipes suggests, but it is not an insignificant point in Weiss's case.[2] For every play inevitably owes its shape, focus, and explanatory powers to a particular political understanding, often as it is idealized in party dogma. In the case of Weiss, it is clearly a political-economic grasp of events that determines the shape of *The Investigation*—not the mere desire to "free the human spirit from bureaucracy or to provide alternatives in society for each individual regardless of party," as Zipes concludes (p. 346). And though documentary dramatists in Germany may well "write with a strong belief that history has too often been written as fiction by the historians," as Zipes suggests, to describe the docudramatist's own poetic license to reshape the past merely as a response to the historians' constructions underestimates both the aesthetic and ideological dimensions of this medium—and the ways they interpenetrate.

The ideological aspects of Weiss's play will be examined here on two levels: both as an "agenda" or consciousness that determines specific representations of events and as the process by which particular versions of reality are represented as naturally true and unconstructed. It is not just that the shape of events as represented in *The Investigation* is determined by the author's economic orientation that makes this play "ideological," for as we have seen, all historical narratives are as determined; but it is because this play exemplifies documentary theater's rhetorical and dramaturgical claims to be so much more than mere representation and figures itself as proof and objective evidence that we submit it to an ideological critique. The aim of this section is not merely to focus on Weiss's unmistakable and openly acknowledged agenda, but it is to explore: (1) how Weiss's Marxist grasp of events has led to his constructions of Auschwitz; and (2) how the documentary dramatic form he both uses and defines accomplishes the ideological effacement and totalization of any explanation of events. Rather than merely isolating the economic model underpinning this investigation of Auschwitz, I concentrate here on how this model has organized events and materials for Weiss, how it manifests and hides itself, whence the rhetoric of this model derives, and where it leads the viewers' understanding.

Though this chapter focuses specifically on both the theory and execution of Weiss's documentary theater, it is also intended as a larger critique of literary realism itself—whether it be "socialist realism," "bourgeois realism," or "documentary realism." For in all cases, the principal aims of such a style are to efface a work's constructedness, in order to foster the illusion of actuality, which rhetorically persuades an audience of a work's objectivity. In this context, we ask here whether documentary realism intends to present facts or an argument as to how these facts materialized in the first place. If it is the latter, then how are the facts used to buttress a particular explanation for events? And in a stylistic vein, how is the idea of fact used to obscure these facts' own constructed nature?

I I

In his preface to *Mythologies*, Roland Barthes writes that "The starting point of [his reflections on current events and popular culture] was usually a feeling of impatience at the sight of the 'naturalness' with which newspapers, art and common sense constantly dress up a reality which, even though it is the one we live in, is undoubtedly determined by history. In short, in the account given of our contemporary circumstances, I resented seeing Nature and History confused at every turn, and I wanted to track down, in the decorative display of *what-goes-without-saying*, the ideological abuse which, in my view, is hidden there."[3] By ideological abuse, Barthes refers to both the false consciousness by which popular events are represented—i.e., their bourgeois assumptions—and the formal means by which events have been passed off as natural and true. Barthes's critical aim in this collection has been to draw back into our apprehension of current events and popular culture the mythological outlines that have, in Derrida's words, "whitened themselves out"[4]—but which have nonetheless continued to structure and interpret the world for us, shaping reality even as they lead us to our philosophical and historical conclusions about reality.

Both Barthes's and Derrida's initial impatience with these hidden formulae of mind seems partly to be a reaction to the very invisibility of "white mythologies"—to the slickness with which they naturalize themselves—and partly, one suspects, a reaction to the gullibility of uncritical readers who continue to mistake the manner in which worldly phenomena are represented and understood for their nature. Barthes and Derrida have thus adapted Marx's critique of bourgeois ideology in order to warn those engaged in the labors of philosophical and historical discourse not to mistake their own creations for independent external realities.

Though Barthes implies, after Marx, that this naturalness of mind and production is primarily a bourgeois phenomenon—bourgeois ideology defined traditionally as that which *does* automatically totalize and thereby perpetuate itself—he seems also to recognize that this epistemic naturalization is not necessarily restricted to the agents of bourgeois culture. In different essays, in fact, he suggests that this whitening-out process may be a reflexive movement in historical and philosophical discourse as well; moreover, any ideology or culture—bourgeois or not—may at times adopt it deliberately as a rhetorical means of self-authentication.[5] As becomes clear, however, even though the "fetishization of the real," in Barthes's words, may have its roots deep in the soil of bourgeois culture, it has been largely the "socialist realists"—critical of bourgeois culture's self-naturalization—who ultimately elevated "realism" from a style to a method, from a means of persuasion to an aesthetic dictate.[6]

Inasmuch as perceived historical precedents and tropes, mythologies, religious topoi, and various narrative forms necessarily frame reality in their own images, Fredric Jameson seems justified in preferring a historical over what he calls an ethical approach to "the ideology of a text."[7] For as Lévi-Strauss, Barthes, and others have demonstrated, the impulse to mythologize history and thus to naturalize and transform it need not always stem from a writer's overt ideological biases or the special interests of a particular social group or class; rather, this impulse is intrinsic to language itself. The ideology of any text might thus be described as a reflexive operation and not as an expressly deliberate function of a writer with an agenda. Once this automatic tendency to naturalize events is acknowledged, however, we might also distinguish between those writers of documentary literature whose texts are reflexively naturalized by a particular religious tradition or cultural continuum and those writers who quite consciously— even conscientiously—employ a documentary rhetoric of fact in order to naturalize, and thereby obscure, a particular subtext.

As bourgeois ideology works by naturalizing its signs in order to appear free, universal, and self-generating, socialist realism and other forms of documentary literature mask and naturalize their own production. And if ideologies work by "repressing the mechanism of their generation," as Terry Eagleton suggests,[8] then so might the rhetoric of fact in documentary realism work to repress the memory of its own construction in order to sanction the particular construction that now gives the "facts" their voice. By presenting itself as *non*ideological, documentary literature enforces its facticity: that is, through its rhetoric of fact, the documentary mode works to obscure its ideological premises precisely in order to be ideological.

Even though a primary concern of ideology criticism has been to deemphasize the element of volition or will in a text's construction and to devalue the supposed deliberate manipulation of reality in ideological writing, we may still remain aware of the ways in which writers can assist the totalization process reflexive in their narrative. Between the social realists' hegemony of reality and bourgeois culture's own naturalization of reality, the generally unselfconscious construction of reality in what we might call "factually insistent" literature has remained so relatively unchallenged by the lay reader that what may have been a reflexive means of naturalizing the world has now been adopted aggressively as its own literary form. That is, literary modes in which the maker's hand and mind are—either deliberately or reflexively—hidden from view, thereby reinforcing the text's seeming naturalness and factuality, have been generically codified in what we have come to call "documentary literature."

As a purely aesthetic strategy by which writers of fiction have traditionally aspired to engage their readers, to move them to pity and fear, or to seduce them into the willing suspension of disbelief, the rhetoric of fact remains an effective, if relatively benign, stylistic device. But as that which would mask its author's hand *as a guide to action* in the world, the rhetoric of fact moves the organizing mythos of documentary narrative from the theoretical sphere of knowledge to the practical realm of applied knowledge. For by inviting action on the basis of its presentation—even if this invitation is only implicit in a text's rhetorical voice—documentary narrrative lends its organizing principles a cutting edge in the world. In asking the reader to act on epistemologically framed experience as if it were natural and unmediated fact, documentary narrative brings the governing episteme of the writer into the world of lived experience.[9] As a literary mode that would mask its seams of construction in order to become the basis for actions in the world, documentary literature seems to share both the process and ends of ideology—and thus might come to be regarded as a fundamentally ideological form of discourse.

In the case of Holocaust documentary literature, in particular, this approach might then lead us to differentiate among: (1) the ghetto diarists whose natural impulse may have been to locate themselves and their experiences in a religious or cultural continuum, in which they perceived themselves as witness-scribes recording evidence against their killers; (2) the survivor-memoirists' attempt to preserve the authentic link between their narratives and experiences in order to reinforce the facticity of events that seemingly defy credibility; (3) the novelists (both survivors and non-victims) who either hesitate to fictionalize real events or would infuse their fiction with the power of the real generated in the fact-fiction ambiguity; and (4) other writers who would conceal their productivity in a documentary text in order to naturalize the specific—and totalizing—shape their particular reconstructions lend Holocaust realities.

Even though the transformations of fact accomplished in all documentary works may be equally severe, each writer's relationship to his text is phenomenologically and, as we have seen, ontologically different from the others'. For unlike the ghetto scribe, the survivor-memoirist, or to a lesser extent, the novelist of the Holocaust, the last writer deliberately masks his interpretation in a conscious attempt to lead the reader beyond mere belief in the existence of a set of events to a belief in a particular version of events. If, after Barthes's critique of the ways popular culture and current events naturalize a society's governing mythoi, one of the principal aims of Holocaust literary criticism becomes to disclose the explaining myths that have shaped representations of the Holocaust, then we might direct our keenest critical attention to the very "works of fact" that are most persuasive of their documentary authority. For they are often also those works that have gone to the greatest pains to mask their organizing mythoi and to lose the memory that they, too, were constructed.

III

One of the most ingenious examples of documentary literature with decidedly more than purely documentary aims is Peter Weiss's play *The Investigation*, which is based on the court and journalists' records of the Auschwitz trials in Frankfurt, 1964–65.[10] On the surface, Weiss openly acknowledges the didactic and polemical function of "documentary theater," locating what he terms a "theater of actuality" in the tradition of the "Proletcult" movement, "Agitprop" of the 1920s and thirties, the experimental political drama of Erwin Piscator, and the didactic plays of Bertolt Brecht.[11] Given this tradition and Weiss's own reasons for writing *The Investigation*, documentary theater necessarily takes sides, as Weiss reminds us (p. 42). But insofar as this alternative theater is intended both to challenge bourgeois political assumptions about Auschwitz and to document events, it remains curious that Weiss would go to such pains to emphasize both the objective quality in this work and its expressly subjective aims. For even though his critical discussion of documentary theater highlights very well the antipositivist side of this and all theater, as a playwright Weiss seems to have exploited the illusion of fact and objectivity generated in documentary theater precisely to mask—not reveal—his work's preassumptions.[12]

Ironically, no critique of realistic representations undercuts the transcendent authority Weiss has generated in *The Investigation* better than Weiss's own. Indeed, Weiss's critical aims in his "Notes Towards a Definition of Documentary Theatre" and the means by which he would perform these aims in his play seem to be hopelessly at odds with one another. For as precise and praiseworthy as his critique of distortion and concealment in the bourgeois media may be, when applied to documentary theatre, it is no less incisive in exposing the ideological lines of his own play's construction. Since these critical questions are essential to our own critique of Weiss, in particular, and of documentary narrative in general, I cite them here in their entirety:

a. Critique of concealment. Are reports in the press, radio and TV slanted to the point of view of powerful interests? What are we not told? Who benefits by the omissions? To whose advantage is it when certain social phenomena are blue-pencilled, modified, idealized?

b. Critique of distortion. Why is an historical figure, a period, or an epoch, eliminated from the history books? Whose position is strengthened by this suppression of historical facts? Who gains from the deliberate distortion of decisive and significant events? How does one recognize the distortions that are made? What effect do they have?

c. Critique of lies. What are the consequences of an historical deception? What does a situation built on lies look like? What difficulties do we have to contend with in searching for the truth? Which influential organs, what powerful groupings will do anything to prevent the truth from getting out? ("The Materials and the Models," p. 41)

In the note to his play, Weiss claims to have distilled the court proceedings into their factual essence, describing his characters as speaking tubes through which he has merely poured the facts of Auschwitz: "Only a condensation of the evidence [*aussage*] can remain on stage. . . . This condensation should contain nothing but facts" (p. xi). As a "theatre of reportage," Weiss writes, "documentary theatre refrains from all invention; it takes authentic material and puts it on the stage, unaltered in content, edited in form" ("The Materials and the Models," p. 41). But in light of the unavoidable subterfuge effected in the process of these facts' selection and arrangement, the sources of these facts, which range from Nazi records to courtroom journalists' notes, and his own profound sensitivity to the bourgeois media's naturalization of such facts, Weiss's insistence on the purity of the facts as he presents them becomes ironic at best and disingenuous at worst. For, as an especially astute and vociferous critic of "concealment and distortion" in the mass media, Weiss has even defined documentary theater as part of a concerted response to an uncritical belief in factual reportage. In fact, by asking in his stinging critique of "concealment and distortion" in the media why historical figures, periods, and epochs *are* eliminated from history and whose position is strengthened by these suppressions of historical facts, Weiss seeks to expose the hidden motives of "those powerful interests" who underwrite the world's press. In this critique, Weiss recognizes clearly that under the guise of journalistic objectivity—a rhetoric of fact in its own right—the mass media also seek to "whiten out" most traces of their own special interests, biases, and ideals.[13]

Of documentary narrative's many rhetorical devices, none is so effectively used as its claim to have been part of the events it would now represent. Weiss suggests both that documentary theater represents "immediate actuality" and that it is, in his words, "a reflection of a segment of that actuality, torn out of its living context" (p. 42). As the documentary rhetoric in novels consists often in the writer's incorporating news reports, handbills, and the like, the basis for documentary theater lies both in its "documenting an event" (p. 41) and in the documents of modern life it uses. In Weiss's notes toward a definition of documentary theater, he even suggests that "Records, documents, letters, statistics, market-reports, statements by banks and companies, government statements, speeches, interviews, statements by well-known personalities, newspaper and broadcast reports, photos, documentary films and other contemporary documents are the basis of the performance" (p. 41). Reminiscent of his earlier work in surrealistic collage, Weiss conceives documentary drama as a pastiche of the fragments of *realia*, the material remnants of the world, out of which a representation is constructed. Though by recognizing later that "This critical selection, and the principles by which the montage of snippets of reality is effected, determines the quality of the documentary drama" (p. 41), Weiss also acknowledges that meaning is constructed in the process as well, no matter how random or accidental the arrangement appears.

But this is precisely the source of such a technique's documentary rhetoric. By reinforcing the sense of whatever link it has to a past reality and then using the "authority" of this link to repress evidence of its own construction, documentary montage like Weiss's invokes itself as evidence not just of the realities to which its parts refer, but of the specific—and apparently natural—shape it now lends these realities. That is, by calling itself a slice of the reality it now signifies, or an extension of it, documentary montage claims rhetorically to be unmediated and determined solely by the larger reality from which it has been torn. In this way, the artifacts of reality are used to authenticate the particular pattern in which they are arranged. And thus, as Weiss writes, "The strength of Documentary Theatre lies in its ability to shape a useful pattern from fragments of reality, to build a model of actual occurrences" (p. 42). A model of actual occurrence built out of the fragments of these same occurrences is suddenly capable of proclaiming itself both representation and part of events. Seemingly self-generated and created in no image other than its own as a fact, the literary document claims a perfect facticity, a kind of antidote to fiction and illusion—even as it remains in itself a most persuasive illusion. This is an essential rhetorical component of any representation claiming for itself the status of object and not just sign.

Like other kinds of documentary literature, *The Investigation* is premised strongly upon the twin figures of witness and evidence. Having both witnessed part of the trials himself and relied on Bernd Naumann's eyewitness reports for the *Frankfurter Zeitung*, Weiss then adapted as well the entire testamentary model itself of the trials. Testimony is thus used here as both artifice and material: technically, the entire play is not only based on courtroom testimony but now represents itself in the figure of this same testimony. And as narrative descriptions of Babi Yar in Thomas's *The White Hotel* may have conjured in readers' minds the familiar photographic images on which they were based, the testimony in Weiss's drama drawn almost directly from journalists' reports similarly recalls for viewers the reality of events as they were recorded in the recent news.

Indeed, as we discover in an interview, Weiss admits to having moved from the film medium to that of the stage precisely because the rhetoric of theater reinforced the illusion of fact. "I moved to theatre [from film]," Weiss said, "because I found that there was always one great lack in film: living contact with the action and the audience. Film seemed two-dimensional, a reproduction of an action, while theatre was closer to the direct action itself."[14] By turning the audience of his play into witnesses,

Weiss takes the entire rhetoric of the stage itself one step further as a technique in documentary drama. As becomes clear in almost every detail of *The Investigation*, Weiss takes pains to create the authority of witness in this play: from his use of free verse (a recessive, more rhetorically natural form than rhymed and metered verse), to the courtroom motif (with its own resonances of proof and evidence), even to his approval of director Erwin Piscator's idea of hanging photographs of the actual defendants over the players' heads as further "documentary" link between his dramatic reconstructions and the events themselves. By thus claiming for his own work the documentary authority he has denied the press, however, Weiss is either ignoring the shape his own ideals have inevitably imposed on the facts, or—more cynically—he has appropriated the ideological process itself, persisting in his own rhetoric of fact precisely in order to mask and thereby naturalize his interpretation of the Holocaust.

Thus, even though Weiss claims merely to condense and arrange the facts, his own political-economic understanding of events has clearly functioned as the arbiter of fact here; we find, for example, that his docu-drama about Auschwitz—where nearly half of the four million victims were murdered solely for having been born Jews—is as *Judenrein* as most of post-Holocaust Europe. That is, Weiss refers neither to *Juden* in this play, nor hardly to *Opfer* (victim), but uses instead the expression *Verfolgten*, a legal term for "those under persecution." Though some critics have hinted darkly at what they suspect is a form of *selbst-hass* or repression of Weiss's own half-Jewishness here, Weiss himself suggests a much more straightforward explanation for his conspicuous omission. In order to "brand capitalism" with the facts of Auschwitz, as Weiss explained to his audience in the program notes, the playwright has written a "documentary drama" that documents not so much the *facts* of Auschwitz but really only his own Marxian conception and interpretation of the facts, a paradigm that simply does not allow for the ethnic identification of the victims. By "distilling" the court record and substituting *Verfolgten* in the play whenever Jews appeared in the actual record, Weiss locates the victims in an a priori dialectic of persecutor-persecuted, in which the persecuted are victims not of antisemitic terror but of monopoly capitalism gone mad.[15]

Whether or not these passages correspond with the court and journalists' records, however, is not the point. For the aim in Weiss's play is not to transcribe the details of these reports but to reassemble them in such a way that they become comprehensible as evidence against capitalism. That is, he systematizes his sources, his evidence, now to make new evidence, not of events but of the criminal link between events and a system, evidence of the model by which he explains events. As a representation of the trial itself, *The Investigation* necessarily remakes it, reconstructing it as any representation will, even the reporters' own. By retaining the courtroom's voice of factuality, however, he is able to lend an implicit authority to his documentary drama. In this way, the details of the court tend to naturalize the very manner in which they have been represented.

At another level, however, Weiss seems to betray his own ambivalent grasp of the actual victims and of himself as a potential victim. In an essay he wrote about his visit to Auschwitz twenty years after the War, Weiss said that Auschwitz "is a place for which I was destined but which I managed to avoid," leaving unclear whether he was destined for Auschwitz as a Jew or as a political prisoner.[16] That it would have been as a victim is clear, but by leaving open the kind of victim he would have been, Weiss may be suggesting both. In the play, he thus merges kinds of victims, allowing each to figure the other:

> Counsel for the Defense: Was the witness
>   politically active
>   before being sent
>   to the camp
> 3rd Witness: Yes
>   It was our strength
>   that we knew
>   why we were there
>   It helped us
>   preserve our identity (p. 110)

But which identity—as Jews or as socialists—is not clear. As Sara Nomberg-Pryztyk figured her victimization as Jew in terms of her prewar persecution as socialist, Weiss seems also to have grasped his own averted victimization both as socialist and as Jew—each now figured in the other's terms.

Had all victims remained completely anonymous in the play, then the omission of Jews might have merely signified the prisoners' loss of their names in the camp, as Weiss suggests in his prefatory note. But in fact, Weiss names explicitly another class of victims—Soviet prisoners of war—who as the only group of victims named in the play come to stand for the unnamed victims of Auschwitz—the Jews—whose specific fate is shared by the Soviets in this play. As the names of the perpetrators are used by Weiss, he tells us, to symbolize an entire guilty system, the Soviet prisoners of war now emblematize all other victims. Through the arrangement of these victims' songs in the oratorio, there is thus a blending of Jewish victims (unnamed) and Soviet POW's (named):

> Judge: Accused Stark
>   how large were the groups
>   you had to conduct to the crematoriums
> Accused #12: On the average
>   150 to 200 head
> Judge: Were women and children among them

> Accused #12: Yes
> Judge: Did you think it right
>   that women and children
>   should be a part of these transports
> Accused #12: Yes
>   The Family Liability Laws
>   were in effect then
> Judge: You did not question
>   the guilt of these women and children
> Accused #12: We had been told
>   they had actively participated
>   in poisoning springs and wells
>   blowing up bridges
>   and other acts of sabotage (p. 148)

In this section, a conventional antisemitic libel is juxtaposed to partisan activities, mixing emblematically Jewish and military "crimes," after which the victims of the gas chambers are named:

> Prosecuting Attorney: Accused Stark
>   in the fall of 1941
>   a large number of Soviet
>   prisoners of war
>   were brought to the camp
>   . . . .
>   What reason
>   was given for the execution
>   of these prisoners of war
> Accused #12: We were dealing with the annihilation
>   of an ideology
>   With their fanatical political organization
>   these prisoners constituted a threat
>   to camp security (pp. 149–50)

In subsuming the extermination of prisoners under the "annihilation of an ideology," the accused effectively links annihilation and a system, substituting "ideology" here for the annihilated people, the Jews. Later on the Soviets are also named accurately by a victim-witness as the first to be gassed at Auschwitz:

> On the 3rd of September 1941
> the first experiments
> in mass killings
> using the gas Cyklon B
> were carried out in the Bunker
> Staff medical orderlies and guards
> brought about 850 Soviet prisoners of war (p. 225)

The first victims of gas come to stand for those for whom the gas was ultimately intended; political and racial killings are thus co-valued here, and made two sides of the same intention.

Later still, the term *Verfolgten* (those under persecution) is substituted for *Juden*, with only an emblematic number to imply specificity; in the same monologue, the Russians are named specifically, not changed from the record:

> 7th Witness: Of the 9 million 600 thousand persecuted
>   who lived in the regions
>   ruled by their persecutors
>   6 million have disappeared
>   . . . .
>   Yet to arrive at the sum total
>   of the defenseless sacrificed
>   in this war of extermination
>   we must add to the 6 million
>   killed for racial reasons
>   3 million Russian prisoners of war
>   shot or starved to death (p. 266–67)

This passage follows instances in which specific numbers and kinds of victims are introduced by the prosecuting attorney in the context of the first gassings:

> Prosecuting Attorney: Accused Stark
>   did you take part in the first gassings
>   which were carried out
>   on Soviet prisoners of war
>   in the first weeks of September 1941
> Accused #12: No
> Prosecuting Attorney: Large-scale extermination
>   of Soviet prisoners of war began
>   in the fall and winter of 1941
>   These resulted in the death of 25,000 men (p. 152)

This dialogue comes at the end of one section, which resumes immediately with the judge's questions concerning further gassings at Auschwitz. The prisoners are a "mixed transport," whose deaths in the gas chambers are minutely described by Stark. Immediately after describing the victims' deaths, Stark explains his conduct this way:

> Accused #12: Your Honor
>   I would like to explain that
>   Every third word we heard
>   even back in grammar school
>   was about

> how they
> were to blame for everything
> and how they
> ought to be weeded out (p. 156)

In its textual position, the pronoun "they" refers to the victims whose deaths have just been described: the Soviet prisoners of war. But in its historical context, "they" must refer to the Jews in Germany, unnamed here but figured nonetheless through another set of victims of the gas chambers. Not only are the unnamed victims thus figured by the Russians, but in this exchange, the Russians are now figured as Jews, their plight represented in specifically Jewish terms. In this way, Weiss seems to have drawn upon the two halves of his own mixed identity as Jew and socialist—each side figured by the other. In effect, the play comes to represent not only his political grasp of Auschwitz but his political grasp of himself as well.

As one set of named victims emblematized other anonymous victims, the names of the accused are used as symbols of an entire "anonymous" system comprising German industrial firms that exploited the slave labor of the camps:

> Prosecuting Attorney: What kind of industries were those
> 1st Witness: They were branch plants
> of I-G Farben
> Krupp and Siemens

These specific names in postwar Germany have come to stand for all West German industry, for capitalism itself: they now stand as well for the system that did in the victims at Auschwitz. "To the author, they (the defendants) have lent their names which, within the drama, exist as symbols of a system that implicated in its guilt many others who never appeared in court" (from prefatory note). The producers of war and the camps are the same:

> 1st Witness: All I knew about the camp
> was that it had to do with
> a large industrial complex
> and that its various branches
> employed prisoners as labor supply
> Prosecuting Attorney: To which of these branches
> did your operation belong
> 1st Witness: We were a subdivision of the Buna Works
> of I-G Farben
> We were engaged in war production (p. 125)

As spoken, this phrase could mean either the production of materials for use during the war or the production of war itself. In this context, the speaker reestablishes a link between German industry, exploitation and murder of victims, and current employees who worked at Auschwitz: though no longer employed by these firms (also named), the defendants still receive pensions from them. And in all of this, of course, we are reminded occasionally of who is prosecuting whom, which side is defending the killers:

> Counsel for the Defense: Who is this assistant prosecutor
>   with his unsuitable clothes
>   It is I believe a Middle European custom
>   to appear in court with a closed robe (p. 268)

Prosecutors are from the Eastern bloc, the defense counsel (and defendants) from the West. The representatives of the capitalist system are on trial by the east; metonymically one system is thus investigating the other, bringing it to justice.

I V

In its context as an alternative—even revolutionary—medium, documentary theater is characterized by Weiss as a "demand for explanations" (p. 41). It is much more than just a demand for explanations, however; it is also an explaining medium in itself. "I wanted a scientific investigation of the reality of Auschwitz," Weiss has said, "to show the audience, in the greatest detail, exactly what happened."[17] In the process, his play necessarily asks questions, as Weiss proposes, and provides answers, reinforcing further the rhetorical—as opposed to practical—aims of his "scientific investigation." Implicit in Weiss's critique of Auschwitz is the assumption that "scientific materialism"—as a "science"—is more objective in its explanations for events than other methods anchored in bourgeois analysis.

To make this argument, however, Weiss would have to accept literally Lukács's contention that "the perspective of socialism enables the critic to see society and history for what they are"—even though "what they are" in any case depends on how society and history are conceived and narrated in the first place.[18] In fact, the tautological character of any realistic writer's claim to transcendent realism is given articulate voice by Lukács himself later in the same essay when he argues that "war can only be understood in its totality if the writer has a perspective which enables him to understand the forces that lead to war . . . " (p. 101). Even though traditional Marxist analysis—as methodology—*is* especially effective at unmasking various ideological forms of "false consciousness," such as law, religion, and myth, when it claims for itself a certain untranscendable status as method, it tends to deny the provisionality of its own power to explain. By calling attention to a text's bourgeois assumptions and their ideological effacement, traditional Marxist analysis implies the capacity to perform a similar operation on itself. By keeping in mind its own self-critical process, Marxist analysis might claim to have more power than other interpretive models to bring its own lines of reference into view, even as it acknowledges the limits of any system to explain its own origins.

But as William C. Dowling has noted in a "critical introduction" to Fredric Jameson's methodology,[19] Marxist analysis thus assumes distinctly theological and idealist dimensions in its own right:

> The problem is not that Marx is implicitly theological—that he offers the Economy as a 'secret' of intelligibility in the same spirit that Christianity offers God and Divine Providence and Hegel offers Absolute Spirit—but that he does so at the very moment he claims to be annihilating all varieties of idealism, including all theology, in the name of a pure materialism that is manifested within human history as the Economy or economic level. In short, Marx may be viewed as perpetrating an unwitting sleight of hand here, claiming the economic as material because the forces and relations of economic production belong to the material world . . . while *within his explanatory system* the economic has the force of an idealist principle of intelligibility.[20]

In claiming for documentary theater the capacity to lay bare realities through its probing, and saying that "All non-essentials, all digressions, can be eliminated to lay bare the basic [historical] problem" (p. 42), Weiss echoes the Marxist credo that art does not imitate reality so much as it makes the real visible. Both propositions would seem to be as naïvely positivistic as the bourgeois historian's insistence that he is merely laying bare the facts of history, not creating them himself. As socialist realism would attempt to reveal conditions, events, and their causes, Weiss would reveal an understanding of history's problem; but neither the socialist realist nor documentary dramatist acknowledges here the constructing of events that attends—even constitutes—their supposed revelation. For we no more lay bare the basic problem of history than we lay bare history itself: both history and its problems are constructed along specific narrative and paradigmatic contours. At best, we might lay bare these contours, and how they both mask and create our understanding of reality.

As it turns out, however, by concealing his approach within such a carefully wrought rhetoric of fact, Weiss not only appears to be passing his interpretive constructions off as fact but seems also to be taken in by them. Inasmuch as the economic explanation for history—even as putative methodology—tends to totalize both itself and reality no less than other forms of interpretation, this in itself may not be so surprising. But in fostering his own rhetoric of fact, Weiss the critic seems to have lost the ability to discriminate not only between his rhetoric and the events but perhaps also between the Nazis' own rhetoric of the camps and the infernal realities this rhetoric was intended to screen. For where the Nazis may indeed have dressed their "enterprise" in the language of raw production materials, management efficiency, and cost-benefit analysis, this capitalist jargon functioned partly as a bureaucratic language by which to operate the camps, partly as a rhetorical veil with which to obscure the actuality of the camps, and partly as a means to justify to the Nazi military establishment the role of the death camps in the war effort itself. In other words, the language of the Wannsee Conference, the work and construction orders, and plans for "relocation" that Weiss relies so heavily upon in his "investigation" of Auschwitz are ultimately less the accurate reflection of the ideological origins of Nazi atrocities than they were a means of concealing the actual aims of such operations.[21] By relying so uncritically on the Nazis' own bureaucratic rhetoric, Weiss seems to have blurred crucial distinctions between the ideological origins of Nazism, the language by which the Nazis implemented their aims, and the critical paradigms for interpreting and representing this period he now brings to bear.

Had he been a more self-critical Marxist, Weiss might have been aware of the fallacy of such a mechanical application of his economic model to Auschwitz and of the contrived causal nexus implicit in his orthodoxy. Instead of claiming for the economic a role as sole determiner of social and historical totality, for example, Weiss might have assigned the economic a particular place within a series of complicated relations constituting the Holocaust. In this way, Weiss might have allowed a multiplicity of meanings and interpretations to issue from his documentary drama, including the religious, political, bureaucratic, and social aspects of Auschwitz. As it stands, however, by enacting an interpretation of historical events in a form of literary discourse—documentary drama—that simultaneously erases the lines of its interpretation, Weiss merely substitutes one totalizing system for so many others. And though he may be no more culpable in this process than other literary documentarists, his method might be regarded as exemplary of the art of ideological effacement. There is a sense in which Weiss has thus elevated the "rhetoric of fact" to its own art form, which by its nature must continue to deny its artfulness, its construction, and its ideological premises.

V

As the healthy sign for Barthes is one that draws attention to its own arbitrariness and artificial status, a healthy critique of the facts of Auschwitz might also convey something of its relative status. But as it turns out, Weiss seems to have appropriated even this critical axiom in order to authenticate still further the lines of his governing myth. In observing that in documentary theater, "objectivity is likely to be merely a concept used by a ruling group to justify its actions" (p. 42), Weiss betrays an exceptionally astute grasp of the rhetorical possibilities in documentary drama, which seems to make him an even more persuasive documentarist. But in the process, he may ultimately be baring his hand in criticism only to cover it that much more effectively again in his play. That is, by proclaiming a certain self-reflexivity on his part, Weiss is seemingly able to resist the ideological distortions of the Holocaust even as he removes the principles of his own distortions from view. In effect, Weiss further reinforces an ideology by claiming an awareness of it: that is, he naturalizes the actual ideological function of his work by having appeared to neutralize it.

If it is true, as Hayden White has suggested, that "one mark of a good professional historian is the consistency with which he reminds his readers of the purely provisional nature of his characterization of events, agents, and agencies found in the always incomplete historical record,"[22] then the reader looking for Holocaust history might be best advised to approach Holocaust documentary literature with special caution. For, in contrast to the quality of self-critique to be found in the most creditable historical accounts, the distinguishing feature of documentary narrative is its relentless insistence on denying its provisionality, not revealing it. Whether it is accomplished ingenuously by the unconscious internalization of the ethos of one's tradition, or conscientiously by the writer on an ideological mission, the effacement from a text of the sign's status as sign constitutes the guiding principle of "factually insistent narrative."

After Hayden White's description of what he calls "figurative historicists" as those writers of history who "remain unaware of the extent to which what they say about their subject is inextricably bound, if not identical with, how they say it,"[23] we might henceforth refer to the writers of documentary narrative as *"figurative* documentarists," who write—and then ask us to accept—their work *as if* it were documentary. This distinction is an important one, for without distinguishing the work's effectiveness in presenting itself as "documentary fact" from its reflexive interpretation of fact, the ingenuous reader risks confusing a work in the documentary style for the documentary evidence it purports to be. And by mistaking the figurative appeal to fact for reality itself and then acting on behalf of what amount to "figurative facts," there is a sense in which we thereby accomplish—or reify—the rhetorical figures of interpretation that have transported these facts from the past moment to the present. In effect, by looking beyond the factual nature of Holocaust documentary literature and focusing instead on the fabulative character of these facts, critical readers can sustain the constitutive ambiguity of "literary testimony," even as they relieve themselves of critical ambivalence; in this way, we might continue to participate in and learn from Holocaust documentary discourse without being drawn intractably into its essential rhetoric.

II.

Figuring and Refiguring the Holocaust: Interpreting Holocaust Metaphor

FIVE

Names of the Holocaust

Meaning and Consequences

Every metaphor is a little myth.

—Giambattista Vico

What, then, is truth? A mobile army of metaphors, meto-
nyms, and anthropomorphisms . . . truths are illusions about
which one has forgotten that this is what they are.

—Friedrich Nietzsche

Who will write a Jewish Musa Dagh?

—Yitzchak Katzenelson

INTRODUCTION

When President Jimmy Carter likened the plight of Palestinian Arabs to
that of blacks in the American South, was he also suggesting that Israelis
were therefore "white racist oppressors," as Edward Alexander believes?[1]
Or was he merely drawing somewhat carelessly on a convenient set of
figures, a known landscape of suffering, with which to grasp a situation
otherwise foreign to him? Inasmuch as he necessarily apprehends new ideas
and experiences in terms of the familiar (Aristotle's justification for metaphor), Carter might not be blamed for groping in his own backyard for an
analogue with which to represent Palestinians' lives; he might be blamed,
however, for extending such a metaphor, or for acting on the putative
equivalences he has created in the figure. Or he might be blamed for failing
to foresee the consequences of his metaphor, that it would eventually take
on a life of its own.

Did American blacks "steal" the Exodus story from Jews to figure their
own emancipation from slavery in the South? Did this make the plantation
owners Pharaohs? And if so, did Jews then steal the blacks' version of the
past back from them by incorporating into the Passover Haggadah the

black gospel version of "Let my people go"? Or did the Jewish labor movement early in this century misappropriate the slavery experience from blacks when its members marched in shackles and referred to their plight not only in terms of, but even as an extension of, the slaves' plight in the American South?

"Jews are not metaphors—not for poets, not for novelists, not for theologians, not for murderers, and never for antisemites," Cynthia Ozick wrote in "A Liberal's Auschwitz."[2] But in fact, Jews are metaphors—for poets, novelists, theologians, too often for murderers and antisemites, and most often for themselves as Jews. For historical memory and ritual commemoration are nothing if not a refiguring of present lives in light of a remembered past. Can any of us know ourselves as part of a people, or the world around us, without grasping both in tropes of our heritage and civilization? We may not like the ways that Jews have been figured traditionally, or the ways Jews are now used to figure other peoples. But in fact, Jewish memory and tradition depend explicitly on the capacity of figurative language to remember the past.

In the case of Holocaust metaphors, we find that figurative language is never entirely innocent and is almost always complicit in the actions we take in our world. How victims of the Holocaust grasped and responded to events as they unfolded around them depended on the available tropes and figures of their time no less than our own responses now depend on the figures available to us in a post-Holocaust era. Like other elements of narrative, the figures and archetypes used by writers to represent the Holocaust ultimately create as much knowledge of events as they would reflect; and like other mediating elements in language, these figures screen as much of the realities as they would illuminate.

The aim of this present section is to explore Holocaust metaphors as they operate on three different levels: first, how events of this period were grasped in the archetypes and paradigms of other epochs during the Holocaust; second, how particular aspects of the Holocaust began to figure other parts of this time within the period itself (i.e., how the Holocaust became its own trope); and third, how images from the Holocaust subsequently came to figure other, unrelated events and experiences for both victims and nonvictims, Jews and non-Jews. The aims here will be to examine how both writers and readers of this literature apprehend events through figurative language, and how we understand our contemporary world in light of the Holocaust figures we inevitably bring to it. Instead of attempting to sanction or legislate particular Holocaust metaphors, the aim will be to see how they have been enacted and what kind of knowledge of both past and present events they create. It is to explore the role of metaphor as an agent in both our knowledge of the Holocaust and our responses to it, the assumption being that particular kinds of knowledge lead to particular kinds of action.

I. NAMING AND UNIQUENESS

In an ironic but significant twist to the cataloguing of historical periods, the massacre of nearly one and a half million Armenians by the Turks between 1915 and 1923 has come recently to be known as the "Armenian Holocaust": it is ironic in that the Armenian massacre has been made to rely for its name on a set of events that postdate it by twenty-five years, and significant in that it is now thus figured for Armenians in the terms of another people's catastrophe.[3] As the Jewish writer Franz Werfel had biblically troped even the number of days at Musa Dagh to read forty instead of the actual fifty-two,[4] succeeding Armenian historians came also to rely on the Jewish reserve of archetypes for their destruction and suffering. That there were certain similarities between the massacres of the Armenians and of the Jews, or that there were also differences came to matter less than the larger continuum of destruction created *in* the naming of these catatrophes, one in light of the other.[5]

Of the different means by which writers and commentators have begun to understand and to interpret the Holocaust, naming it—along with the metaphorical process at the basis of naming—would thus seem to be the most reflexive. Through an elaboration of the terms *sho'ah*, *churban*, and Holocaust, it may be possible to illustrate how the names we assign this period automatically figure and contextualize events, locating them within the continua of particular historical, literary, and interpretive traditions. In this process, we are reminded as well of our inevitable reliance on past terms and events in order to know "new" experiences. And by recognizing the reflexive understanding constructed for us in the naming process, we remain aware of the reciprocal exchange between past and present when each is figured in terms of the other. The names of this period are, in this view, the opening metaphors by which we come to grasp the events of the Holocaust.

In their first applications to unnamed events, terms like "holocaust," "*sho'ah*," or "*churban*" necessarily evoked other destructions in order to frame the catastrophe of European Jewry during World War II. Unlike English or Armenian cultural lexicons, however, Jewish tradition already contained not only a set of possible precedents and terms like *churban* or *sho'ah* by which to know the latest destruction, but also ritual days of lament, during which all catastrophes—past, present, and future—are recalled at once.[6] Whether or not the destructions of the First and Second temples, the quelling of the Bar Kochba rebellion, and the massacre of Europe's Jews are equivalent events, upon sharing the same name, each event is automatically grasped in light of its namesake.

With its roots deep in specific historical disasters like the destructions of the First and Second temples, the Hebrew term *churban* suggested itself immediately to Jewish writers describing the unfolding massacre in Europe early in 1940. At the same time, however, its Yiddish echo (*churbm*) and explicitly religious resonances made *churban* less appealing among Labor Zionists in Palestine writing about the situation in Europe. As a result, the term *sho'ah* was adopted as a deliberate alternative, it seems, to designate the latest, unprecedented murder of Jews. Uriel Tal has thus cited a collection of eyewitness reports on the mass killings published in Hebrew under the title *Sho'at Yehudei Polin* (*sho'ah* of Polish Jews) in 1940.[7] Other early references to *sho'ah* in this context include that by poet Shaul Tchernikowsky in his paper "The Command of the Horrible *Sho'ah* That Is Coming over Us," delivered at a conference of Hebrew writers and poets gathered in the Jewish Agency offices in Jerusalem in 1942 expressly to address the European catastrophe (p. 48). Later that year a conference attended by four hundred rabbis proclaimed that "the *Sho'ah* that European Jewry was undergoing was without precedent in history." And in 1943, the historian Benzion Dinur "stated that the *Sho'ah* . . . symbolized the uniqueness of the history of the Jewish people among the nations" (pp. 48–49).

Because they perceived events in Europe as completely unprecedented, neither secular nor religious Zionists in Palestine were content to call this merely the "third *churban*." For this might have located events directly in a succession of previous destructions, even as it suggested the divine scheme of sin and retribution that explained every *churban*. By locating these events in a long line of destructions, *der driter churbm* seemed not only to justify the current catastrophe but also to level its significance and to deny its historical and political uniqueness, consequences of naming that directly contradicted the writers' reasons for citing the growing destruction in the first place. Even though *sho'ah* still resonated a biblical order, as a less specific—and thus more flexible—term than *churban*, it seemed to allow for new meanings. By calling the unfolding European catastrophe *sho'ah*, these arbiters of a national response relied upon a figure that would mark events as part of Jewish history even as it avoided comparisons with specific precedents created in such a trope.

For these early writers, the Hebrew term *sho'ah* thus reverberated both the destruction of Israel by surrounding nations (Isa. 6:11, 10:3, 47:11 and Zeph. 1:15) and the humiliation of Babylon, echoes consistent with the Zionists' view of both the Jews' general situation in the *galut* and their specific circumstances during the war. So even though the Deuteronomic concepts of divine retribution and judgment are still implicit in *sho'ah*, historians, writers, and even theologians in Israel have tended to cultivate more its roots of desolation and metaphysical doubt than its more pious echoes of sin and punishment. As Uriel Tal has also demonstrated, the term itself has thus acquired new meanings in its contemporary usage as well as shaped new experiences in light of its biblical past.

Where there were names in Hebrew and Yiddish for the annihilation of European Jewry, in which events were already figured and understood, there was no "ready-made" name in English. Like the Armenians, English-speaking writers and historians who perceived these events separately from their World War II context were moved to adopt a name by which events would be known in their particularity. First used in a purely descriptive or figurative sense, according to Gerd Korman, it was not until sometime between 1957 and 1959 that the English term "holocaust" came to refer specifically to the murder of European Jews.[8] And even then, this particular usage depended upon the community of users, with non-Jews hesitating to distinguish between the Jews killed "in the war" and the other "war victims." That is, because they did not perceive the difference between kinds of victims, many non-Jewish historians were unwilling to grant these events the independent "selfhood" their own name would give them.

Like *sho'ah*, the English term "holocaust" derives from more broadly descriptive, generic references to disaster (usually by fire), without reference to specific past conflagrations. But like *sho'ah* and *churban*, "holocaust" also carries a certain theological load in its etymons, which has led some writers to question its appropriateness as well. Derived from the Greek *holokauston*, which literally means "whole burnt," it referred in the Septuagint specifically to sacrifice by fire, assonant with the Hebrew term for sacrificial offering, *ola*. Wary of the archaic Christian notion of a Jewish calvary in the Holocaust, many Jewish writers and theologians continue to resist this term altogether. For as problematic as the theological implications underpinning *sho'ah* or *churban* may be, they are still more consonant with Jewish tradition than the resonances of sacrifice and burnt offering in "holocaust."[9]

The salient point here is that unlike the English term "holocaust," the terms *sho'ah* and *churban* figure these events in uniquely Jewish ways, which simultaneously preserve and create specifically Jewish understanding and memory of this period. And as the names for this period reflect what was already known about events, even before they happened, they will continue to create Jewish understanding and memory in future events as well. As one of the first hermeneutical moves regarding an event, its naming frames and remembers events, even as it determines particular knowledge of events. It is not a matter of borrowing a name from one era to obfuscate the nature of events from another, but rather to grasp the unfamiliar in familiar terms. That events from this time would be contained under the rubric of other names like "Patriotic War" (in Russia), "Hitler-time" (in Germany), or "World War II" (in America) tells us as much about the particular understanding of this period by the namers as it does about the events themselves. The differences among names also explain the great gulfs in understanding between different nations and people, reflecting disparate experiences of the period as well as the different shapes respective national mythologies and ideologies necessarily confer on events. Every language's name thus molds events in the image of its culture's particular understanding of events. Naming these events is thus inevitably to conceive of them, to constrain as well as to create conditions for acting on events.

With these considerations in mind, the question of the Holocaust's uniqueness becomes somewhat of a red herring. On the one hand, only when the events of the Holocaust are brought into a continuum of some sort can sense be made of them; on the other hand, all comparisons tend to belie the unique character of events. That is, on the basis of the historical valence of the Holocaust, it may certainly be considered a unique set of events, but given our own limited resources for understanding and interpreting these events, the sense we make of them may never be unique. Historical events are never exactly like one another; nor do they often occur for the same reasons. While the events are new, our names for events and the meanings they make are necessarily old. Only if we allow new and unprecedented events to corrupt in their image the old and available frames of reference we bring to them can we begin to create unique meaning.

Though the sheer extremity of the Holocaust makes it even less like any other event, it was never the quality of its sheer terror or unlimited suffering that set it aside from other catastrophes but the meaning of this suffering, its causes and effects, what has been called the intentionality of the Holocaust, that makes it so different. Inasmuch as these qualities of uniqueness are measured in the language and figures we bring to events, we might shift the emphasis here away from the intrinsic uniqueness of the Holocaust to the ways it is inevitably figured by other calamities—and inevitably used to figure post-Holocaust suffering. For even though these events were indeed like no others, as soon as we speak of them, or respond to them, or represent them in any fashion, we necessarily grasp them in relation to other events; even in their unlikeness, they are thus contextualized and understood in opposition to prevailing figures, but thus figured nonetheless.

As a historian searching for a cause-and-effect sequence as well as understanding, Yehuda Bauer has also recognized the problematic nature of the Holocaust's uniqueness, the limits and necessity of knowing the Holocaust within the continuum of historical understanding, and the literary conventions in which this understanding is subsumed. On the one hand, he writes, "if what happened to the Jews was unique, then [the Holocaust] took place outside of history, and it becomes a mysterious event, an upside-down miracle, so to speak, an event of religious significance in the sense that it is not man-made. . . . On the other hand, if it is not unique, then where are the precedents or parallels?"[10] It is neither completely unique nor entirely precedented, Bauer concludes. The problem then becomes both the writers' and the readers', who are dependent on language and its implicit continuities for the means to represent discontinuity and uniqueness.

Though many have suggested that the Holocaust writer's task has been to reconcile experiences with traditional Jewish beliefs and paradigms, one wonders how deliberate such a reconciliation can ever be. For merely by living and perceiving events in "the Jewish grammar," through a reflexive application of Jewish tropes, precedents, and paradigms, the writer locates events in a Jewish continuum, understands them in Jewish ways. In fact, given the reflexivity of such knowledge and understanding generated in traditional forms and language, the problem may not be how to reconcile the Holocaust with Jewish figures and traditions so much as it is to know events outside of a Jewish grammar of being.

Short of creating an entirely new word, without any previous meanings, associations, assonances, or even rhymes, naming events must inevitably deprive them of their ontological particularity. For until they are named, compared, or interpreted, they continue to exist outside existing traditions. So even though persuasive arguments can be made on the basis of "historical valence" to affirm the uniqueness of the Holocaust, what finally makes it so important in history is precisely the kinds of meaning that accrue from its location in history, in language, and in the figures of its names. As events, those that occurred in Europe between 1933 and 1945 were unique in kind, number, and effect; but they are still always already known in relation to other events, other times and places, always understood and responded to in light of those figures which now enunciate this period.[11]

The issue here is not whether it is possible to generate new responses to catastrophe in the frame of the ancient archetypes, but rather how it has been done, to what effect for both the lives of the victims and for our understanding of the events, and to what extent both events and the archetypes by which we have known events are transformed in the process. For even with the "dangers" of archetypal thinking so apparent, there are ultimately no alternatives: to think about, to remember, and to express the events of the Holocaust is either to do so archetypally or not at all.

II. THE CRITICS OF METAPHOR

In a literary-critical era when the fundamental metaphorical character of language, thinking, conceiving, and writing is fully acknowledged, it thus becomes all the more puzzling when critics persist in trying to know the Holocaust without recourse to metaphor, as if it were possible to write about it, talk about it, or even narrate its history without figurative language. Rather than looking for the Holocaust outside of metaphor, therefore, I would suggest that we find it in metaphor, in the countless ways it has been figured, colored, distorted, and ultimately cast as a figure for other events— all for the ways that each figure brings further understanding to both the events and to ourselves in light of events.

The problem with Holocaust metaphor became apparent first to the victims themselves, who in trying to represent events "as they happened" and in their uniqueness were constantly frustrated by language that seemed simultaneously to lead away from events and to analogize them. For even if the realities of the camps and ghettos were unprecedented, the available language and figures to describe them were not. Part of the problem, however, stems from the assumption that the writers' task is only to relate "the facts" of the Holocaust, without the meaning in these facts necessarily created in metaphor. Since the movement in metaphor seemed to transport writers and readers away from the facts (as opposed to toward the meaning in them), figurative language was perceived as somehow incompatible with the transmission of factual information. As language was perceived to displace the events to which it was supposed to refer, figures and metaphors also seemed to substitute one experience for another—ultimately diverting attention from, not focusing it upon, the facts.

For writers and subsequent critics, the "lie" in any Holocaust metaphor thus became a lie about the Holocaust itself. "There are no metaphors for Auschwitz," Alvin Rosenfeld has written, "just as Auschwitz is not a metaphor for anything else. . . . Why is this the case? Because the flames were real flames, the ashes only ashes, the smoke always and only smoke. If one wants 'meaning' out of that, it can only be this: at Auschwitz, humanity incinerated its own heart. Otherwise the burnings do not lend themselves to metaphor, simile, or symbol—to likeness or association with anything else. They can only 'be' or 'mean' what they in fact were: the death of the Jews."[12] Though as we see here, even Rosenfeld necessarily figures events ("humanity incinerated its own heart"), thereby suggesting a meaning in the death of the Jews. For whether or not one wants meaning in Auschwitz, it is automatically created the instant its smoke and ashes are represented— that is, figured—for us in language.

As he suggests in another essay, however, it may not just be the arbitrary creation of meaning or transformation of facts that is most troublesome in metaphor but the averted glance implied in it. The "function of metaphorical language of this kind," Rosenfeld suggests, "is to compare one thing with another not so much from an urge to get at the first but to get rid of it."[13] In some ways, in fact, this assertion reminds us of the impulse by writers to confine their language and figures to those of the camps and ghettos themselves. Part of this impulse may stem from a traditionally positivist attitude toward metaphor as frivolous and merely decorative, a trivializing influence—not a frame for difficult concepts and realities. In fact, even among contemporary theorists of metaphor, the potential for transcendence of and escape from reality still occupies some of the discussion.[14]

For example, Karsten Harries has noted that "Metaphor no longer has its telos in reality. It . . . invites us to take leave from familiar reality, but not for the sake of a more profound vision of what is. Instead metaphors become weapons directed against reality, instruments to break the referentiality of language, to deliver language from its ontological function and thus to confer on the poets' words a magical presence that lets us forget the world."[15] This is not to say, however, that the obverse is also true, that there might not also be a certain avoidance of reality in the concentration of detail and nonmetaphoric language, which is tied closely to the avoidance of the cumulative meaning of reality. In this context, José Ortega y Gasset actually suggests a link between the "avoidance of reality" in metaphor and the avoidance in what he calls "infra-realism." "Both satsify the urge to escape and dilute reality," he writes. "Instead of soaring to poetical heights, art may dive beneath the level marked by the natural perspective. How it is possible to overcome realism by merely putting too fine a point on it and discovering, lens in hand, the microstructure of life can be observed in Proust, Ramón Gómez de la Serna, Joyce. . . . [The procedure] simply consists in letting the outskirts of attention, that which ordinarily escapes notice, perform this main part in life's drama" (pp. 35–36).

Since the transmission of facts in Holocaust writing still dominates this literature's function for so many writers, and since metaphor cannot directly transmit these facts, many critics still regard metaphor as not only ineffective but even dangerous for representing the Holocaust. In purporting to present the facts, they would say, Holocaust metaphors can ultimately do no more than falsify the facts and, therefore, deceive the readers. The dilemma implicit in these objections to metaphor stems from the writers' dual recognition of their unavoidable dependence on the metaphorical qualities of language to transmit facts to the reader and of the qualities in metaphor by which readers are transported away from these facts to something else. In striving only to see the likeness between the Holocaust and the figures by which we know it, however, the reader once again neglects the interpretive activity and tension in the movement between parts of metaphor. But once the reader consents to make the leap between language and referent, and to partake in what Ricoeur calls the "calculated error" in metaphor,[16] even as he resists being deluded by this error, the language and metaphors by which we come to events tell us as much about how events have been grasped and organized as they do about events themselves. Rather than seeing metaphors as threatening to the facts of the Holocaust, we must recognize that they are our only access to the facts, which cannot exist apart from the figures delivering them to us.

Indeed, to leave Auschwitz outside of metaphor would be to leave it outside of language altogether: it was known, understood, and responded to metaphorically at the time by its victims; it has been organized, expressed, and interpreted metaphorically by its writers; and it is now being remembered, commented upon, and given historical meaning metaphorically by scholars and poets of the next generation. If carried to its literal end, an injunction against Auschwitz metaphors would place events outside of language and meaning altogether, thereby mystifying the Holocaust and accomplishing after the fact precisely what the Nazis had hoped to accomplish through their own—often metaphorical—mystification of events.

In fact, rather than attempting to quantify the uniqueness of the Holocaust as a means of disputing metaphor, or sanctioning metaphor altogether, the critic might be better served by exploring the interpretive aspects of metaphor and their consequences for both the victims and for our understanding of these events now. In this vein, we turn not just to the obfuscations of metaphor but also to the illuminations of events both by the tropes and archetypes victims brought to their predicament and by those now based in the Holocaust, through which a post-Holocaust generation has come to understand its own world. In between and linking these two metaphorical moves is the use of the Holocaust as its own trope or archetype, the point at which it became its own point of reference as well as a point of reference for all subsequent pain, suffering, and destruction.

III. CONSEQUENCES OF METAPHOR

Unlike other literary problems, however, this question of metaphor, precedent, and analogue implies consequences that go far beyond literary texts alone. For as scholars of Holocaust history have already suggested, it may have been precisely this understanding of the Holocaust as nothing more than the continuation of traditional antisemitism that blinded both Jews and the rest of the world to the actual gravity of events, and that left them so unprepared in the face of the Nazi threat. Yehuda Bauer has written that "Jews reacted to present threat with reference to past experience; what they were threatened with were persecutions, pogroms perhaps, hunger, economic destruction. It was this threat they were trying to combat" (p. 10). Apprehending, interpreting, and then understanding new experiences in terms of the previously known is an inevitable—if eternally problematic—aspect of knowing anything. But by creating particular meanings and screening from view other aspects of their predicament, this "flaw" in the metaphorical process held dire consequences. "Both perpetrators and victims drew upon their age-old experience in dealing with each other," writes Raul Hilberg. "The Germans did it with success. The Jews did it with disaster."[17]

In addition to Zionist, religiously orthodox, Marxist, and biblical models of mind that determined understanding of events leading into the Holocaust, remembered historical events themselves also seem to have constituted a governing mythos of sorts. In *The Jewish War Front*, for example, the Zionist revisionist leader, Vladimir Jabotinsky, specifically warned that if the Armenian massacres of twenty years before were not taken into account by the Allies in their response to Hitler, Germany's war against the Jews would end in the their annihilation.[18] And as the Armenian massacres constituted a particular historical "paradigm of possibilities" for Jabotinsky, the Holocaust itself has hardened into its own guiding mythos for many of the survivors' and post-Holocaust generation's responses to the current world. Where the shtetl Jews during the Holocaust may have initially perceived their lot in terms of a ghastly—but relatively limited—pogrom, many of the survivors—their understanding of Jewish persecution now enlarged to include the enormity of the Holocaust—tend to perceive new persecutions in terms of the "permanent pogrom" they have known.[19]

The intrinsic danger in the act of knowing anything at all, of course, is that our actions are inevitably based in the epistemological transformations of events engendered in knowing one thing in light of another. As Robert Alter has warned in this context, "super-imposing the images of past murderers on present adversaries turns every enemy into a potential Hitler. [T]o invoke the Holocaust as the supreme paradigm of the historical experience of the Jewish people is to preclude the idea of political bargaining and concessions, for every potential advantage granted to one's opponent, whatever might be given in exchange, will be seen as a paving stone on the road to extinction."[20] The consequences of interpetation would thus lead in two directions: back into the events of the Holocaust and out of the Holocaust into a world that is now understood in light of it.

In some ways, it is as if regions of the imagination that had been effable only through their objectification in metaphor were now suddenly real partly because of metaphor. After the Holocaust, we might ask whether by making something imaginable through metaphor we have also made it possible in the world. That is, to what extent does "imaginative precedent"—the kind we effect in metaphor—prepare the human sensibility for its worldly reification? This is not to say that metaphor makes its own reification likely, but one might still ask to what extent, for example, the repeated figurative abuses of the Jews in Nazi Germany prepared both killers and victims for the Jews' literal destruction. Was it, in fact, any easier for the Germans to use Zyklon-B (roach gas) to "exterminate" the Jews after having equated them figuratively for so many years with *Ungeziefer* (vermin)? If the soldiers who poured quicklime down the sewers in Warsaw to kill Jews in the uprising there could write home that they were busy "liquidating vermin," then it would seem that the imagination can be subjugated—as well as liberated—by metaphor. For once the distinction between figurative and literal language was lost, language and metaphor ceased to function as the arbiter of thought and became its tyrant instead.

It is ironic then that so many critics of Holocaust literature would emphasize the literal or positivistic aspects of metaphor in their arguments. For the danger in metaphor lies precisely in this puncturing of its figurative life. Though perhaps it is because the life of a metaphor—once thus punctured—is never the same in these critics' eyes that they object to it so strenuously. In fact, the Nazi literalization of metaphor during the Holocaust may have destroyed the possibility of innocent figuration thereafter. "In closing the space that formerly mediated between violent words and violent deeds," Alvin Rosenfeld has suggested, the Nazis effected nothing less than the death of language itself (p. 135).

What once might have been "only" a literary problem—the so-called death of language—now bears directly, however, on the post-Holocaust world. For in the survivors' eyes, a once-literalized metaphor seems to invest in all subsequent metaphors their own potential for realization: figurative speech thus becomes haunted by the implicit threat of its actualization. The Israeli survivor of the Holocaust, for example, may find it nearly impossible to dismiss as mere figuration the Arab war cry "We will turn the sea red with Jewish blood" after parts of the European sky were quite literally turned black with Jewish ashes. The rhetorical phrase after the Holocaust is no longer innocent but is now condemned to carry the ominous threat of its literalization.

In this light, we may never be able to isolate the purely "literary" levels of response to events from the more "worldly" responses; for insofar as both literary and practical responses share common archetypal assumptions, they may never be wholly separable. In fact, as David Roskies suggests in another context, during the Holocaust the literary and practical may even have been fatally interdependent:

> The Holocaust was the most demonic of conspiracies between literature and life. Designed as such by the Nazis (one of Hitler's professors had studied at the Hebrew University in Jerusalem), it was perceived by the Jews as a return to the hoary past. This, of course, raises a host of painful questions as to the role that the memory of past destruction played and continues to play in the politics of Jewish survival. Would the Nazis have succeeded in deluding Jews into repeating past responses had it not been for a tradition that constantly rehearsed the destruction? Or shall we say that without a patterned, collective response to catastrophe, all Jews might ultimately have perished? And is it possible to generate new responses in the post-war world when the enemy still chooses the holiest day of the calendar to launch its attack?[21]

As Roskies painfully acknowledges, the Nazis themselves thus demonstrated a frighteningly profound grasp of both "archetypal thinking" and its practical implications. Self-trained as "Hebraicists" in order to annihilate the "Hebraic people," the Nazis seemed to understand all too well this historically minded—which is to say analogically minded—nature of the Jews. By reinstituting the Renaissance ghetto, the medieval yellow star, and the seventeenth-century Jewish councils, for example, the Germans "thereby created a world that was both utterly terrifying and strangely familiar" (p. 191). And then by coordinating actions with the Jewish calendar, they further inflamed this same archetypal thinking and understanding among their victims. All of which not only encouraged the victims to perceive their circumstances in light of the past and the ancient archetypes but also encouraged paradigmatic response to and understanding of their predicament. By thus lulling their victims into analogy, as it were, by re-creating all previous persecutions, the Nazis were actually able to screen from view *the difference* of the present persecution until it was too late.

IV. INHERITED AND CHOSEN METAPHORS

Whether or not it is ever possible to generate new responses to catastrophe in the frame of the "ancient archetypes" might thus constitute one of the essential questions in this section on Holocaust metaphor. For even with the dangers of archetypal thinking so apparent, there may be no alternative: to think about, to remember, and to express events is either to do so archetypally and figuratively—or not at all. As long as events continue to enter the languages of the Jews, they continue to be incorporated into a Jewish continuum and to be understood in inescapably Jewish ways. Thus, it has made little difference how dissimilar or unrelated separate catastrophes in Jewish history have been, once they enter the traditional paradigms that give them meaning. And as is apparent throughout Jewish literary history, events in Jewish history and their literary representations have always been incorporated as paradigmatic points of reference used to organize current catastrophes. In this way, ancient biblical legends—like the destruction of Sodom and Gomorrah, the Akedah, or the Exodus—as well as legendary accounts of more recent events like the destructions of the First and Second temples, as well as relatively modern events like the Crusader massacres, the Chmielnicky pogroms, and the Ukrainian pogroms all become archetypal events by which new disasters are measured and understood.

Even as these archetypes are invoked in the traditional literature, however, they are qualified—even recast—as efficacious paradigms. Both Roskies and Alan Mintz have thus found in their examinations of scriptural archetypes that even though earlier figures were indeed recalled by the survivors of destruction, it was not always for their intrinsic appropriateness, but often for their perceived *in*adequacy as analogues: "Is there any agony like mine?" asks the ravaged figure of Jerusalem in Lamentations (1:12), to which the scribes have answered, "The chastisement of my poor people / Was greater than the punishment of Sodom, / Which was overthrown in a moment, / Without a hand striking it" (Lam. 4:6).[22] That is, even the scribes of Lamentations found themselves simultaneously dependent on past destructions for their figures and resistant to them.

The same tendency is evident in nearly every other literary representation of Jewish catastrophe. For example, even though the Akedah was most commonly recalled as archetype for representing the Rhineland Crusader massacres of the eleventh and twelfth centuries in both the Hebrew Chronicles and in the poetry of this era, it is often invoked for its inadequacy as a figure for understanding such suffering. To a great extent, part of the response to catastrophe has thus always been a self-reflexive questioning of the available archetypes to frame it—a quality in modern literature many have mistakenly deemed exclusively modern.

Although several critics have suggested that one of the innovations of Holocaust literature is precisely the manner in which it would mock and subvert the traditional forms and archetypes its writers have called upon, Roskies finds that this tendency to question accepted figures has always in itself been part of the tradition. By considering the earliest—i.e., scriptural—responses to catastrophe, Roskies shows (after Michael Fishbane) that to a great extent, the *Widerruf* of Paul Celan or the symbolic inversion of figures in Chaim Kaplan's diary is actually part of the tradition itself. The instances of archetypal doubt in Lamentations thus exemplify what Fishbane describes as "inner-Biblical midrash," a correction or modification of a traditional interpretation now codified in the biblical text.[23] In this light, the bitter recriminations and outcries against God, as well as the many subversions and repudiations of traditional figures in works by Bialik, Halpern, Sutzkever, Katzenelson, Kaplan, and the rest are all—inescapably— located within the tradition itself. Roskies even concludes that "inverting Scripture can [thus] be seen as a means of *keeping* the faith" (p. 19, emphasis mine).

As Roskies is quick to add, however, once the scribes do any kind of violence to the sacred texts—through either gentle mimicry or outright rejection—the parodied text is never quite the same, for "it would always carry with it the pain of that momentary defiance" (p. 69). By absorbing this parody, the sacred texts are thus enlarged and enriched—even reinvigorated—and the potential for parody is simultaneously codified. At this point, Roskies distinguishes between what he calls the "sacred parodists" and the modern "sacrilegious parodists" of the tradition. On the one hand, even though the survivor-scribes of Lamentations may have lamented bitterly, questioning the efficacy of the figures and archetypes available to them, they ultimately accepted the covenantal framework of guilt, punishment, and retribution; that is, while they may have questioned the paradigm, they accepted the meaning it conferred on their catastrophe. On the other hand, Roskies tells us, "the modern writers use parody to unmask the artificiality of the accepted conventions and to argue for radical change" (p. 69).

Taken further, however, this distinction may become less palatable for Roskies. For even though the moderns may indeed reinvigorate the routine archetype by forcing new and extreme experience into its frame, thus perhaps radically changing it, unlike the sacred parodists of the past, the moderns repudiate both the mere figure of the archetype and the meaning it imposes on experience. That is, they may have used the traditional paradigms because they were the only ones available, even as they attempted to discard the meanings and explanations attending these same archetypes. More fully elaborated, this difference between "sacred parodists" and "sacrilegious parodists" suggests the possibility of using the forms of faith while simultaneously rejecting the tenets of the faith, retaining the shell of the archetype while disposing of its meaning. The modern writers may, by necessity, be part of the tradition, but contrary to Roskies's suggestion, they are not necessarily keeping faith in it.

This leads to a further point concerning the activity and the intentionality of metaphor and archetypal thinking. At one point, Roskies writes that, for the early rabbis, "ideally, the choice of archetypes would fulfill a triple purpose: to give the immediate events a biblical sanction, thereby to alert God to the grand design of history, and to assure the survivors of their own place on the continuum" (p. 23). But as have others before him in a more contemporary context,[24] Roskies implies here that these archetypes and the particular meanings they lend events are a matter of choice, that they are "willed" somehow, and that specific archetypes are chosen because they are more appropriate than others. Extended further, however, this formulation also suggests that the rabbis (or any of the subsequent scribes) could have "chosen" not to locate events archetypally, not to assure their own place on the continuum. But in fact, neither the ancient rabbis nor the ghetto scribes may have been consciously attempting to make catastrophe fit into a priori patterns of Jewish history, or choosing to remain within the tradition as a collective act of faith, or "arguing for the tradition," as Roskies suggests, so much as they were necessarily resorting to the only system of myths, precedents, figures, and archetypes available to them. In giving catastrophic events a narrative form at all, the rabbis reflexively imposed upon them the unity and coherence that come automatically with any language and narrative. That is, it may always be less a matter of the rabbis' and scribes' "keeping the faith" when they write events as they do, than it is a matter of "the faith keeping them."

For inasmuch as the scribes who question the tradition are necessarily obligated to do so from within it, with recourse only to its pool of archetypes and interpretations, they may never actually choose to be in or out of the tradition. By suggesting, however, that an individual can be "cut off from the sustaining archetypes, from the exalted messianic schemes . . . , from the communal saga, from the past, from his own set of inherited symbols," Roskies implies that one can cut oneself off from one's tradition, or leave it behind somehow. But in fact, the individual "cut off from the sustaining archetypes, his past, and his inherited symbols" might only exist hypothetically as the emblematic modernist or freethinker, or in fiction as "*der Mann ohne Eigenschaften.*" For only the desire to cut oneself off from the tradition and all of its cumbersome, informing, and constraining myths might be represented and speculated upon in writing; inasmuch as language and narrative are essential parts of any tradition, however, this desire to be "cut off" can never actually be enacted in writing.

And as we may not enact this cutting off in writing, we find that we may not be able ever to represent the tremendum, the caesura, the traumatic breach we infer in the events of the Holocaust. As writing tends to stitch the writer into the forms and conventions he might be attempting to cut himself off from, it also tends to mend perceived breaking points in history,

creating unities and continuities, causes and effects, preserving the archetypes at the expense of discontinuity. In this sense, even the Holocaust can
never lie outside of literature, or understanding, or telling. For as the "end"
of history, tradition, or archetypes, the Holocaust falls outside all paradigms
of knowledge: it becomes unknowable. But as long as we name the events
of this period, remember them, or figure them in any form, we also know
them—however poorly, inappropriately, or dangerously. In this way, the
Holocaust may not be a breach in knowledge, or in history, or in the continuum so much as it is a traumatic breach in our uncritical belief in the
kinds of knowledge we have of it. After such a breach, we may stand hum-
bled in our limited repetoire of archetypes and figures and the tentative
understanding they bring to the Holocaust—but we continue to know the
Holocaust by these figures nevertheless.

SIX

The Holocaust Becomes an Archetype

Evoke not Ezekiel, evoke not Jeremiah . . . I don't need
them!. . .
. . . I don't compare myself to the prophets—
But all the martyred Jews taken to their death, the millions
murdered here—

—Yitzhak Katzenelson

I

It is ironic that once an event is perceived to be without precedent, without
adequate analogy, it would in itself become a kind of precedent for all that
follows: a new figure against which subsequent experiences are measured
and grasped. As writers grew increasingly frustrated and dissatisfied with
their traditional lexicon of destruction, they became more likely to figure
the most horrible events not in terms of the ancient past but in the tropes
of their current disaster. The figure of the "Holocaust Jew" thus seems to
have been born of events themselves, coming to epitomize for both Jews
and non-Jews the embattled victim, the sufferer and martyr. Among its
many reapplications by nonvictims to unrelated events, the Holocaust and
its Jewish victims have thus figured suffering Russians in Yevgeny Yevtushenko's poetry; gulag prisoners for Andrei Sinyavsky; poets for Paul
Celan; Angela Davis for James Baldwin; psychic pain for Sylvia Plath; and
Palestinian refugees in the poetry of contemporary Israeli writers.

The process is inevitable, for as new experiences are necessarily grasped
and represented in the frame of remembered past experiences, "incom-
parable" experiences like the Holocaust will always be made—at least rhetorically—comparable. Though this process is both creatively used and
viciously abused, because it is also a reflexive literary operation for knowing
or representing anything at all, the discussion here will focus not on these
writers' poetic license to others' suffering but rather on the meanings created and reflected in such figures. It will explore the understanding of
oneself and of others that is created and reflected in the figure of the
Holocaust Jew in the writing of both victims and nonvictims.

No longer satisfied merely to invoke—and thereby rebuke—the ancient
tropes for their perceived inadequacy, writers in the ghettos and camps

relied increasingly on images drawn from their immediate experiences to figure other parts of the Holocaust. There came a point when the only analogue perceived not to betray a particular set of events was that anchored in the equally horrible experience of the day before. Thus, in the diaries and poetry written during events, the ancient archetypes were steadily displaced by more recently acquired figures—including those culled from the pogrom poems of three decades before—until only the figures drawn from contemporaneous events seemed adequate to the current tragedy. For writers such as Chaim Kaplan, Yitzhak Katzenelson, and Avraham Sutzkever, the deportation of children on one day became the only possible paradigm by which the deportation of children two days later might be represented. So even if the Holocaust itself would not become archetypal for other disasters until it was used afterwards to figure them, earlier parts of it did become archetypal for subsequent parts. In this way, the Holocaust might be said to have become "its own archetype."

Among several scribes of the ghetto who turned to their own experiences for poetic figures of the Holocaust, perhaps none exemplifies the self-conscious displacement of past archetypes by contemporaneous figures better than Yitzhak Katzenelson. Aware that he has indeed "invented a Jewish people" in his monumental elegy, *Song of the Murdered Jewish People*, Katzenelson necessarily reimagines an entire people, for whom "Only their sufferings are true. Only the pain / Of their slaughter is true and great indeed. . . . "[1] Every victim's face, every murdered Jew is thus figured in the eyes of the writer's lost family. Having been concentrated by the Germans into the Warsaw ghetto, the Jews there began to concentrate for Katzenelson the figure of all Jews and their situation in Nazi-occupied Europe: in their image, Katzenelson found the means by which to figure all other Jewish victims of the Nazis, even the potential victims in America and the Yishuv.

Once in his field of vision, his murdered wife and son never leave it, and all subsequent suffering is perceived in the shape and visage of his murdered family. An emanation of himself, his family becomes a base archetype in whose image Katzenelson would represent all Jewish suffering in the Holocaust:

> —How can I sing? How can I lift my head?
> My wife, my Benzionke and Yomele—a baby—deported . . .
> They are not with me, yet they never leave me.
>
> (P. 13)

> Look! Look! They all stand around me, endless throngs,
> A shudder goes through me—
> All of them look with Ben Zion's and Yomke's sorrowful eyes.
> All of them look with the sad eyes of my wife.
>
> (P. 19)

The point of his greatest, most inconsolable pain becomes the reference point for his figures, for the other millions—which can only intensify, not relieve, his own suffering.

With all avenues of escape cut off, with every Polish city of refuge now mirroring the other cities' hopelessness, Katzenelson walls his language and figures into the ghetto as well:

> Where are my dead? O God, I seek them in every dunghill,
> In every heap of ashes . . .
> . . . heaven that is as deaf as the dunghill earth.
> . . . .
> . . . O Wagons, speak! . . . the only ones present at the funeral.
> O you coffins, you carried them alive on their last journey.
> . . . .
> Warsaw packed with Jews like a synagogue on Yom Kippur . . .
> (Pp. 14, 32, 37)

The city itself is now distilled in a Jewish figure. Dead Jews are now figured as live Jews, the living as already dead. The result is a reciprocal exchange between living and murdered people, wherein the living have already begun to assume the aspect of death:

> Dead Jews stood among dazed living ones—
> Pressed together, the dead stood erect, unable to fall,
> No one could tell the living from the dead.
> . . . .
> The dead Jew's head swayed as if it were alive . . .
> (P. 28)

Even Adam Czerniakow's suicide is incorporated as a figure here, a dead man leading a condemned people, none of whom are able to tell the dead from the living:

> . . . The dead chairman sits in his chair—
> With eyes closed, his head tilted, he sits at the head—
> . . . .
> Mr. Chairman? You? You called us? There's a meeting!
> . . . .
> . . . Don't say anything! He's alive, though dead . . . What now?
> Open the meeting—ten! Yes, ten! . . . Silent and pale sat
> The *Kehillah* council around the green table . . . They sat—

The chairman at the head, then the members of the council.
....
All of them listened . . . As if the dead chairman conducted the meeting—

(P. 35)

As he uses these parts of disaster metonymically to figure the larger catastrophe around him, Katzenelson rejects possible alternative tropes from
without the ghetto, elevating individual instances around him to allegorical
proportions, even as they remain linked concretely to events themselves.

As have numerous other poets and writers, when Katzenelson recalls
the ancient archetypes here, it is almost always to mock their inadequacy
as appropriate figures. But in addition to this repudiation of traditional
tropes, Katzenelson conscientiously displaces them with his and his people's
own suffering, a move often implied in poetic responses to the Holocaust
but rarely represented so explicitly as it is here:

A great throng [of murdered Jews], a huge crowd, O how huge!
Far greater than Ezekiel's valley of bones.
And Ezekiel himself would not have spoken to the murdered of trust and hope
As in bygone days, but would have wrung his hands *like me*.
Like me he would cast back his head helplessly . . .

(P. 17)

Rather than figuring his pain and suffering in biblical terms, Katzenelson
deliberately casts the figure of himself backwards in time to refigure the
archetypes themselves, now revised in light of his new unparalleled pain.
Not only does he reject and displace the old archetypes, but he would recast
them altogether in the figure of his current suffering.

Evoke not Ezekiel, evoke not Jeremiah . . . I don't need them!

Why? Because he has now adopted his own experiences and the suffering
of Jews around him as archetypes. In reference to a small Jewish child in
the ghetto, Katzenelson writes,

. . . Isaiah! You were not as small, not as great,
Not as good, not as true, not as faithful as he.
(P. 40)

Isaiah is no longer the model for this child, but he is now compared to the
child of the Holocaust—and found wanting. Because "The world never
saw such children before . . . they never existed on earth" (p. 40), these

children are now the new Jewish standard against which all past and future Jewish suffering will be measured.

> . . . I don't compare myself to the prophets—
> But all the martyred Jews taken to their death, the millions murdered here—
>
> (p. 53)

The millions of murdered have not only displaced the prophets but in their newly acquired status as archetypes, they become prophets in themselves. It is a realm where the Treblinka death camp itself is made plural:

> . . . the rest deported to the Treblinkas—
>
> (p. 67)

and thus becomes a figure for other camps. This is explicitly the point at which events within events become their own archetypes, the point at which they become eternal figures, displacing all that came before as archetypes of suffering, establishing themselves as the new archetypes of suffering.

By figuring the end of the Jewish people in the pillar of cloud and fire of its beginning, Katzenelson simultaneously neutralizes the hope, faith, and joy implicit in their beginning and ironically finds closure in it:

> The end. At night, the sky is aflame. By day the smoke coils and at night it blazes
>   out again. Awe!
> Like our beginning in the desert: A pillar of cloud by day, a pillar of fire by night.
> Then my people marched with joy and faith to new life, and now—the end, all
>   finished . . .
>
> (p. 82)

When the ultimate trope of beginnings is used to figure the end, its meaning is forever altered in the poetic act, its figure forever corrupted, making it unavailable now as trope for other beginnings only, but always a simultaneous figure for endings as well.

Fearful that only "imaginary Jews" will exist after the extermination of every last flesh-and-blood Jew, Katzenelson enumerates them nevertheless, as if to ensure that they continue to exist in some form, even the figurative.

> They are no more! Don't ask overseas about Kasrilevke, Yehupetz. Don't.
> Don't look for Menachem Mendels, Tevye the dairymen, Nogids, Motke thieves.
>   Don't look—
> They will, like the prophets, Isaiah, Jeremiah, Ezekiel, Hosea and Amos from the
>   Bible,

Cry to you from Bialik, speak to you from Sholem Aleichem and Sholem Asch's books.

(p. 84)

He recognizes the simultaneous displacement and regeneration of Jews in these figures, that books and poetry become then the metonymical remnants of the Jewish people. For when the Jews in their literality "are no more!" they will live in the figures left behind by the writers, imaginary Jews now imagining others.

I I

Where Katzenelson was ultimately murdered at Auschwitz as a Jew, the Polish writer Tadeusz Borowski finally survived Auschwitz as a non-Jew. Arrested as a political prisoner, Borowski experienced Auschwitz as a death camp only for the others who marched on, the Jews. He had nothing in common with Katzenelson except for what now appears to be a shared tendency to seal the language of his stories tightly into the realities of the camps. Once concentrated in Auschwitz, Borowski thus concentrated his language as well, keeping his writing figures as walled into Auschwitz as he was. And like Katzenelson, he seemed also to seal himself and his mind, his grasp of all the world, into figures deriving from his experiences in Auschwitz.

On the one hand, as Sidra Ezrahi observes, Borowski seems to avoid metaphor whenever possible, precisely not to escape the realities he would chronicle, as well as to prevent the reader from averting his glance.[2] Thus, when he uses metaphors to describe Auschwitz realities, he draws them pointedly from the same world. Rather than risking a dilution of these experiences, or an escape or transcendence of them through metaphor, Borowski would concentrate the reader's mind now on the realities through metaphor, doubling the impact (not mitigating it) through analogue. As Ezrahi shows, the camp "library" in Borowski's words, is thus "locked up tight as a coffin," a "dark gusty wind, heavy with the smells of the thawing, sour earth tossed the clouds about and cut through your body like a blade of ice," and "empty pavement . . . glistened like a black leather strap."[3] In this way, even if metaphor does divert the reader away from the initial object, he is still left with another contemporaneous image; by remaining camp-referential, these metaphors keep both the writer's and the reader's mind fenced into the camp.

Through this kind of figuring, Borowski also reflects a consciousnesss that in itself has become subject to the norms of the camp. "The camp has been sealed off tight," the narrator begins. "Not a single prisoner, not one solitary louse, can sneak through the gate" (p. 29). Once sealed into the camp like this, Borowski represents a world in which the natural phenomena of Auschwitz, the rules of the camp, become his own rules: both mind and bodies are sealed into the camp, as are the figures by which Borowski eventually represents the camp in his stories. As Borowski's narrator had adapted to the laws of the camp, internalizing its figures, methods, and vision all in order to survive within it, he retains the new rules and code afterwards, as reluctant to abandon his recently acquired vision as he was his prewar naïveté in the camp. These experiences and images turn out also to be the referential sources of his postwar understanding as well. Though he has been liberated physically from the camps, Borowski will never be liberated from the tropes and figures of the camps, by which he represents and seems to grasp the postwar world: he remains locked within the concentration camp of his mind.

"A certain young poet," Borowski writes, "a symbolic-realist, says with a flippant sarcasm that I have a concentration camp mentality" (p. 176). That is, the knowledge and figures in his possession would now possess him. As the stories placed in the camps are about the painful transition, wherein past figures seem broken and inappropriate, and new ones need to be learned, then the postliberation stories betray the readjustment to a normal world—one that Borowski's narrator finds suspect: "[C]oncentration-camp existence . . . had taught us that the whole world is really like the concentration camp; the weak work for the strong, and if they have no strength or will to work—then let them steal, or let them die" (p. 168). In fact, if anything, he now seems to have the figural paradigm to reinforce many of the political beliefs for which he was arrested in the first place.

"At this point," the narrator says in "The World of Stone," "I must confess that, although since the end of the war I very rarely force myself to polish my shoes and almost never shake the mud off my trouser turn-ups, that although it is a great effort for me to shave my face, chin and neck twice weekly, and although I bite off my fingernails in order to save time, and never, never hunt after rare books or mistresses, thus relating the deliberate senselessness of my own fate to that of the Universe, I have recently begun to leave my house on hot summer afternoons to go for long, lonely strolls through the poorest districts of my city" (pp. 177–78). By taking the laws of the camps outside, the narrator allows its figures to order both his behavior and the post-camp realities around him. "And I can see as distinctly as if I were looking in a mirror the ruins" (p. 178), he writes, recognizing that the world has indeed taken the shape of his mind and is now nothing more than a reflection of himself, of the broken figures of mind he projects onto it.

Possibly because Borowski perceived a particular poverty in both the traditions and civilization that spawned Auschwitz in the first place, he avoided invoking the names and icons of his civilization for his descriptions of camp realities. But when he left Auschwitz, it became clear that his mind—his meaning-making capacity—was still interned. The camp and its realities became his new tradition, his new mythos; he was reborn in the world with a new set of expectations. The world was now remade automatically in the shape of Auschwitz: it became his "home" in many more ways than he anticipated in "Auschwitz, Our Home." In a way, his incarceration might thus be said to have lasted from 1943 to 1951. These figures, these metaphors began to function as part of a deeply personal mythology by which both inner and outer worlds were organized, understood, and ultimately responded to. The outer world in this way became an extension of the camps—a world he could now never leave. Walled in by his governing tropes, Borowski killed himself, by gas in 1951, yet another extension perhaps of camp figures.

In becoming its own figure for Borowski, the Holocaust also became a referential topos for both past and future events. Trapped now within the "concentration-camp of his mind," Borowski's narrator reflexively grasps former history and civilization in the bedrock tropes of his own experience as forced slave laborer at Auschwitz. For the politically conscious speaker, these experiences and their resulting figures may not have scarred his vision so much as they actually lend him greater insight into past history. "Only now," he writes, "do I realize what price was paid for building the ancient civilizations. The Egyptian pyramids, the temples, and Greek statues—what a hideous crime! How much blood must have poured on to the Roman roads, the bulwarks and the city walls. Antiquity—the tremendous concentration-camp where the slave was branded on the forehead by his master, and crucified for trying to escape! Antiquity—the conspiracy of free men against slaves!" (p. 131). Not only has the writer's future been turned into a great camp of the mind, but so has the past of his heritage: all he knows is now apprehended—and thereby reorganized—in the figures of captor and slave, oppressor and oppressed.

I I I

When the ancient archetypes are perceived as inadequate frames for current history, even while they are still used to figure events, the reciprocal movement between figures and events grows more complex. Instead of grasping a current crisis only in terms of the Akedah, for example, we find that the paradigm of the Akedah itself is retrieved in light of present history: it is recast and reunderstood in light of new experiences, taking on new, often startling, meanings and significance. In fact, as Elie Wiesel seems to have found, his Holocaust experiences have as great an effect on the ancient archetypes as the archetypes have had on his understanding of new experiences. In his collection of post-Holocaust midrashim, *Messengers of God: Biblical Portraits and Legends*, Wiesel rereads, reinterprets, and then represents the traditional legends and archetypes in light of the Holocaust— a process that may not turn every Holocaust victim into a Job, but does turn Cain and Abel, Isaac and Job all into Holocaust victims.[4]

Even though Wiesel suggests that only now—after the Holocaust—can he understand these biblical legends, by retelling them in the figure of his own remembered experiences, he reinterprets them, which in the midrashic tradition brings new understanding to old stories. As a disciple of his tradition, Wiesel remarks that "his aim is not to plunge into historical exegesis . . . but to reacquaint himself with the distant and haunting figures that molded him. He will try to reconstruct their portraits from Biblical and Midrashic texts, and eventually insert them into the present" (p. xi). But in fact, by reconstructing these texts now, Wiesel may not be inserting them into the present so much as he necessarily inserts present memory into these past legends. All of these portraits are thus redrawn in the image of the teller and his Holocaust experiences.

Only in such a rereading informed by the Holocaust can he find in Cain and Abel "the first genocide" and write that "Abel is an obvious victim. . . . Every victim throughout the ages was and is meant to recognize himself in him" (p. 46). For it is not just that victims come to Abel as a figure for their own victimhood, but as Wiesel does here, victims now create other victims in these stories by figuring them as such. That is, Abel may not figure Wiesel's plight so much as Wiesel figures Abel's own story in his retelling of it. In fact, by calling the Cain and Abel story "the first genocide," Wiesel first refigures the legend and then allows it to inform his own experience: his midrash is as much about Wiesel's reservoir of figures as it is about the Cain and Abel story.

Of all his midrashim, however, it is his retelling of the Akedah—i.e., the binding of Isaac—in "The Sacrifice of Isaac: a Survivor's Story" that illustrates most clearly his own reorientation toward the past archetypes. Where the Akedah has traditionally been invoked as a paradigm for unexplained tragedy and test of faith, Wiesel now invokes (if implicitly) a new referential paradigm—the Holocaust—to explain the Akedah. As much as "this strange tale is about fear and faith, fear and defiance, fear and laughter," for Wiesel, it is also "about" the Holocaust. In retelling the story, Wiesel's attention is now drawn to words in the Hebrew (e.g., *le'olah*) that have in themselves recently accumulated the weight of memory in Greek and English words (*holokauston* and Holocaust) derived from them. "Take your son and bring him to Me as an offering," Wiesel writes, quoting the biblical passage. "The term [for offering] is *ola*, which means an offering that has been totally consumed, a holocaust" (p. 71). *Le'olah* did not mean "holocaust," of course, until Wiesel retranslated it in the figure of its own linguistic future. It is now impossible for Wiesel to read or to retell the Akedah without hearing the echo of "holocaust" in *le'olah*. Wiesel thus rereads and translates the command "Kahk na eth binkha eth yekhidkha asher ahavta eth yitzhak [ve'ha'aleu sham]" as "Take your son, your only son, whom you love and bring him to me in holocaust" (p. 74)—a version that reflects and creates a significance available to this story only after the midrashist's own experiences in the Holocaust.

In his discussion of others' readings of the Akedah, Wiesel reminds us in another way of the corrigibility of an archetype like the Akedah. Where traditional commentators "preferred to imagine Isaac shaken but alive, spending the unaccounted for years at a Yeshiva," darker readings suggest that in descending Moriah alone (*Vayashav avraham el nearav*), Abraham has not avoided the tragedy after all. That the Akedah, which is technically only the *binding* (not the sacrifice) of Isaac, should be used through the generations as an archetype for catastrophe might suggest, in fact, that this ominous version is more widely accepted than commonly assumed. There is a way in which catastrophic experiences may thus always predispose the tragic interpretation of this text. For in light of the innumerable "bindings" that eventually turned into actual "sacrifices," even the traditional commentators may have found it difficult to read this story without their own catastrophes in mind. If it is true, as Wiesel suggests, that the "popular imagination—collective memory—adheres to the tragic interpretation," it may be because in the figure of these other writers' experiences, Isaac was not saved, just as too many of their contemporaries had not been saved. Once again, only the tragic reading of the Akedah makes it appropriate as an archetype for the subsequent tragedies in Jewish history: if the Akedah is appropriate, it is because it has been interpreted in the figure of later experiences.

"We have known Jews," Wiesel writes, "who, like Abraham, witnessed the death of their children; who like Isaac, lived the Akedah in the flesh; and some who went mad when they saw their fathers disappear on the altar, with the altar, in a blazing fire whose flames reached into the highest of heaven" (p. 95). When Auschwitz is the altar, and father, son, and altar are all consumed as an offering, then it follows that "All the pogroms, the crusades, the persecutions, the slaughters, the catastrophes, the massacres by sword and the liquidations by fire—each time it was Abraham leading his son to the altar, to the holocaust all over again" (p. 95). At the end of his retelling Wiesel refers clearly to an Isaac reconstructed in the figure of himself, the child-survivor: "Isaac. . . never freed himself from the traumatizing scenes that violated his youth; the holocaust had marked him and continued to haunt him forever" (p. 97). The Holocaust has "marked" Isaac because it now figures Isaac; it haunts Isaac because it now haunts the post-Holocaust teller of his legend.

At Yad Vashem Holocaust Memorial Authority in Jerusalem, Nathan Rapoport's statue of Job stands near the entrance to the art museum. But as we might expect in this context, this sculptural interpretation of Job is literally marked both by the experience of the sculptor and by the context itself: Job has a concentration-camp number on his left forearm. The sculptor Rapoport has only literalized here the figurative survivor Wiesel finds in Job after the Holocaust. In "Job: Our Contemporary," Wiesel acknowledges one-half of the equation: "Whenever we attempt to tell our own story, we transmit [Job's]" (p. 211). What Wiesel leaves out, however, is that in retelling Job's story, or Cain and Abel's story, or Isaac's in these commentaries, Wiesel necessarily transmits his own story as well—in the interpretive figures from the Holocaust framing his midrashim.

In neither Wiesel's nor Borowski's case is there a calculated effort to find equivalence between past and present stories, but rather only the reflexive equivalence created once they re-view antiquity through eyes now informed by new experiences that are so strong as to overwhelm and displace other figures. Experiences, stories, and texts of the ancient past remain the same in themselves; but their meanings, their echoes, causes and effects, and their significance all changed with the addition of new experiences in the lives of these texts' interpreters. The understanding is genuine, as are the conclusions survivors like Wiesel and Borowski draw; this is part of the reciprocal exchange between minds that simultaneously figure and are figured by Holocaust experiences.

I V

Before turning to the "Holocaust Jew" as a figure in non-Jewish writing, we might consider briefly this figure in Jewish writing itself—and what it means for Jewish self-knowledge. For as has become painfully apparent, a part of the generation of Jews growing up in Europe and America after the Holocaust was forced by events to identify as Jews only in relation to Holocaust suffering. Jean Améry (aka Hans Maier), for example, the son of a Jewish father and Christian mother in Austria before the war believed he was Christian until the Nuremberg laws defined him as Jewish, after which he was treated "as a Jew," after which he came to know himself as a Jew—if now, only as a "Catastrophe Jew."[5]

But for other writers like Philip Roth, there is something pernicious in such Jewish identity, and so he mocks it in his stories, particularly in *Goodbye Columbus and Other Stories* and in parts of his trilogy, *Zuckerman Bound*. In the third part of this collection—*The Ghost Writer*—Roth's protagonist Zuckerman is a young writer accused by his family of betraying his "faith" and his "people" in a story he has published about family squabbles over money. In a parodic replay of too many real-life critical responses to Roth's own work, Zuckerman's family and even a judge who supported his admission to the university condemn the young writer for the unflattering "Jewish types" in this story. "Can you honestly say that there is anything in your short story that would not warm the heart of a Julius Streicher or a Joseph Goebbels?" asks Judge Wapter.[6] If the young writer wants to know what Jews are really about, the judge suggests, he should go see the Broadway production of *The Diary of Anne Frank*. All argument is thus quashed by this dark injunction to remember the Holocaust through the figure of Anne Frank.

By extension, they seem to be telling him, if you know nothing else about being Jewish, know Anne Frank, now a two-sided metonymy for both

Jewishness and Holocaust. For as Roth recognizes, Anne Frank has become for many in his postwar generation without other Jewish memory a kind of martyrological icon, dying so that a new generation of Jews might live— and identify—*as* Jews. Her name in lights and her face on the cover of every weekly magazine would now remind postwar Jews that she died some-how for them; without any other Jewish memory or knowledge, this gen-eration will remember that Anne Frank died for being Jewish. In Roth's story, this leads the imaginative Zuckerman to fantasy about ways he might reauthenticate himself as a Jew in his family's eyes and to reenter the family of the Jewish people.

He accomplishes this by turning a mysterious researcher he meets at his literary mentor's home into Anne Frank, falling in love with her, and then in his fantasy, taking her home to Mom and Dad:

> Throughout breakfast, my father, my mother, the judge and Mrs. Wapter were never out of my thoughts. I'd gone the whole night without sleep, and now I couldn't think straight about them or myself, or about Amy [the re-searcher], as she was called. I kept seeing myself coming back to New Jersey and saying to my family, "I met a marvelous young woman while I was up in New England. I love her and she loves me. We are going to be married." "Married? But so fast? Nathan, is she Jewish?" "Yes, she is." "But who is she?" "Anne Frank." (Pp. 157–58)

Is she Jewish? Is she ever.

Simultaneously exemplifying and pilloring the postwar notion of what it means to be an "authentic Jew," Roth would work his own revenge against those who would hate him for hating his Jewish self. For Zuckerman is marrying not just Anne Frank here but the Holocaust itself, attempting to participate vicariously in the one experience that unequivocally defined Jews for his generation. He would thus wed both himself and his Jewish identity to *the* Holocaust Jew—thus becoming the kind of "authentic Jew" his parents wanted in their son, and the kind of Jew Roth's critics seem to have wanted in the writer. In smashing the ceremonial glass underfoot at his wedding, Zuckerman would have recalled the destructions of the Tem-ple and of the Holocaust, now joining them together as well in his marriage. In his imagination, the young writer thus reauthorizes himself as a Jew by appending himself to the ultimate Jewish figure: Anne Frank, who is now considered authentically Jewish only through her own victimization in the Holocaust. For as Sander Gilman observes, "What happened to the Jews of Europe in the decade before became the pattern against which Roth's American Jews, those who so freely wield the label of 'self-hating Jew' against the writer, measure themselves."[7]

If in the eyes of his family and community, the young Zuckerman could in effect marry back into his people by marrying Anne Frank, then in his own search for Jewish identity in *The Prague Orgy*, he returns to the Old

World itself in order to retrieve a little of the persecution—qua Jewish identity—missing in his American dream. Visiting with Czech émigrés in New York, Zuckerman squirms in his own comfort: as a writer, an artist, and a Jew, Zuckerman begins to crave adversity. In Czechoslovak émigrés and citizens, Zuckerman thus finds a new class of oppressed victims, many identifying variously, figuratively, and fictitiously as Jews. In fact, in Eva Kalinova he even finds the Czech actress who played Anne Frank in Prague and who was then persecuted herself, not for being Jewish but for merely *playing* Jewish. So upon hearing about a lost Holocaust manuscript, Nathan Zuckerman embarks on a literary-Jewish mission, as much it seems to put himself at risk as to recover a piece of the Holocaust: by searching for a remnant of the Holocaust, in the homeland of his people's past, he might at last regain some of the Jewish memory of persecution lost to him in America. If he cannot write Holocaust literature, through no fault of his own, then he might at least be its literary midwife.

Indeed, once in Czechoslovakia, Zuckerman finds that the new victims there specifically are the writers, an exciting prospect. If Zuckerman cannot suffer as a Jew, then perhaps he might as a writer: "I imagine Styron washing glasses in a Penn Station barroom, Susan Sontag wrapping buns at a Broadway bakery, Gore Vidal bicycling salamis to school lunchrooms in Queens—I look at the filthy floor and see myself sweeping it."[8] Prague becomes Zuckerman's remembered Jewish homeland, its writers the new Jews, defined now by their suffering. And the

> national industry of the Jewish homeland, if not the sole means of production (if not the sole means of satisfaction), [is] the construction of narrative out of the exertions of survival . . . [next] were the jokes—because beneath the ordeal of perpetual melancholia and the tremendous strain of just getting through, a joke is always lurking somewhere, a derisory portrait, a scathing crack, a joke which builds with subtle self-savaging to the uproarious punch line, "And this is what suffering does!" . . . That such things happen—there's the moral of the stories—that such things happen to me, to him, to her, to you, to us. That is the national anthem of the Jewish homeland. By all rights, when you hear someone there begin telling a story—when you see the Jewish faces mastering anxiety and feigning innocence and registering astonishment at their own for-titude—you ought to stand and put your hand to your heart. (Pp. 761–62)

In this story, of course, Roth would only mock an American Jewish boy's attempt to produce Jewish identity through a quest for (not escape from) persecution. As he might have come back into the Jewish fold through his marriage to Anne Frank, Zuckerman would now through his recovery of a lost Holocaust manuscript become irrevocably a Jewish literary hero, another notion mocked by the realism of history's literal players:

> The marvelous Zuckerman brings from behind the Iron Curtain two hundred unpublished Yiddish stories written by a victim of a Nazi bullet. You will be a

hero to the Jews and to literature and to all of the Free World. On top of all your millions of dollars and millions of girls, you will win the American prize for Idealism about Literature. And what will happen to me? I will go to prison for smuggling a manuscript to the West. (P. 770)

At the end of his quest, of course, Zuckerman finds his Holy Grail, this remnant of the Holocaust; it is in Yiddish, however, so he cannot read it. As an American Jew, he speaks English and will therefore never know "first-hand" the terror of his people's past. In fact, he even fails at being well persecuted and is finally mocked in his adventures by a smirking customs officer, who unceremoniously expels the writer and dismisses him with, "Zuckerman the Zionist agent. . . . An honor . . . to have entertained you here, sir. Now back to the little world around the corner" (p. 784).

V

If Anne Frank represented all that was Jewish for Zuckerman and his family, it should not be surprising that she would also figure so prominently in non-Jewish writers' own meditations on Jewish identity. Shortly after suggesting in his essay on Anne Frank's diary that Anne Frank "has been made into a spokesman against one of the grand crimes of our age, and for her race, and for all its victims, and for the victims (especially the children) of all the tyrannies of this horrifying century," John Berryman thus muses, "Suppose one became interested in the phenomenon called religious conversion."[9] It is not only religious conversion per se that engages Berryman here, however, but also "the conversion of a child into a person," the becoming of Anne Frank's self in a world that would not let her self develop because she was Jewish.

As Berryman raised the possibility of religious conversion in his essay on Anne Frank, six years earlier he had considered in an essay on "The Mind of Isaac Babel" the possibility that literary meaning is both created and grasped through the reader's identification with a narrator. After asking how one arrives at a fuller meaning in a Hasidic anecdote by Martin Buber, Berryman suggests that "Identification is probably the chief means. . . . " It is not that the reader identifies specifically with Buber here, but rather with the Jewish spirit of the story:

> The identification that occurs in serious works of the imagination takes place at deep levels of the mind or spirit. The identification is very incomplete—few people still sane have ever felt for a moment that they *were* Hamlet or Don Quixote—but may be profound and lasting, because learning has accompanied it: learning what it is like to be, or pretend to be, another person. (P. 126)

The fine line between empathetic identification and actual conversion fascinated Berryman—and became in itself a kind of no-man's-land in which he lived and wrote. That it was within a specifically Jewish context determined the kind of self-understanding and self-representation his powers of identification would create.

As one who considered for years a literal conversion to Judaism, Berryman entertained first the notion of a figurative conversion—not to Judaism as such, but to Jewishness, to aspects of being as if one were Jewish. To be Jewish in Berryman's mind, however, was inextricably tied to the persecution Anne Frank had come universally to represent. "In my old story," Berryman noted later in reference to his short story "The Imaginary Jew," "a confrontation as Jew is resisted, fought, failed—at last is given into *symbolically*. I identified at least with the persecution. So the 'desire' [to become Jewish] . . . is at least 25 years old."[10] Later in his life, as he contemplated an actual conversion, he thus acknowledged that part of him he already understood as Jewish: the persecuted part.

As he illustrated in this story, Berryman recognized that it may always be a short step between figurative and literal Jews: the line between them remained as titillating for Berryman as it was vague. In fact, it seems that at the end of his life, he was half-convinced that as an imaginary Jew in his work, he had already taken the first step toward literal conversion, a process he was apparently mapping in an unfinished manuscript he called "The Jewish Kick." It was almost as if he recognized to some degree that even as a convert to Judaism, he might have remained forever a figurative Jew: his Jewishness would always still be defined only insofar as he saw himself—and others saw him—*as* a Jew. It is almost as if he wondered: at what point is one a Jew after conversion, and to what extent is a convert always becoming Jewish? Insofar as conversion may always be a figurative kind of transformation into being Jewish, it exemplified for Berryman the possibility of understanding—even re-creating—oneself in the Jewish figure.

Half-pleased by the thought that his own name, "Berryman" would be thought Jewish (p. 241), the poet considered the many ways he had already arrived. "I become a Jew—the wonder of my life—it's possible!" he exclaimed. "Rabbi M. is coming at 2:30 . . . Left and came to my room and incredibly thought of *becoming a Jew*" (p. 240, his emphasis). Having had a Jewish wife, Berryman bore a Jewish son, a nexus, he realized, that made him a Jewish father, if only through patrilineal ascent. In naming his second daughter from a third marriage to an Irish woman Sarah Rebecca, he even seemed to affirm (if only figuratively again) that he regarded himself somehow as a Jewish father. In his wonder at "becoming a Jew," Berryman thus recalled all the ways in which he already was a Jew. "*All* has pointed HERE," he wrote (p. 240).

Throughout his essays, poetry, and fiction, Berryman alternately idealizes what he perceives as Jewish traits—e.g., teetotaling, love of learning, and penchant for suffering—and then identifies with his idealizations. As his biographer and critics have already noted, even though both Berryman and his narrators had figured themselves as Jews at several levels, it was the suffering—even dead—Jew who preoccupied Berryman. "The most sustained and obsessive identification in *The Dream Songs*," James Bloom writes, "appears in the twelve-poem sequence that mourns Delmore Schwartz 'the new ghost/ haunting Henry most . . . the Hebrew spectre.' Henry laments: 'I can't get him out of my mind, out of my mind.' "[11] As Bloom goes on to note, it is the "Hebrew spectre's" identity the speaker of these poems attempts to appropriate. Of the many ways to remember Delmore Schwartz, Berryman's narrator focuses on his Jewishness and his death, each now cleaving to the other in the poet's mind.

In his brilliant short story "The Imaginary Jew," written in 1945, in the midst of revelations of the death camps, Berryman thus explored the shaded area between being and imagining oneself in the frame of a persecuted Jew. "The second summer of the European war I spent in New York," the story opens. "I lived in a room just below street-level on Lexington above Thirty-fourth, wrote a good deal, tried not to think about Europe, and listened to music on a small gramophone, the only thing of my own except books in the room."[12] As did other "confessional writers," Berryman began his meditations by weighing the effect the outer world would have on his inner world, with his verse and his writing representing a kind of intersection between worlds.

Coming from the South, says the narrator, he began his education without any clear idea of what a Jew was. He then found that as he mixed with them, and got to know who Jews were, he also got to know himself: part of his education included knowledge of the Jews and knowledge of himself in light of the Jews. Indeed, he found upon inquiring that about one-third of his friends at college were Jewish, that they knew they were Jewish, were disliked and excluded for being Jewish, and "that what in short I took to be an idiotic state was deeply established, familiar and acceptable to everyone. This discovery was the beginning of my instruction in social life proper—construing social life as that from which political life issues like a somatic dream" (p. 361).

As further word of German persecution of the Jews filtered into the country (and his consciousness), he became in 1933 a Jew-lover. In this he is a little apologetic (a self-hating Jew-lover perhaps?) and even professes a kind of genetic egalitarianism wherein he remained "spectacularly" unable during his life to identify Jews as Jews, he said. But as a Jew-lover, he

> thus denied the presence of obvious defects in particular Jews, feeling that to admit them would be to side with the sadists and murderers. Accident allotting me close friends who were Jewish, their disadvantages enraged me. Gradually, and against my sense of impartial justice, I became the anomaly which only a partial society can produce, and for what it has no name known to the lexicons. In one area, but not exclusively, "nigger-lover" is cast in a parallel way: but

for a special sympathy and liking for Jews—which became my fate, so that I trembled when I heard one abused in talk—we have no term. (P. 361)

This was the narrator's state of mind when he joined a heated discussion of America's possible entry into the European war one muggy night in Union Square. Upon asserting that Roosevelt had in fact helped Franco by nonintervention, the narrator is suddenly turned upon by an Irishman, "What's that? What are you, a Jew?" and then he is ignored altogether. When he tries again to speak,

"Shut up, you Jew," said the Irishman.

"I'm not a Jew," I said to him. "What makes—"

. . . "I don't give a damn what you are," he turned his half-dark eyes to me, wrenching his arm loose. "You talk like a Jew."

"What does that mean?" Some part of me wanted to laugh. "How does a Jew talk?"

"They talk like you, buddy."

"That's a fine argument! But if I'm not a Jew, my talk only—"

"You probably are a Jew. You look like a Jew."

"I *look* like a Jew? Listen," I swung around with despair to a man standing next to me, "do I look like a Jew? It doesn't matter whether I do or not—a Jew is as good as anybody and better than this son of a bitch—" I was not exactly excited, I was trying to adapt my language as my need for the crowd, and my sudden respect for its judgement, possessed me—"but in fact I'm not Jewish and I don't look Jewish. Do I?"

The man looked at me quickly and said, half to me and half to the Irishman, "Hell, I don't know. Sure he does."

A wave of disappointment and outrage swept me almost to tears, I felt like a man betrayed by his brother . . .

"You look like a Jew. You talk like a Jew. You *are* a Jew," I heard the Irishman say. (P. 365)

As the speaker realizes, however, whether or not he is an actual Jew, he has in fact become an imagined Jew, though not by choice. Being treated as a Jew, being addressed as a Jew, he now felt *like* a Jew, but a Jew defined now only in relationship to others, specifically here in the context of his argument with the Irishman. Alone, he was not a Jew, except as he might now relate to the world as its victim, as its "Jew." But unlike other confessional writers who also identified literarily as Jews, and who also killed themselves, Berryman sustains a completely self-conscious awareness of the figurative nature of his Jewishness. In fact, as becomes painfully clear to him, it is precisely the point at which a figurative Jew is reified that the danger begins.

For as he concludes, it is always only the figurative Jew that antisemites hate—i.e., the imaginary Jew of their minds—but once acted upon, the figure is reified, and real blood flows:

> In the days following, as my resentment died, I saw that I had not been a victim altogether unjustly. My persecutors were right: I was a Jew. The imaginary Jew I was was as real as the imaginary Jew hunted down, on the other nights and days, in a real Jew. Every murderer strikes the mirror, the lash of the torturer falls on the mirror and cuts the real image, and the real and the imaginary blood flow down together. (P. 366)

Although Berryman the poet knew many Jews and admired what he regarded as "Jewish traits" (e.g., storytelling, argumentation, interpretation), the "imaginary Jew" figured only one kind of "Jewish knowledge" for Berryman: victimization.

The Holocaust Jew was not yet a figure in its own right when Berryman wrote his story, but it might be said that with knowledge of the Holocaust in mind, this figure accrued added weight and gravity. For he understood that the figurative Jew—the victim—was necessary for the actual victimization of the Jews. Though this "incident" might have occurred any time, at any place, as Berryman notes, it seems only to have become significant for him at the end of the war, in light of the Holocaust. From speaking like a Jew to being persecuted as one, Berryman suggests that it is the "figure" of the Jew that is always chased, always killed—though when this figure is killed, so too is the literal Jew on whom the figure was projected. There are consequences to being even a figurative Jew, Berryman seems to realize. Even if Berryman and other figurative Jews have nothing to do with the Holocaust, these events and the figures they have spawned may ultimately have much to do with those, like Berryman and Plath, who came to see themselves *as if* they were Holocaust Jews.

SEVEN

The Holocaust Confessions of Sylvia Plath

Every man is a Jew.

—Abram Tertz (Jewish psuedonym for Andrei Sinyavsky)

All poets are Jews.

—Paul Celan

We all of us, grave or light, get our thoughts entangled in metaphors, and act fatally on the strength of them.

—George Eliot

I

Of the many poetic references to the Holocaust by nonvictims, those in Sylvia Plath's last book of poems, *Ariel*, remain among those most bitterly contested. For unlike John Berryman, who became an imaginary Jew in order to explore the idea of antisemitism, or Anne Sexton, who explicitly represented the impact of Auschwitz on herself, or even Yevgeny Yevtushenko, who called himself (and all Russians) Jewish in order to remember Babi Yar, Sylvia Plath represented herself—her inner life—in the figure of the Holocaust Jew. Whether or not these poets and other nonvictims like William Heyen, Charles Reznikoff, Irving Feldman, and Barbara Helfgott Hyett can be read as Holocaust poets may be debatable.[1] Sylvia Plath's case is more straightforward: she is not a Holocaust poet, simply because she does not write about the Holocaust. She writes about herself figured as a Holocaust Jew, among other contemporary images of suffering. As poets like Abraham Sutzkever, Yitzhak Katzenelson, Nelly Sachs, and Paul Celan inevitably figured the Holocaust in the shapes of unrelated events, Plath has now figured her own—outwardly unrelated—life in the image of the Holocaust itself.

Alvin Rosenfeld is therefore correct to question the assumption that Plath's poems can "expose the atrocity of the age through exposing self-inflicted wounds,"[2] echoing Edward Butscher, who writes on this point:

"There is no way that the poetry of an American girl writing from the remote perspective of the 1950's could ever capture the actual, brutal reality of the Holocaust."[3] But then, to some extent, this would also be true of any young American-born poet, boy or girl, Jewish or non-Jewish, writing safely in the fifties, including Heyen, Reznikoff, Feldman, or even Randall Jarrell, to name a few of the American poets who have responded most eloquently to the Holocaust. But unlike these poets, who attempted to capture—or at least, respond to—aspects of the Holocaust, Plath has not tried to reimagine these events in any way. The Holocaust exists for her not as an experience to be retold or described but as an event available to her (as it was to all who came after) only as a figure, an idea, in whose image she has expressed another brutal reality: that of her own internal pain.

This chapter on Plath is not intended to cast new light on the events of the Holocaust, but rather to explore the ways in which the poet's world and personal experiences are perceived and represented in light of the Holocaust. Specifically, it is to examine how the Holocaust—once it became its own archetype and entered the public imagination as an independent icon—also became a figure for subsequent pain, suffering, and destruction. In this discussion of Plath, I would like to shift our critical emphasis away from the poet's "right" to Holocaust imagery, in order to explore: (1) how Holocaust imagery functions in non-Holocaust poetry; (2) how its figures organize and create meaning in the poet's world; (3) the possible consequences of Holocaust figures for the poet who uses them; (4) the implied understanding of the Holocaust revealed in the poet's figures; and (5) the community of metaphor implied in the poet's Holocaust figures. For even though Plath's poems are not about the Holocaust, her Holocaust tropes do reveal indirectly her own grasp of events, even as they organize and project meaning onto the realities of her inner life. In working to externalize her internal world, Plath found it inextricably tied to public figures like the Holocaust, which may have oppressed her imagination even as they gave it form.

During the months preceding her suicide, it may thus be impossible to discern at what point images of the Holocaust entered her imaginative world and then, taking root there, at what point every domestic scene, every daily bump and bruise evoked in her images of mass suffering. For it was in this period that the events of the Holocaust broke into the public domain and became not just public knowledge but public memory. Between April and December 1961, when the Eichmann trial in Jerusalem riveted public and media attention on the heretofore neglected details of the Holocaust, Plath was pregnant (after having miscarried in February) and moving to Devon from London with her husband, Ted Hughes. Between Eichmann's conviction in December 1961 and his execution in April 1962, Plath lived and wrote in Devon in their new country home, which she left in September after discovering Hughes's infidelity. Between September and December 1962, in her darkest hours, Plath wrote "Mary's Song," "Lady Lazarus," and "Daddy," her so-called Holocaust poems. She killed herself by gas on the morning of 16 February 1963 in her London flat.

Both *Ariel* and the autobiographical novel she was completing at the time, *The Bell Jar*, are rife with allusions to Jewish suffering, not all of them from the Holocaust. In both the poems and her prose, personal experiences and domestic objects accrue the weight of historical significance: both the day-to-day objects in the world and pain itself had lost all innocence. "Don't talk to me about the world needing cheerful stuff," she wrote to her mother. "What the person out of Belsen, *physical or psychological*, wants is nobody saying the birdies go tweet-tweet, but the full knowledge that somebody else has been there and knows the worst, just what it is like."[4] Even though she distinguishes one who has actually been through Belsen from one who was there only psychologically (i.e., imaginatively), the fact that one of them was literally in Belsen oppresses the other all the same. Through an imaginative association, she simultaneously reflects and creates a link between her private pain and a much more vast and overwhelming *Weltschmerz*.

Plath's use of victimized Jews as figures did not begin with Holocaust Jews, as such, but with other historically and literarily victimized Jews. In choosing the name "Esther" for the speaker of her autobiographical novel, Plath figures herself implicitly as the Jewish queen who kept her Jewishness secret until Haman plotted to destroy her people, at which point she became the deliverer of the Jews. The opening trope for the protagonist's identity thus resonates with both potential Jewish victimhood and Jewish deliverance from oppression. As she introduced herself in the trope of Esther, she would introduce the story of Esther's mind through the figure of other—peripherally Jewish—suffering. Her autobiographical novel, *The Bell Jar*, opens with:

> It was a queer, sultry summer, the summer they electrocuted the Rosenbergs, and I didn't know what I was doing in New York. I'm stupid about executions. The idea of being electrocuted makes me sick, and that's all there was to read about in the papers—goggle-eyed headlines staring up at me on every street corner and at the fusty, peanut-smelling mouth of every subway. It had nothing to do with me, but I couldn't help wondering what it would be like, being burned alive all along your nerves.
>
> I thought it must be the worst thing in the world. . . . I kept hearing about the Rosenbergs over the radio and at the office till I couldn't get them out of my mind.[5]

Though the Rosenbergs "had nothing to do with her," she couldn't get them out of her mind; and once they entered and then occupied her mental world, coming as the opening obsession of her "autobiography," they had everything to do with both her and her representations of herself. She was suddenly unable to "know" or write herself without reference to the Rosenbergs.

As public victims, the Rosenbergs assumed tropic dimensions by which Plath introduced and thereby framed her New York experiences—and ultimately by which she knew her own pain. Not only are the Rosenbergs' deaths suggestively represented by Plath in the Holocaust figure of being "burned alive along your nerves," but in an earlier poem, she also recalls her own electroshock therapy in the figure of their deaths:

> By the roots of my hair some god got hold of me.
> I sizzled in his blue volts like a desert prophet.[6]

Having wondered "what it would be like," Plath finds the closest parallel in her own torture. Jews, Jews as victims, and her own perceived victimhood seem to have melded together first in her imaginings of the Rosenbergs and then again in her reimagined electroshock therapy—the figure yoking two separate life realities together. After empathizing with others' pain and suffering, knowing it in the figure of herself, she now began to know herself also in their figures as well.

Of history's innumerable victims, what aspect of the Jews' victimization during the Holocaust lent this catastrophe to Plath's imagination more than others? Why is she not Armenian here, or a black slave, or a Russian from the Gulag? The choice of the Holocaust Jew as a trope here by Plath has less to do with its intrinsic appropriateness than it does with its visibility as a public figure for suffering. As was the case to some extent with the Rosenbergs' execution, the salient aspect of the Holocaust was its wide public knowledge, its place as a figure in the public mind. Where figures of destruction had traditionally taken generations to enter the literary imagination, being passed down an epoch and a book at a time, in America's mass media of the fifties and England's of the sixties, generations of inherited memory were compressed within the space of months. Images selected by the media for their spectacular and often horrifying qualities became the most common figures of all. For the writer and poet immersed in letters and media, as Plath was, these figures seem to have become a kind of currency by which she traded her ideas with the rest of the world, literally absorbing the shape of these figures only to return them to the public sphere with her own imprint on them.

In fact, as Alvarez reminds us, the "Holocaust Jew" was not Plath's only figure for victimhood. Mixing metaphors slightly in an early version of "Lady Lazarus," Plath drew also upon the Japanese victims of the atomic bombs. Again, it was not for any actual correspondence between these kinds of suffering, but as Alvarez suggests in the case of the Japanese, it may only have been for the rhyme. The figure of victimized Japanese was presumed already to be part of an available figural lexicon, which she now searched for the right sound:

> Gentlemen, ladies
>
> These are my hands,
> My knees.
> I may be skin and bone,
> *I may be Japanese . . .*

" 'Why *Japanese?*' [Alvarez] niggled away at her. 'Do you just need the rhyme? Or are you trying to hitch an easy lift by dragging in the atomic victims? If you're going to use this kind of violent material, you've got to play it cool . . . ' She argued back sharply, but later, when the poem was finally published after her death, the line had gone."[7] As Alvarez acknowledges in retrospect, however, she *did* need the rhyme, even if her allusion to the Japanese was not quite relevant. Form and sound may have thus influenced her choice of metaphors at this point, not just the supposed meaning created in such allusions.

In the cases of both Japanese and Jewish figures, mass and anonymous suffering were drawn from the war period, an era contemporary with her own life. Her historical memory was thus constituted both by history books and classical poetry, as well as an infusion of images from the mass media, from newsreels, newpapers, and radio, which create public figures and icons not by using them as figures so much as by saturating the imagination with them. For Plath, it may have been important that events were drawn from the era of her own life, if not from the experiences of her own life. In this way, she shared the era of victimhood, victimized by modern life at large as the Jews and Japanese had been victimized by specific events in modern life.

In Plath's case, her metaphors are built upon the absorption of public experience by language itself, experience that is then internalized and made private by the poet, used to order her private world, and then reexternalized in public verse. If "The public horrors of Nazi concentration camps and the personal horrors of fragmented identities become interchangeable," as Arthur Oberg suggests,[8] it is not because they are actually analogous; it is just that the movement between public and personal horrors is at once historical and private. As long as these images of the Holocaust are public, they inevitably enter the private imagination at some level, where they are invariably evoked to order personal experiences. To use the camp experience as a "ready-made modern example" (Alvarez's words) of one's personal pain need not be a conscious or deliberate act, but only a way of knowing one's inner life in the language and figures of an outer world. In fact, we might ask here if it is ever possible to separate "private" from "historical" worlds, insofar as we may neither express our private lives without recourse to public (i.e., historical) language, nor know history except by ordering it privately. In embodying the extremity of this reciprocal exchange between the private and historical realms, Plath's poems seem not to "exploit atrocity" so much as they merely draw upon a public pool of language that is necessarily informed by atrocity.

Thus, in "Mary's Song," a "Sunday lamb crack[ing] in its fat" suddenly turns sacrificial as the speaker glimpses it through the oven window. The fire that "makes it precious" becomes

> The same fire
>
> Melting the tallow heretics
> Ousting the Jews.
> Their thick palls float
>
> Over the cicatrix of Poland, burnt-out
> Germany.
> They do not die.
>
> Grey birds obsess my heart,
> Mouth-ash, ash of eye.
> They settle. On the high
>
> Precipice
> That emptied one man into space
> The ovens glowed like heavens, incandescent.
>
> It is a heart,
> This holocaust I walk in,
> O golden child the world will kill and eat.[9]

From associations that reveal more her imaginative preoccupations than her sense of self, she moves suddenly from peering inside her oven to entering it—at which point, it seems to enter her. The Jews' pall floats over and through her, and they do not die but obsess her heart. Even the ambiguity of her syntax (is she addressing a golden child or describing one who will be killed and eaten?) seems to reflect the confused exchange between her associations; she moves from seeing, to figuring what she sees, to entering her metaphor as both agent and victim of it.

Like her other poems, "Mary's Song" is not about the Holocaust, but it still betrays some understanding, a particular figure, of it. She has, after all, recalled only certain images, which in themselves reveal her personal access to them. In "Mary's Song," it is not the personal pain of the victims she draws upon, or the mass murder, or the history of Jewish persecution, but rather, it is an idea of victimhood and sacrifice of innocents that constitutes the core of her figure. She did not thereby suffer "as a Jew" so much as she represented her suffering through her own grasp of how (even why) Jews suffered. And as Edward Butscher hints, this vision is necessarily Christian: "Like the victims of Hiroshima, Sylvia suffers innocently for the crimes of others" (p. 322). That is, she suffers martyrlike, Christlike, and in her mind, Jewlike for others' sins: through this figure and its exchange with her own victimhood, Plath's Holocaust seems to be a kind of calvary.

In this way, she also reveals a surprisingly acute sensitivity to the paschal valences in a "lamb cracking in its fat [that] sacrifices its opacity," seemingly conscious of the etymological resonances of sacrifice and burnt offering in her reference to "this holocaust I walk in." But by making herself the sacrifice here, she also betrays her own limited understanding of the figure of Jewish suffering itself: again, it is a particularly Christian remembrance of events automatically figured by her idea of a "holocaust" as a sacrifice of Jews, however innocent. So even as she uses a knowledge of the Holocaust to figure her pain, her own victimhood, this knowledge itself is necessarily prefigured in an essentially Christian frame.

In "Lady Lazarus" and "Daddy," the contours of her own grasp of the Holocaust Jew are less exposed than the manner in which the figure itself organizes, expresses, and perhaps even inflames her private pain. On "Daddy," Plath has said, "The poem is spoken by a girl with an Electra complex. Her father died while she thought he was God. Her case is complicated by the fact that her father was also a Nazi and her mother very possibly part Jewish. In the daughter or in her imagination, the two strains marry and paralyse each other—she has to act out the awful little allegory once over before she is free of it."[10] The salient point here is that Plath did not believe in the literality of her figures: the poem is spoken by a girl (not written by one), and it is the speaker's (not her own) father who is a Nazi and whose mother is Jewish. The irony here, however, is that by "acting out the awful little allegory once over [to be] free of it," neither the speaker nor the poet seems to have freed herself of it but has only incorporated the allegory and its pain all the more deeply. Indeed, as I will suggest, insofar as these figures lay in some measure at the base of her unhappiness, she may have simultaneously represented them and used them to represent herself.

> An engine, an engine
> Chuffing me off like a Jew.
> A Jew to Dachau, Auschwitz, Belsen.
> I began to talk like a Jew.
> I think I may well be a Jew.
>
> The snows of the Tyrol, the clear beer of Vienna
> Are not very pure or true.
> With my gypsy ancestress and my weird luck
> And my Taroc pack and my Taroc pack
> I may be a bit of a Jew.
>
> I have always been scared of *you*,
> With your Luftwaffe, your gobbledygoo.
> And your neat moustache

And your Aryan eye, bright blue.
Panzer-man, panzer-man, O You—

The Nazis had nothing to do with her feelings of oppression at the hands of her father (he now a figure for her husband), but she was oppressed just the same. In fact, given the reciprocal transfer of imagery between men in these lines, Plath may even be going beyond her personal relationships to husband and father to suggest the larger experiences of women at the hands of men. She might have used slave and master, or even czar and Jews; but insofar as the speaker began in the figure of a Jew, she saw fit to see it through. Whether she became a Jew because her father was already "Nazi-like" or turned her father into a Nazi because she already identified as a Jew may never be clear, but it is possible that one side of the equation ultimately determined the other, thus completing itself. For once she became a "bit of a Jew," both speaker and poet began to know and to represent her world in "the Jewish way."

On the one hand, Plath recognized somewhat self-consciously that she needed her own authentic life experiences as both writing material and as her prospective pool of tropes: "How could I write about life when I'd never had a love affair, or a baby, or seen anyone die?"[11] On the other hand, she also allowed herself an inheritance of what might be called cultural or literary memory: in reading about others' experiences, she seemed to make them her own. So even though she thought that her poems came "immediately out of [her own] sensuous and emotional experiences," she wrote, "I cannot sympathise with these cries from the heart that are informed by nothing except a needle or a knife or whatever it is" (p. 64, Newman). Her psychic pain and the pain of Holocaust victims might thus be linked temporally in her mind, and as such might have been linked causally, as well.

When Plath explained in a BBC interview that "personal experience shouldn't be a kind of shut box and mirror-looking narcissistic experience . . . [but rather] it should be generally relevant, to such things as Hiroshima and Dachau" (p. 64, Newman), she seems to have been arguing for just this reciprocal exchange between outer and inner realities, the inevitability of knowing each in terms of the other. By "generally relevant," Plath may have suggested not just that personal experience should be generally relevant to Hiroshima and Dachau, but that these historical icons had been overly relevant to her own personal experience. That is, it may never be clear to what extent she derived her pain from the knowledge of Hiroshima and Dachau or merely relied upon these public experiences to figure her pain.

Once imagining the suffering of others in order to represent her misery, the poet may have found herself unable to cross back into safe territory. Reaching for the most extreme of all possible figures to objectify her pain (to allegorize and thereby relieve it, as she has said), Plath may have found that rather than merely projecting her pain outward through such public figures, she has actually injected them into the matrix of herself, turning her inner life into a "concentration camp of the mind."[12] In attempting to find a worldly correlate or objectification for her psychic torment, turning to the "Jewish kind" of pain, Plath has thus refracted her private pain through the images of Auschwitz, magnifying and possibly even aggravating this pain further. Instead of objectifying her suffering and thereby relieving herself of it through allegory, she has internalized the allegory as her own, intensifying the consequences of this figure for both self and poetry.

Thus, in addition to finding what Alvarez has called "the ready-made modern example of hell on earth," Plath may also have found that these facts lay in some measure at the root of her psychic pain and seemed therefore that much more appropriate in its expression. It may be difficult to determine at what point

> a cake of soap
> A wedding ring
> A gold filling

become linguistic currency by which subsequent agony is measured, and at what point these images actually incite the pain they are then used to express. In this context, it may not be so surprising that as pieces of an overwhelmingly painful modern reality, these images floated so near the surface of her imagistic repetoire. In Plath's case, one might even wonder if it was her belief in the realities whence she pulled her figures that contributed to her inner torment. Perhaps it was the realization that there was an external equivalent—and much more—for her pain and that it was visited on millions of other humans, that her metaphors had been more than metaphors, which lent her own inner pain such an urgent sense of gravity.

I I

In his early essay on Holocaust literature, A. Alvarez warns that in his experience, he had "personally known half-a-dozen suicides or near-suicides; and each prepared his act with a fierce immersion in the literature of the camps."[13] Seeming to echo Steiner's note that "he who handles this material does so at his peril," Alvarez may also have in mind the poet Plath, who did not immerse herself in the literature of the camps, so much as she immersed her *self* literarily in the figures of the camps. As misguided and even dangerous as it is to speculate on such cause-and-effect relationships, Alvarez cannot help but raise the question of the kinds of consequences a poet's work holds for herself. "[F]or the artist himself art is not necessarily therapeutic," he writes. "[H]e is not automatically relieved of his fantasies by expressing them. Instead, by some perverse logic of creation, the act of formal expression may simply make the dredged-up material more readily available to him. The result of handling it in his work may well be that he finds himself living it out."[14] At issue here is not Plath's believing in the literality of her own tropes and then "living them out," but that it may be difficult to separate how she understood herself from how she represented—i.e., figured—herself. How much her figures reflected the speaker's understanding of herself and how much they created a kind of understanding after the fact may be impossible to determine, though there seem to be consequences for the poet in either case.

Elaborating still further on this possibility, the psychoanalyst and survivor Dori Laub also asks:

> Does the artist or the patient . . . simply use the modern metaphor, the one that is specific to his times, to express his own personal conflict, dread and despair? Is it a mere external vessel that is tailor-made to his inner fantasy world? Or, is this inner world already strangely affected by the actuality of atrocity-events and therefore uniquely sensitive, bearing a particular affinity to such specific themes? Have we already assimilated our historical actuality to our unconscious inner life and do patients therefore readily give expression to it, when the therapeutic ambience allows this to happen?[15]

Laub's primary concern was the manner in which a patient's figures both reflected and framed psychological conflict, character and symptom formation, and the psychotherapeutic process itself. But by asking here whether one's inner world is strangely affected by the actuality of atrocity events, he suggests that the figures poets and patients use to express their inner lives function simultaneously as source and as figure of psychic pain— for both survivors and for nonvictims who only know of such horrors but never experienced them directly. As other experiences functioned as figures for the Holocaust, shaping comprehension and expression of specific events, the Holocaust itself would now function as a guiding figure for other events, especially the realities of inner life that are possibly generated by knowledge of the Holocaust.

Breaking Plath's figurative identity as Holocaust Jew into its metaphoric and metonymic parts suggests a further basis of her appropriation of this imagery. For at the metonymical level, where we "simultaneously distinguish between phenomena and reduce one to the status of a manifestation of the other,"[16] it becomes possible to grant the difference between parts of the figure even as we sustain one's relation to the other. In this case, the massive suffering of the Jews becomes appropriate as a trope for the poet's pain precisely because it was also an agent of it. Rather than the two kinds of pain bearing on each other in the purely object-object relationship of metaphor, she may have conceived them to function in a "part-whole" relationship to each other. Taken still further, Plath's pain might thus even become an extension of the original Jewish suffering (not just a parallel of it), an empathetic link she would codify in becoming a "Holocaust Jew."

As speculative as it is to infer a causal connection between Plath's metaphors and the pain of her inner life, given the disturbing mortality rate of those, like Plath, who were possessed by the Holocaust, a further observation seems in order. All of us working in the literature have colleagues—both survivors and nonvictims—who have been broken by the knowledge of events. In fact, among the actual survivors, many suffered mortal wounds to the spirit and, unable to repair the damage done to their trust in the world, eventually died by their own hand. Beginning with prominent Jewish leaders like Samuel Zygelboim in London, who attempted to draw attention to the Jews' plight with his suicide, and Adam Czerniakow in the Warsaw ghetto, who seemed to accept a burden of guilt for the deportations of his community; extending to the Polish non-Jewish survivor Tadeusz Borowski, to the self-described "Holocaust Jew," Jean Améry, to the survivor-poet Paul Celan, and survivor-novelists Piotr Rawicz and Primo Levi—all suicides—enunciating their pain seems not to have kept them from despair (as Camus suggested), but may only have deepened it. Of the generation of non-Jewish poets who identified literarily as Holocaust Jews, the numbers are also disquieting: John Berryman, Randall Jarrell, Anne Sexton, and Sylvia Plath all killed themselves after representing themselves literarily in light of the Holocaust. This is not to concretize a cause-and-effect relationship between the poets and their figures, but only to acknowledge the potential consequences in such figures for the poet's understanding of both herself and the world around her.

Of Sylvia Plath and John Berryman, Alvin Rosenfeld has written: "While their suicides . . . also mediate between us and their books, one senses no historical determinism behind the personal anguish that must have led them to take their lives; the pressure to which they succumbed seems to have been biographically generated, its pain not larger than a single life" (p. 18). We might ask here, however, to what extent anyone is able—or unable—to assume for himself "historically determined" pain, and if we can ever satisfactorily distinguish between "historically determined" and "biographically generated" pain. For it seems that as long as we incorporate the historical by sharing common pools of knowledge with history's sufferers, a reader's biographically and historically generated pain may never be entirely separable. That is to say, by reading and listening to the stories of the camps, to what extent did Plath make these stories her own? Instead of asking whether a writer coming after the Holocaust should be traumatized by a memory she may have inherited only literarily, we might ask to what extent the writer was traumatized by her literary historical memory of the Holocaust.

In the Aristotelian tradition, E. D. Hirsch affirms not just the possibility, but the necessity, of knowing the present moment in terms of previously known types when he suggests that "one would never invent or understand a new type of meaning unless he were capable of perceiving analogies and making novel subsumptions under previously known types."[17] For Sylvia Plath, the previously known type was the suffering of the Holocaust, known to her only through its literary figuration, which then framed (and perhaps contributed to) her own psychic misery. To question whether or not the suffering of the Holocaust should be cast as a type implies that we have some sort of legislative control over which events figure others, which events enter consciousness. But once the events of the Holocaust enter language— even through more authentic means like diaries and memoirs—they assume certain typological dimensions, as we have seen in the survivors' own work. That the previously known pain of the Holocaust was not known firsthand by Plath makes it all the more typological, all the more dependent on the forms and figures of the media by which Plath has come to these events. Thus, it was as a *type* that the collective suffering of the Holocaust entered Plath's poetry, along with other types like Lazarus and Lesbos, and it was as a type that she represented it. At what point she chose these types to exemplify her pain, at what point they organized her inner world for her, and at what point they aggravated her torment may always be difficult to say.

"All poets are Jews," Paul Celan has written, quoting Russian poet Marina Zwetajewa—a figure Alvin Rosenfeld accepts as meaning "all poets write out of a harried condition, and none so much as those Jewish writers . . . who have written in German."[18] Here the critic grants that there is a Holocaust Jew, a figurative Jew, confirmed repeatedly by other Jewish writers as a literary type. Thus, Nelly Sachs would write that being a Jew had nothing to do with obedience to "Mosaic law, but to endure suffering and fear. All human beings who suffered became Jews. . . ."[19] Thus, one of Edmond Jabès's speakers would castigate the prisoners around him, soon to be scattered throughout the death camps, "as if in the name of the Lord to His assembled people: 'You are all Jews, even the anti-Semites, because you are all marked for martyrdom!' "[20] And thus, even Uri Zvi Greenberg, the most uncompromising of Jewish nationalists, suggests that because "to this, our disaster . . . / There are no other analogies,"

> For every cruel torture that man may yet do to man in a Gentile country—
> He who comes to compare will state: He was tortured like a Jew.
> Every fright, every terror, every loneliness, every chagrin,
> Every murmuring, every weeping in the world
> He who compares will say: This analogy is of the Jewish kind.[21]

Because the suffering of the Holocaust was not like anything else, it became a referent, a standard, by which subsequent suffering would be measured. In groping for metaphors with which to express her private pain, Plath has thus reached for the most extreme figures imaginatively available to her: those "of the Jewish kind."

I I I

"In none of the essays devoted to praising Plath," writes Irving Howe, "have I found a coherent statement as to the nature, let alone value, of her vision."[22] The nature of her vision, however, is necessarily metaphorical, as is the nature of anyone's vision; its value comes in the understanding such a vision reveals or creates. She sees the world, her place in it, and her private agony in the figure of some experience—ocassionally literary (Lesbos, Lazarus), occasionally personal, and often in a blend of the two. How to separate her vision, the value of her vision, and the figures by which she would simultaneously grasp and represent her vision may well be beyond us. But to what extent figures of the Holocaust framed her vision, even inspired it, might still suffice as one of many points of critical departure for reading her poetry.

For the most part, the critics of Plath's Holocaust figures object primarily to the want of apparent empirical connections between Plath's life and the death camps, as well as to the "impropriety" of her borrowing from what they consider the emotional "reserves" of the Holocaust. Alvin Rosenfeld asks whether there are any contact points between the sufferings of the girl with the Electra complex and those endured by the victims of Hitler, "a sufficient similarity to draw them into valid analogy" (pp. 177, 179). But this approach assumes only one basis for metaphor—the preexisting properties two disparate experiences have in common, which Kant called "actual" (*angemessen*)—and neglects the "underlying" (*unterlegt*) similarity created by the poet in her metaphors. For there may be no more external "symmetry between the sufferings of the little girl" and those endured by the victims of Hitler than between Eliot's evening and his "patient etherised upon a table." But in neither case does the poet attempt a literal analogy: these are only figurative comparisons, one thing seen in light of another. The question might be changed from "Should the Holocaust be used as a public image of reference?" to "How has the Holocaust been used as a public image of reference?"

Like Rosenfeld, Irving Howe finds the implied comparisons in such figures "utterly disproportionate"; but in addition, he also suggests that these comparisons are deliberately made, that "Plath *tries* to enlarge upon the personal plight, give meaning to the personal outcry, by fancying the girl as victim of a Nazi father." For reasons to be explored later, the figure of Plath as a Holocaust Jew may just not work for Howe. But it seems to be the calculated effort to enlarge her pain at the expense of the Holocaust that actually galls the critic. "There is something monstrous, utterly disproportionate, when tangled emotions about one's father are deliberately compared with the historical fate of the European Jews; something sad, if the comparison is made spontaneously" (p. 232). It is the willed aspect of Plath's figure that Howe cannot abide, even though the will to make meaning out of her pain seems acceptable. But as did the poets before her in actually writing about the Holocaust, Plath may not have chosen these figures so much as they possessed her. There may indeed be something sad if these "comparisons" are made spontaneously, as Howe suggests, but this something sad may have more to do with our tragic reservoir of atrocious figures than with their spontaneous use.

The last and most biting criticism of Plath in this context, however, is not that her figures are merely disproportionate or deliberately exploitative, but that she may be ethically at risk in such metaphors. "Does any writer, does any human being other than an actual survivor have the right to put on this death-rig?" asks George Steiner.[23] To which we might answer, no more so than any of us has the right to compare our lot with that of the Jews escaping Egypt, or the destruction of cities in wartime with that of Jerusalem in 587 BCE. We do not put on these "death-rigs" because they fit, but because they are the remembered archetypes in our language by which we grasp our current lives. In fact, in writing that "Auschwitz and Belsen lodge at the centre of our current lives and sensibilities like the energized, malignant void of a Gnostic vision" (p. 305), Steiner recognizes the force of events like these to assume archetypal proportions. But when he asks in addition, "In what sense does anyone, himself uninvolved and long after the event, commit a subtle larceny when he invokes the echoes and trappings of Auschwitz and appropriates an enormity of ready emotion to his own private design?" Steiner evokes the moral high road. "Subtle larceny" and "right" suggest a moral crime against the victims—"stealing their deaths as well as their lives"[24]—by Plath, when the actual crime may be committed by the memory in public language itself. For as Robert Alter reminds us in a slightly different context, "[L]anguage is the one artistic medium that develops perceptibly through historical time . . . and thus literature is before all others the memory-laden art, the one that resumes its past in the very act of exploiting its full resources for the expression of the present."[25] To deny language its "memory load" accumulated in historical time would be to deny literature its own historical consciousness.

Ultimately, however, there may be only one dimension to Plath's Holocaust figures that actually mitigates between them and her critics: the "community of metaphor." In addition to a metaphor's cognitive meaning, Ted Cohen writes that there is also a certain implied "cultivation of intimacy in metaphor," in which the maker and reader of metaphor must both share several basic assumptions. "Three aspects are involved: 1) the speaker issues a kind of concealed invitation; 2) the hearer expends a certain effort to accept the invitation; and 3) this transaction constitutes the acknowledgement of community."[26] If for some reason the reader chooses not to accept the invitation—because of some kind of conflicting knowledge that interferes with the movement in metaphor—the "community of metaphor" cannot be established.

In the case of Plath and her critics, her invitation to metaphor is refused on several grounds: there is, in fact, a serious preexisting conflict in "community knowledge" between what Plath knows and what most of her critics know. Cohen's work is again helpful here:

> The sense of a close community results not only from the shared awareness that a special invitation has been given and accepted, but also from the awareness that not everyone could make that offer or take it up. . . . *[A]ll literal use of language is accessible to all whose language it is. But a figurative use can be inaccessible to all but those who share information about one another's knowledge, beliefs, intentions, and attitudes.* (P. 7, emphasis added)

As we've seen with Steiner, Rosenfeld, and Howe on Plath, there was from the beginning a disinclination to believe in the metaphors constructed with Holocaust imagery, a resistance to the movement between a Holocaust icon and a personal state of mind. The figures were either taken literally as empirical comparisons, in which case they were perceived as false analogies, or seen as so loaded with pathos as to be intrinsically exploitative. In either case the ability to accept these invitations to metaphor rests upon completely different—and perhaps irreconcilable—assumptions regarding the Holocaust, one's personal connection to it, and one's definition of it *as* a collective catastrophe. For even though the language is indeed shared, the weight, charge, and meaning assigned to terms like Auschwitz and Belsen by the different reader and writer communities could be no more disparate.

Plath wrote her poems as a non-Jew—on whose sensibility the Holocaust seemed to have a terrible effect—to others in "her community of metaphor," for whom the Holocaust was also principally a figure, a universal point of reference for all kinds of evil, oppression, and suffering. For the community of Jewish readers, however, these events are inevitably grasped in all their literality (recall Rosenfeld's emphasis on the reality of events), often in relation to the specific fate of families. In fact, for this community of readers, Plath's mere attempt to personalize events necessarily contradicts the larger perception of these events' essence *as* collective, as a catastrophe because it was the destruction of an entire people, and not one person. Plath's personalization of events thus ignores the immense communal weight by which they have been grasped immediately by Jewish writers. Where Auschwitz and Belsen are symbols of suffering for Plath—public ones, which carry no "sacred" charge—they are for the Jewish community at once symbols of specifically Jewish suffering (the Holocaust defined as a Jewish catastrophe) and realities they either experienced firsthand or to which they are connected by the suffering of loved ones.

When evaluated by Cohen's criteria of "metaphor-community"—i.e., knowledge, beliefs, intention, and attitudes—Plath and her critics clearly begin and end in two entirely different worlds. It may not be just a matter of one community's unwillingness to take the metaphoric plunge with Plath, but essentially an inability to do so, given the meaning and understanding they already bring to part of the metaphorical equation. For those outside the closed community of metaphor, Plath's figurative claims may forever be read as patent and somewhat illegitimate hyperbole. In effect, as one who is not related to the Holocaust on any level other than her literary identification, Plath is perceived to lie outside the community of her own tropes. For if Plath's pain is not perceived literally to be part of the larger pain of Jewish suffering, then even the figurative force of her metonymical connection loses its authority.

Thus, it is not a matter of Plath's having been Jewish or not, for as a Jewish writer, she probably could not have used these figures this way: her entire grasp and knowledge of them would not have allowed it, just as it does not allow her critics to accept these figures. In fact, it may be difficult to find an example of a Jewish writer using the collective suffering of the Holocaust as a figure for explicitly personal suffering, unrelated to war or military persecution. This is not to say that Holocaust figures aren't used at all, for indeed they are used widely in contemporary Jewish writing about non-Holocaust events, but never in regard to purely personal suffering.

There is, in fact, a compelling parallel between "confessional poetry" and the testimonial mode of Holocaust literature: for what is confessional poetry if not that which emphasizes its personal authenticity and link to material over all else? As testimony to the poet's private pain, confessional poetry depends for its power—its authority—on personal authenticity, as do so many other kinds of literary witness. But just as the interpretive truths in Holocaust literature are undermined by a misguided emphasis on eye-witness authority, so too are the truths of confessional poetry when judged on these grounds alone. In Plath's case, rather than disputing the authenticity of her figures, we might look to her poetry for the ways the Holocaust has entered public consciousness as a trope, and how it then informs both the poet's view of the world and her representations of it in verse.

Entered as it was onto the "public record" during the Eichmann trial in Jerusalem, a time when images of the camps flooded the media and commanded world attention as they had not since the war, the Holocaust necessarily began to inform all writers' literary imagination as a prospective trope. In this way, it is also sustained in public memory, as part of a larger realm of experiences constituting language itself. It is therefore surprising that its figurative use should then be critically sanctioned and made unavailable to all those for whom the Holocaust was not "authentic" experience. For in absorbing these experiences and making them its own, language might be said to remember experience long after all of its authentic witnesses are gone. Rather than attempting to constrain the Holocaust's impact on our understanding and current representations of the world, the critic's task is to examine how the Holocaust has mattered. For by allowing these images to figure current experiences, writers and critics sustain events in consciousness and measure their impact at the same time. To remove the Holocaust from the realm of the imagination, however, to sanctify it and place it off-limits, is to risk excluding it altogether from public consciousness. And this seems to be too high a price to pay for saving it from those who would abuse its memory in inequitable metaphor. Better abused memory in this case, which might then be critically qualified, than no memory at all.

EIGHT

When Soldier-Poets
Remember the Holocaust

Antiwar Poetry in Israel

As soon as he tells me about the binding of Ishmael
I tell him about the binding of Isaac.

—Mordechai Goldman

I

Of the centuries of historical archetypes for suffering accumulated in Hebrew, those generated during the period of the Holocaust have begun to
overwhelm all others. Due partly to the sheer enormity of events, partly to
the great proportion of Holocaust survivors in Israel (nearly one-half the
population in 1948), and partly to the central negative place of the Holocaust in Zionist ideology as the ultimate consequence of Jewish vulnerability
in the Diaspora, images and figures from the *Sho'ah* have all but displaced
their historical precedents. Not only has the *Sho'ah* begun to figure retro-
actively all pre-*Sho'ah* catastrophes—lending them significance they could
not otherwise have had—but it has also become a standard in Jewish literature by which all kinds of post-Holocaust calamities, Jewish or not, are
now measured.

The impulse to represent other people's suffering in the language and
archetypes of one's own tradition is hardly new. As we have seen in the
case of Franz Werfel's novel of the Armenian massacres—*The Forty Days of
Musa Dagh*—for example, the actual fifty-two-day siege there is refracted
through the archetypally biblical (i.e., Jewish) forty days. With yet another
set of figures available to Jewish writers after the Holocaust, it seems inevitable that victims of post-Holocaust calamities would thus be grasped by
Jewish writers—especially survivors—in the images of Holocaust suffering.
When Elie Wiesel makes pleas on behalf of massacred Cambodians, Vietnamese boat people, forgotten Armenians, South African blacks, or even
on behalf of humankind as potential victim of a nuclear holocaust ("all the
world is now Jewish in the face of nuclear holocaust," he has said), it is not

to diminish the suffering of Jews or to exaggerate that of contemporary victims.

When another survivor tells us in a video interview that the first image after the Holocaust to rekindle her own pain and evoke almost total empathy was that of the Vietnamese boat people with no place to land, she intends no equivalence, but reflects the only understanding of such events available to her. After the Holocaust, she tells us, she cannot sit still while these people suffer; she insists that they be rescued, that they be taken in, as she and her family were not.[1] These analogies need not stem from a desire to find moral equivalence or to suggest an equality in the proportions of suffering. But rather, they may originate largely from the genuine empathy for new victims that is generated by the memory of one's own victimhood.

As natural as it is for survivors in Israel to apprehend current persecutions in light of their past experiences, however, this tendency eventually cuts two ways. On the one hand, as victims of both contemporary P.L.O. terror and past Nazi atrocities, Holocaust survivors in Israel reflexively grasp their new killers in the figures of remembered Nazis: the P.L.O. is perceived as an extension of Hitler, whose aim is to finish the Nazis' job. On the other hand, when survivors perceive other people as victims, they tend also to see them in light of their own past victimization. As a result, both survivors and their children in Israel have turned to what amounts now to a national memory of the Holocaust to represent the suffering of others: not to find correspondence between kinds of suffering, but to represent it in the only language at hand. Merely by writing of enemy soldiers' experiences or of the Palestinians in Hebrew, contemporary Israeli poets necessarily evoke a language latent with the Jews' own suffering.

In the reflections of writers and soldiers at Kibbutz Ein Ha-horesh after the Six-Day War in 1967, Israelis explored the extremely complicated relationship between collective Holocaust memory, their reasons for fighting in the war, and their understanding of the enemy. Twenty-two years after World War II, their proud Zionist education notwithstanding, Israeli soldiers came inevitably to see themselves as little more than another generation of Jews on the brink of a second great massacre—and responded in battle as if the life of an entire people depended on every fire fight. As Muki Tzur describes waiting for the beginning of this war, in fact, it grows clear that his inherited memory of the Holocaust constituted his primary reason for fighting, the impetus driving him and his comrades—all now identifying figuratively with the generation of survivors preceding them: "We tend to forget those days before the war, and perhaps rightly so—yet those were the days in which we came closest to that Jewish fate from which we have run like haunted beings all these years. Suddenly everyone was talking about Munich, about the holocaust, about the Jewish people being left to its own fate."[2] Questioned later by a slightly incredulous Abba Kovner, who led the Vilna partisans during the Holocaust and came to Israel in the Zionist belief that by definition, Israel made the possibility of another Holocaust "unthinkable," another soldier revealed that not only was it thinkable, but it was in fact the governing thought underlying his very *raison d'être* as a soldier:

> It's true that people believed that we would be exterminated if we lost the war. They were afraid. We got this idea—or inherited it—from the concentration camps. It's a concrete idea for anyone who has grown up in Israel, even if he personally didn't experience Hitler's persecution, but only heard or read about it.
> . . . Did you really get the feeling that extermination could happen here? [asks Kovner].
> . . . Yes, certainly. I think it's an idea that everyone in Israel lived with. (Pp. 217–18)

This is the great irony of the Israelis' grasp of their predicament. On the one hand, only a people fighting another Holocaust will survive with Israel's tenacity. But on the other hand, the sabra has been educated to believe that Israel is the only safe haven for Jews in the world, the only guarantee against another Jewish Holocaust, and that "holocausts" happen only in the Diaspora. Thus, the soldier is compelled to fight by the memory of what happened in the diaspora, precisely and paradoxically because it could also happen in Israel.

But this is not the Israeli's only double-bind. Of more serious consequence is that expressed by Muki Tzur at the end of his opening meditation:

> We know the meaning of genocide, both those of us who saw the holocaust and those who were born later. Perhaps this is why the world will never understand us, will never understand our courage, or comprehend the doubts and the qualms of conscience we knew during and after the war. Those who survived the holocaust, those who see pictures of a father and a mother, who hear the cries that disturb the dreams of those close to them, those who have listened to stories—know that no other people carries with it such haunting visions. *And it is these visions which compel us to fight and yet make us ashamed of our fighting . . .*
> . . . We carry in our hearts an oath which binds us never to return to the Europe of the holocaust; but at the same time we do not wish to lose that Jewish sense of identity with the victims. (Pp. 38–39, my emphasis)

Having carried the memory of his people's past victimhood into battle in order never to be victimized again, the Israeli discovers the source both of his strength and of his weakness as *victor*: the same figure of victimization that motivates him as a soldier also compels extraordinary sympathy for his defeated enemies, now grasped in the figure of his own people's defeats.

In fact, as long as the dual memory of Jewish martyrs and heroes remains the predominant ideological trope in Israel, her soldiers cannot lose their sense of identity with the victims, as becomes clear first of all to the soldiers themselves:

> I felt uneasy about being a victorious army, a strong army. If I had any clear awareness of the World War years and the fate of European Jewry it was once when I was going up the Jericho road and the refugees were going down it. I identified directly with them. When I saw parents dragging their children along by the hand, I actually almost saw myself being dragged along by my own father. This was perhaps one of the immediate experiences that brought an association with the war years. It wasn't so noticeable in times of action, but just at those moments when we felt the suffering of others, of the Arabs, against whom we fought. This was perhaps the tragic thing, that the identification had to be with the other side, with our enemies. (Pp. 216–17)

This soldier was not drawing an equivalence between Arab and Jewish refugees, much less one between the circumstances of these two wars. But merely by witnessing his enemies' flight, he has necessarily seen (i.e., understood) it in the only terms available to him: that of his own family's past deportations. In fact, the most amazing part of this passage may not only be that he has reflexively grasped his enemies' predicament in a Jewish figure, but that he has actually now grasped his own remembered past in terms of the Arabs' flight from their towns. In the reciprocal flow between past and present experiences, between his and his enemies' defeats, each is now framed by the other; the reality of the Arab refugees before this soldier's eyes have shaped the remembered image of his own past, even as it is cast alternately in the figure of the Jews' remembered past.

This movement between past and present persecution, between the compulsion to fight and the shame of fighting, exemplifies Israel's own ambivalent need to remember the Holocaust and to forget it: it is simultaneously the reason for the Jews' life in Israel—for the state itself—and that which incites empathy in them for their new, defeated enemies. The consequences of these figures can only be speculated upon: at what point does this memory, and the subsequent empathy it generates for a defeated enemy, weaken the resolve to fight further, and at what point does it make Israel stronger? Always struggling with this dilemma, Israel found in 1982 a renewed tension in it, represented now by her soldier-poets in their antiwar poetry.

I I

Where the memory of the Holocaust—and the analogies implicitly created in the memory of one destruction in light of another—spurred Israeli soldiers to fight for survival in 1948, 1967, and 1973, something strange happened in 1982 in Lebanon. When Prime Minister Menachem Begin responded to a reporter's questions about Israel's bombing of Beirut, he reflexively asked: "And if Hitler himself was hiding in a building with 20 innocent citizens, you still wouldn't bomb the building?" The Prime Minister was immediately challenged by Holocaust historians Yehuda Bauer and Ze'ev Mankowitz, and by novelist Amos Oz, among others, who answered, "No, Mr. Prime Minister, your example is not an equivalent . . . "; "Beirut is not Berlin."[3] In fact, one of the distinguishing characteristics of the antiwar poetry flowing from Lebanon during and after the war was precisely this repudiation of Holocaust figures as justification for the war, even as the poets simultaneously embraced such figures as the primary means for representing victims of this war—especially the children.

During this protracted war and even after the Israeli withdrawal from Lebanon, poetry and essays, handbills and posters thus appeared throughout Israel responding to the war with both explicit and oblique references to the Holocaust. Two collections, in particular, *Border Crossing: Poems from the Lebanon War* and *Fighting and Killing without End: Political Poetry in the Lebanon War*,[4] illustrate the sheer impossibility of representing or reading about contemporary destruction and suffering without recourse to both the most traditional figures in the liturgy as well as to those more recently acquired during the Holocaust. But as dominant as the Holocaust had been before 1982 as an image of survival, it was now handled ironically in reference to the Israelis' situation in Lebanon. For the first time, Jewish suffering was not the principal object of Israel's war poetry. Instead of recalling traditional Jewish archetypes to figure the deaths of Israeli soldiers or the condition of bereaved families at home, Israeli poets of the Lebanon War recalled such figures more often to depict the death and suffering of others, especially that of Arab children. The Holocaust was now being used not as an image for Jewish suffering, but as an anti-trope for it.

In a poem that was printed and distributed widely during the war, Efraim Sidon thus conjures remembrance of the Holocaust explicitly to discard it as justification for the war in Lebanon. He begins with a mock pronouncement of guilt on the heads of the children for their own fate:

> I accuse the children in Sidon and Tyre
> Whose numbers are still uncounted
> Three-year-olds, seven-year-olds, and others of all ages,
> Of the crime of living next door to terrorists.
> If you hadn't lived near them, children,
> You could have been students today.
> Now you will be punished.
>
> (*Fighting and Killing*, P. 124)

He then continues by accusing the women and mothers who lived near the terrorists, as well as the houses that sheltered terrorists, and ends by blaming everyone in Lebanon for the Holocaust itself, for which all there will be punished:

I accuse the residents of Lebanon—all of them.
For the Nazis' mistreatment of us in the World War.
Because from generation to generation, everyone must see himself
As if he were destroying Hitler
Always, always
And that's what Begin is doing.

I accuse you all!
Naturally.
Because I am always, always the victim.

(P. 124)

By completing the Passover obligation "from generation to generation, everyone must see himself" with "As if he were destroying Hitler," the poet acknowledges the command to remember, even as he repudiates it through its mocking extension. Sidon would literalize the figure of the Holocaust here, stretching the linkage to its breaking point as argument for the war, precisely in order to invalidate the figure as a basis for military action.

Just before their afterword to *Fighting and Killing without End*, the editors have reproduced a poster in which Chaim Nachman Bialik's "Upon the Slaughter" is printed in Arabic and Hebrew, side by side, overlaid on an Israeli map of Beirut. In this graphic way, the poster forces the reader quite literally to read the map of Sabra and Shatilla between and through the lines of Bialik, the national poet. It also literally refigures Jewish experience in Arabic, with its own pool of references, allusions, and tropes—even as it incorporates into Bialik's own lines the suffering of Palestinians. For once "Upon the Slaughter" is used to represent another pain (as it was by writers in the Vilna and Warsaw ghettos), it not only organizes the pain of others but also absorbs—and thereby remembers—it, as well.

As the greatest test for Abraham's faith had been his aborted sacrifice of Isaac, the least bearable kind of suffering in Jewish tradition seems always to have been that of children. Where a breaking point had been reached for Bialik in his response to the Kishinev pogroms in the now axiomatic lines from "Upon the Slaughter"—

Who cries Revenge! Revenge!—accursed be he!
Fit Vengeance for the spilt blood of a child
The Devil has not yet invented . . .

—and for the ghetto scribes describing the murder of children during the Holocaust, it seems a breaking point of sorts had been reached for Israeli poets faced with responding to the suffering of children in their midst. It was here, therefore, that they simultaneously reached for and disposed of their own greatest national responses to destruction. Specifically, it is the murdered children in Lebanon that simultaneously provoked the bitterest antiwar verse by Israel's soldier-poets and recalled the figures of Holocaust children.

As it was the slaughter and deportation of children in the Holocaust that seemed to break all sustaining archetypes for writers in the ghetto,[5] it seems often to have been the suffering of children that moved several of the Israeli antiwar poets to question their own accepted lexicon of war-related suffering—and then implicitly to compare the child-victims of the War in Lebanon with the child-victims of their own memories. Even though the "R.P.G. kids" of the P.L.O. proved to be as lethal to the Israeli soldiers as the P.L.O. regulars, the crises of conscience they provoked may have been more traumatic still; for they destroyed in the Israelis both a perceived sanctity in children as well as the belief that they were fighting a conventional war. Ultimately, the R.P.G. kids also incited an even deeper hatred for an enemy that would use its children as both protective shield and frontline soldiers. On the other hand, however, as children, the R.P.G. kids were regarded in the tradition as victims, in this case, of both enemy and friendly soldiers.

Almost every figurative allusion to the Holocaust in this poetry thus begins with an image of suffering children. In fact, at some level, it seems to have been just this unprecedented prospect of having both to fight children (as R.P.G. kids) and to find them massacred in Sabra and Shatilla that broke Israel's resolve in this war and turned so many soldiers against it. For we find once again that even as the memory of Jewish children murdered in the Holocaust compelled Israelis to fight, it seems also to have paralyzed them as soldiers sympathetic to suffering children.

In becoming archetypal points of reference within events of the Holocaust, remembrances of besieged ghetto fighters, brutalized children, and death camps have hardened into icons themselves. As a single image from the Holocaust, the young boy with his arms upraised and surrounded by laughing German soldiers has come to distill several aspects of this era at once—particularly the fear, helplessness, and courage of the victims and the heartless barbarity of the killers. But once this icon is pulled loose to stand on its own for a whole set of events, it lends itself to easy transfer as an emblem, used to organize meaning in other events as well. In this way, not only has the young boy come to signify the innocence of Holocaust victims, but he has now been adopted archetypally by former victims to grasp currently suffering children.

In his 1982 "satirical cabaret," *Ha-patriot*, Hanoch Levine thus features a Palestinian child standing center stage, his arms upraised, surrounded by laughing Israeli soldiers—possibly the most explicit comparison until then between Jewish suffering in the Holocaust and the Arabs' condition on the West Bank. As the most recognizable symbol in the iconography of Jewish suffering, this studied pose on stage provoked outrage among survivors, though most condemned not so much the comparison between children as the implied suggestion that Israelis now behaved like Nazis. For as unacceptable as the Nazi-Israeli analogue might have been, the explicit figure of the child as victim has, in fact, remained an unshakable motif in Jewish representations of suffering—Jewish and non-Jewish alike.

Like other traditional Jewish archetypes used by the poets of the Lebanon War, however, that of Levine's child is recalled simultaneously to figure a Palestinian child's situation in the West Bank and to dismiss the use of Holocaust imagery as justification for such a situation. It was probably this second aspect of the comparison that led to the following lines' elision from the play by a board of censors; the image itself of the little boy was already part of Israel's iconographic vocabulary and could not be denied. In this scene, the main character, Lahav, speaks to his own murdered mother as he holds a revolver to the little boy's head:

He will avenge your blood and the blood of our murdered family, as then, mother, when your little brother stood alone in front of the Germans, at night, in the field, and the German aimed his revolver at his head, and your little brother, trembling with fear, said (and he sings as he aims the revolver at the little boy):

> Don't shoot
> I have a mother
> she is waiting for me at home.
> I haven't eaten yet.
> Dinner.
> Don't kill me.
> I am a child.
> I am a human being like you.
> What did I do?
> What difference would it make to you
> if I yet lived?[6]

Standing next to the little boy, Lahav figuratively gives voice to the Palestinian child in front of us, even as he literally speaks for a murdered Jewish child, who would have been his uncle. By yoking this Holocaust icon, his personal memory, and the figure of the Palestinian child into one moment, the playwright simultaneously reflects and compels Jewish understanding of the Palestinian child.

I I I

Almost as if to intensify his words' terror-filled past before applying them to the present, Tzvi Atzmon thus recites one calamity after another in his poem "*Yizkor*" before ending the litany with slaughtered Arab children. Although the *Yizkor* prayer is recited on neither of the ritual days of remembrance (*Yom Hasho'ah* and *Tesha B'av*) recalling national catastrophes, it has come through custom to be associated with the dead of the Holocaust, primarily as an engraved icon on Holocaust memorials and monuments. *Yizkor* ([God] will remember) and *Zakhor* (Remember!) have both become liturgical words for remembering not just the dead but, by extension, the era and circumstances in which loved ones have died.

In his poetic *Widderuf* of the *Yizkor* blessing, Tzvi Atzmon expands on this latter sense to include not the individual names of deceased loved ones (as would be the tradition), but the larger, collective death of a people— and then it is not just to remember the dead, or even that they have died, but specifically how they died.

In Eretz Israel arose the Jewish people
Who had been forcibly exiled . . .
Pursued and tortured and sold into slavery, and expelled from France, Portugal,
    from England . . .
Raped, beaten, sacrificed . . . , drowned . . .
Murdered in broad daylight, in the crusades, in the black plague, in the revolutions
    of the cossacks, and in the darkness of the inquisition.
Kidnapped, incarcerated, massacred, stoned
And defiled in pogroms, and cursed for murdering God
And for drinking children's blood.

                                                   (Fighting and Killing, p. 12)

As the personal *Yizkor* prayer has been expanded in Holocaust Remembrance Day services to encompass the collective passing of a people, Atzmon expands the focus of memory to include also how a people has died. Once the focus of memory is changed, remembrance of a kind of death becomes its own figure.

And then, as is the point of departure for the other poets, it is the death of children that stops the poet's voice, which makes him recall here again Bialik's lines, "Vengeance for the spilt blood of a child, / The Devil has not yet invented." He catches himself, stutters and repeats:

And the revenge upon every small child will cry out.
And suddenly
Got up in the morning and saw
Got up in the morning and saw
Children who were shot when the sun rose
And real blood, not just a libel.
Arab children, without half a consolation.

The murdered children simultaneously oppress the poet and inspire him to remember them in the *Yizkor* prayer. That they are killed by Christians may, in fact, only exacerbate the figure's memory of traditional anti-Jewish persecution. But this is real blood, not a blood libel as it had been traditionally and as Begin had described the accusations against Israel, and these were real Arab babies now slaughtered at Sabra and Shatilla.

At the end of the poem, Atzmon incorporates a line and a half of *Hatikvah*—the Israeli national anthem—only to cut off literally the Jewish part of its spirit:

> In Eretz Israel arose the Jewish people
> On the history of two millennia
> And as long as within the inmost heart a spirit: I am accused!
>
> > (P. 12)

Having incorporated Arab chidren into this catalogue of anti-Jewish terror, the poet provides an immediate figural context for them. And in so doing, Atzmon would rewrite both the national anthem and the prayer for the dead—refiguring both in order to make Arab children part of collective Jewish memory.

Of the many references to children, the most haunting and explicit come in the poems of Dalia Ravikovitch, who not only condenses the figure of the Holocaust in the image of suffering children but then also uses the children of Arab refugees metonymically to figure the condition of their people at large. Although Ravikovitch does not explicitly refer to the Holocaust, it remains difficult to read several of her poems without the associations created for us in the memory and language of the Holocaust. In "Exit from Beirut," the speaker commands the refugees to

> Take the rucksacks
> And the household bric-a-brac
> And the books of the Koran
> . . . .
> And children scurrying like chickens in the village.

At which point, the poet interjects:

> How many children do you have?
> How many children did you have?
> It's hard to watch over kids in a situation like this.
> . . . .
> Put into sacks whatever isn't fragile,
> Clothes and blankets and bedding
> And something as a souvenir
> Perhaps a shiny artillery shell
> Or any utensil that comes in handy

And the rheumy-eyed babies
And the R.P.G. kids.

And then in a language that is both forever corrupted by its application to the Jews in Nazi Germany and laden with Jewish memory of expulsion with no destination but the sky, the poet simultaneously recalls and creates a new "voyage of the damned," leaving little doubt as to the source of her figures:

We want to see you sail in the water, sail aimlessly
Not to any harbor or shore
They will not receive you anywhere
You are banished human beings
You are people who don't count
You are people who are superfluous
You are nothing but a handful of lice
Stinging and itching
To madness.

(*Fighting and Killing*, pp. 65–66)

Speaking on behalf of all Israelis in this ironic inversion, the poet would thus avenge the Jews' past suffering by condemning their present enemy-refugees to suffer *as* Jews.

Finally, in "One Cannot Kill a Baby Twice," Ravikovitch overlays imagery drawn almost directly from Bialik with language infused by the Holocaust; and again, children provide both the essential locus of horror and motivation for the poem.

Upon sewage puddles in Sabra and Shatilla
There you transferred masses of people
Great masses
From the world of the living to the world of the dead.

Night after night.
First they shot
After that they hung
Finally they slaughtered with knives.
Terrified women appeared in haste
Above a dust hillock:
"There they slaughter us,
In Shatilla."

A delicate tail of a new moon was hung
Above the camps.
Our soldiers illuminated the place with flares
Like daylight.

"Return to the camp, march!" the soldier commanded
The screaming women from Sabra and Shatilla.
He had orders to follow.
And the children were already laid in filthy puddles
Their mouths wide open
Calm.
Nobody will hurt them anymore.
One cannot kill a baby twice . . .

(Fighting and Killing, pp. 55–56)

The soldiers are only "following orders," and it happens if not in broad daylight then beneath the light of the soldiers' own flares. One cannot kill a baby twice, it turns out, except in memory and the figures memory lends contemporary experiences; in this way, the children in Bialik's poem and those remembered from the Holocaust die again and again in every subsequent child's murder.

After the explicit references to the Holocaust by soldiers in the Six-Day War, later allusions may seem both a little oblique and, at times, even arbitrary. Occasionally, references seem to come only in the reader's own specific knowledge of events, in projections of Holocaust memory onto more general suffering. But in fact, it is partly in memory of events that analogy and metaphor are created in the first place. For the memory of Hebrew is so tenacious that its words may always resonate past experiences; an expression like "we didn't see and we didn't know" is so burdened with past violence that it becomes impossible to recite innocently in Israel: it can only be repeated ironically.

To this day, it seems that the rest of the world has confused genuine Israeli empathy for the victims of the Sabra and Shatilla massacres with culpability in the killing itself. When 400,000 Israelis marched in Tel Aviv to protest the killings, the world mistook a profound expression of sympathy for the victims and outrage at the killers for a demonstration of guilt. In its craving for the facile symmetry of persecuted turned persecutor, the world seems to have ignored the capacity of one people to feel—if only figuratively—the pain of another. The world has not understood that an outpouring of grief like this might have been spawned as much by the memory of past Jewish suffering as it was by the massacre itself of Palestinians by Christians.

For memory of the past is not merely passed down *mi dor le dor*—from generation to generation—but it is necessarily regenerated in the images that transport it from one era to the next. The past is thus recalled in present figures no less than contemporary events are refigured in light of past events. In this exchange between past and present, every generation simultaneously inherits and transmits memory—which now becomes in itself a series of analogues linking events to one another. Rather than attempting to legislate the inevitable framing of present crises in the figures of the past, we might recognize that historical memory itself may be invigorated by this framing. In the end, reimagining contemporary and past historical crises—each in terms of the other—may ultimately be the only way we remember them.

III.

Texts of the Holocaust:
A Narrative Critique

Introduction

At the heart of this inquiry into Holocaust narrative has been the assumption that we cannot know this—or any—era outside the ways it is transmitted to us in its representations. While suggesting a critical approach to Holocaust narrative that might encompass all of its texts—including literary, graphic, and memorial representations—I have focused until now only on written responses. Like literary and historical narratives of the Holocaust, however, its other texts also recall both events and the national myths, religious archetypes, and ideological models along whose contours remembrance has been constructed. Meaning and understanding of the Holocaust are simultaneously reflected and created in the various texts and contexts now shaping events.

In order to extend this critique to the rest of Holocaust studies, therefore, I have expanded the range of Holocaust texts to include here not just diaries, memoirs, fiction, drama, and poetry, but also selected cinemagraphic testimony, memorials, and museums. This concluding section on "Texts of the Holocaust" is not intended as an exhaustive compilation of extraliterary responses, which would also include paintings, music, photography, and liturgy, among other media. But rather, based as it is in a semiotic reading of cinemagraphic and memorial texts, this final section is meant to suggest the potential value of this approach for interpreting all representations and texts of the Holocaust—past and future, literary and graphic. In the process, "Texts of the Holocaust" should also illustrate both the varieties of understanding every medium brings to events and the essential continuity of Holocaust studies over several disciplines. By examining the performance of memory as it is textualized in both memorials and cinemagraphic narrative, this section proposes itself as a model for further study of Holocaust representations. Instead of closing this book, "Texts of the Holocaust" might thus open the area of Holocaust studies to further inquiry, ensuring that study of the Holocaust continues in itself as a form of memorial work.

Making Holocaust video testimony at Yale. *(Photo courtesy of Yale University Office of Public Information.)*

Survivor Simon Srebnik's silences amidst his former villagers in Chelmno tell part of his story in *Shoah*. *(Photo courtesy of New Yorker Films.)*

In the symbolic graveyard at Treblinka, 17,000 granite stones recall both individuals and Jewish communities wiped out at the death camp here. Erected in 1964; designed by sculptors Adam Haupt and Franciszek Duszenko. *(Photo: Monika Krajewska.)*

The monument at Auschwitz-Birkenau stands at the end of the rail line. Erected in 1967; designed by P. Casella, J. Jarnuskiewicz, J. Palka, and F. Simoncini. *(Photo: James E. Young.)*

Ruins of crematoria and gas chambers still stand at Auschwitz-Birkenau. *(Photo: James E. Young.)*

At Dachau, rows of symbolic foundations refer to the barracks that once stood there. *(Photo: James E. Young.)*

Memorial sculpture at Majdanek. Erected in 1970; designed by Wiktor Tolkin and Janusz Dembek. *(Photo: James E. Young.)*

At Majdanek the crematorium and guard towers still stand, and a mausoleum covers ashes of the murdered, all visible through the opening in the great sculpture's base. *(Photo: James E. Young.)*

Tombstone monument built at the site of the old Jewish cemetery in Sandomierz by survivors after the war. *(Photo: Monika Krajewska.)*

Broken tombstone retaining wall at the Jewish cemetery in Warsaw. *(Photo: James E. Young.)*

The break in Jewish memory in Kazimierz is represented both by fragments and by the gap in the wall. Designed by Tadeusz Augustynek.
(Photo: Monika Krajewska.)

Warsaw Ghetto Monument. *Left*,
bas-relief, eastern face; *right*, western
face. *(Photo: Foto-Ruch.)*

NINE

Holocaust Video and Cinemagraphic Testimony

Documenting the Witness

The film is made around my own obsessions; it wouldn't
have been possible otherwise.

—Claude Lanzmann

I. FILM AND NARRATIVE

Memory rarely comes in a long and twisting narrative skein but more often
in freely associated moments, kernels of time around which events gather
and accrue significance. By inviting a Holocaust survivor's recollections and
then filming them, the makers of video and cinemagraphic testimony simultaneously (and paradoxically) preserve broken fragments of memory
even as they stitch them together into a continuously unfurling scroll: a
kind of celluloid *megilla*. These high-tech testimonies are now being taped,
catalogued, indexed, edited, and transcribed in video archives at Yale,
UCLA, and Gratz College, among other repositories. From these archives
they are distributed for use in classrooms and on television, for courses
devoted specifically to Holocaust history and literature, as well as for more
general courses in oral history, psychotherapy, and literary testimony.

By examining video and cinemagraphic testimonies as texts that are as
constructed as literary testimony, we can keep in mind the ways that formal
elements of film media create meaning and explanations in the survivors'
stories. For every medium brings its own generic properties to bear on the
material it transmits: each shapes as well as reflects particular events. Literature remembers events differently from photographs, paintings differently from plastic monuments, museum exhibitions differently from video
testimony. This chapter will explore some of the ways in which memory,
understanding, and meaning of the Holocaust are constructed and reflected in video testimonies; more specifically, it will examine the process
itself of testimony, appealing to the literal etymological sense of *testificare*—
or, the "making of witness."

Though critics like Lawrence Langer have warned against the search for literary or moral unity in Holocaust literature and video testimony,[1] a survivor's memories are necessarily unified and organized twice-over in video testimony: once in the speaker's narrative and again in the narrative movement created in the medium itself. For like literary narrative, whether it is elicited by sympathetic listeners or commanded by the tradition, video testimony sutures time and space, yoking events together to create continuities and new insights, cause-and-effect relationships, and historical meanings. Implicit in the lateral movement of film and video is a sense of sequence, a linear causality that suggests explanations for events: underlying every testimony—in its beginning, middle, and end—is a particular understanding of events. Like the literary testimony of Holocaust diaries and memoirs, video and cinemagraphic testimony is thus dependent on the formal properties of narrative and textuality that frame testimony and lend it voice.

In Holocaust video testimony, therefore, at least two levels of narrative intersect: that of the film—its lateral movement, its editing, its juxtaposed images—and that of the survivors' own story, which then becomes a narrative within a narrative. The tendency to slip from one narrative level to the other in video testimony becomes a natural one; for inasmuch as the content of the video seems to be the survivor's story, his narrative seems to determine the structure of the entire text, even though the story itself is necessarily contained within the larger narrative of the video medium. In this light, the content of Holocaust video testimonies might be regarded as a combination of the survivor's story, the telling of the story, and the audiovisual taping of testimony.

The documentary film-maker Frederick Wiseman once remarked in an interview that "One of the things that intrigues me in all [my] films is how to make a more abstract, general statement about the issues, not through the use of a narrator, but through the relationship of events to each other through editing."[2] As both the director of events in his films and editor of their representation, Wiseman understood profoundly his role as both documentary craftsman and maker of witness. He grasped that merely by juxtaposing strips of film in any order at all, he generated cause-and-effect sequences and suggested theories for explaining events that he seemed only to be documenting. Through its lateral movement, the film (not the speaker in it) thus narrates events—and in so doing, creates particular knowledge of them.[3]

Sharing this view, Annette Insdorf suggests in her discussion of Holocaust documentary film that for this reason there can be no unmediated testimony in film. Disputing André Bazin's ingenuous assertion that the lens (called *objectif* in French) intervenes between reality and viewer only as an impassive, nonliving agent, Insdorf reminds us that "framing, camera angle, lighting, and proximity to subject all result in different images: the subject might be the same, but the camera placement determines whether it seems insignificant, threatening, or neutral."[4] When we add to these conditions the time and place of filming, questions asked by interviewers, the state of a survivor's mind on a particular day, current events invoked as analogies, or even subtitles and translations, we find that the aim of filmed testimony can never be to document experiences or to present facts as such. But rather it is to document both the witness as he makes his testimony and the understanding and meaning of events generated in the activity of testimony itself.

Like other narrative, Holocaust video testimony necessarily begins and ends somewhere, thereby framing and enclosing the survivor's experiences for both speaker and viewer. "Start at the beginning," suggests the interviewer, at which point the survivor must determine where this beginning came. Was it when the family moved to Germany from Russia after World War I, or when they heard on the radio that Hitler was appointed chancellor, or was it *Kristallnacht*? Was it when the community was deported to the ghetto, or when they arrived at Auschwitz? Or does one's personal memory of the Holocaust actually begin on a collective basis centuries before, in the *Churban* of the First and Second temples and subsequent pogroms? And where then does one's testimony end? At liberation from the camps, or on one's arrival in Israel? When the tape runs out, or when the interviewer grows tired? Can memory ever have closure? Depending on where the beginning and end of testimony come, particular premises, conclusions, and meanings are created for the whole of testimony. In this context, we recall that like the literary memoirist, the survivor in video testimony also begins testimony with full knowledge of the end, which inevitably contextualizes—and occasionally figures—early experiences in terms of later ones. Some memories are given elaborate voice, while others from before and after the block of testimony remain unrecorded altogether.

Lawrence Langer has found that all of these testimonies are different, not because every experience was completely unique, but because each "story" depends on the numerous personal and structural patterns that have framed it: "Even when witnesses have been in the same labor, concentration, or death camp," Langer writes, "the details of recollection are modified by so many distinct factors—memory, personality, extent of loss, duration of imprisonment, health, moral attitude, depth of spiritual commitment—that no unified view emerges from the testimony."[5] By unified view, Langer means a universal view shared by all the victims, which would seem to make these experiences similar, when these tapes seem to confirm exactly the opposite. But in fact, when witnesses share the same *Weltanschauung*, their respective grasps of experiences are relatively similar: not because the experiences were the same, but because the narrators often share the same traditions and language used to describe experiences. In this way, disparate events told in the same figure are unified in their expression, united by a common vision of experience.

For even though Langer suggests that many of these video testimonies are "without symbolic dimensions or legendary resonance, unmodified by literary precedent,"[6] these narratives are necessarily as dependent on the myths, figures, and ideologies comprising the survivors' world and language as literary testimonies are. Can one tell the story of two young girls hiding for months beneath a trap door covered over by a manure pile (Langer's example) without allegorical resonance to the Jews' condition in Europe during the Holocaust? And as eloquently bare as some of these testimonies are, others are as strikingly figural. "When the sun came up [at Auschwitz]," intones one clear-eyed woman, "it was not like the sun. I swear to you it was not bright ... It was black to me."[7] Even if this survivor had never heard Paul Celan's "Todesfugue," the listener cannot avoid the literary allusion to the poem's first words, "Black milk of daybreak ... ," itself a classic figure for the grotesqueness of this time. In these testimonies, the speakers necessarily figure their experiences as the images on the video screen inevitably figure the speakers themselves.

II. INTERPRETING THE TESTIMONIAL IMAGE

Many survivors have chosen after the war to speak and to tell their stories only in English, which they regard as a neutral, uncorrupted, and ironically amnesiac language. Having experienced events in Yiddish, or Polish, or German, survivors often find that English serves as much as mediation between themselves and experiences as it does as medium for their expression. In video and cinemagraphic testimonies, this on-camera simultaneous translation of events from memory into language and from one language into another is strikingly evident in ways lost to literature. Part of the video text here is precisely the visual record of this entry of memory into language, the search for the right words, and the simultaneous interpretation of events in this search for language.

This process is perhaps best exemplified in Claude Lanzmann's film *Shoah*, where all layers of translation are left intact on screen. Indeed, the effect at times is that of a multilingual echo-chamber, in which experiences seem almost to be in search of a language. In *Shoah*, Lanzmann asks the questions in French, they are translated by an interpreter into Polish, Yiddish, or Hebrew, answered in one of these languages, translated back into French, and then in this country flashed onto the screen in English subtitles. In the process, questions and answers are thus literally repeated three times in different translations (i.e., interpretations) for the viewer. Even though each language brings a slightly different twist to the testimony, it is almost as if no single language were finally adequate to the task. At least part of the text here is both this repetition and seeming reformulation of events in language, as well as the events' apparent flight from language.

Another important part of the text is the on-screen interpretation of questions and answers by Lanzmann's translators. Though Lanzmann attempts to frame his questions as directly and as unambiguously as possible, they are often laden with irony and even sarcasm that may well have antagonized the witnesses, had they not been rephrased by his interpreters. As it turns out, his interpreters screened the answers as well, attempting to relate only that which seemed pertinent to Lanzmann's question. The mediaries in this case are clearly interpreters: rendering the French into an acceptable Polish question, receiving a reply to a Polish question, and then reinterpreting it back into the frame of the French original, even editing it slightly to conform with the perceived intent of the original question.

It is not merely a story or narrative being recorded in cinemagraphic and video testimony, but the literal making of it: the painful and deliberate choice of words, selection of details and memories, the effect of these details on the speaker, and then the effect of these details on the narrative itself. We watch as experiences enter speech: that point at which memory is transformed into language, often for the first time. Where writers necessarily break silence in order to represent it, in video testimony silence remains as much a presence as the words themselves; silence that cannot exist in print except in blank pages is now accompanied by the image of one who is silent, who cannot find the words. Unlike literary testimony, video testimonies can also represent *not* telling a story, the point at which memory will not enter speech. We are witness to the speaking and to the not speaking, to the choice of whether to go on or not. Unlike written narrative, which tends to collapse the spaces between words and ideas, in video testimony the pauses and hesitations in the telling of a story remain intact. The sense of incoherency of experiences, the associative nature of reconstructing them, the visible groping for terms and language are all preserved in video and become as much a part of the textual content of video testimony as the survivor's story.

And as Lawrence Langer has observed, that the speaker of these stories is completely involved in the telling of them "is immediately and visibly evident."[8] That is, we quite literally watch the narrator organize his testimony, edit it, and retell it until he is satisfied. We are able to see the telling act itself, its starts and stops, its essential provisionality. We remain aware of the search for language when it does not just come, of the automatic figures when they come easily, of the self-reflexivity of the narrators when they are affected by their own narrative. In all of this, we remain excruciatingly aware of the ontology of testimony, that witness is quite literally being made before our eyes.

The process of remembrance, of construction, of editing, of formulating ideas, and the search for order—which remains mostly invisible in literary texts—gives the video testimonies a painful self-awareness and reflexivity missing in literary testimony. In fact, this sense of self-reflexivity is animate in the tellers themselves: that is, they often seem to respond to the sound and meaning of their own words as they talk, even making slight corrective movements in tone as they proceed. They seem to be their own audience at times, reflecting on what they have just said, turning it back over in their minds, sometimes seeming to wonder what to do with their own stories.

At times the survivors seem almost to guard themselves against their stories, approaching remembrances warily, circling them as if measuring the impact their words will have not just on the listener but on themselves. There is a point at which these memories are still part of the survivor's inner life, still an inner wound; if, in watching these memories pass from the private to the public sphere, we also feel some of the pain in this transition, we may understand something more about the consequences of both the experiences and the telling of such experiences.

In the testimonial image, we also perceive traces of a story the survivor is not telling; these traces are in his eyes, his movements, his expressions— all of which become part of the overall text of video testimony, suggesting much more than we are hearing and seeing. We grasp here that memory is being transmitted not merely through narrative but by body movements and behavior as well. In fact, here we realize that there are kinds of testimony available to us only in video or film, kinds of testimony that we must ourselves witness. In *Breaking the Silence*, Eva Fogelman's film about the children of survivors and the relationships with their parents, we discover that the children have inherited a particular understanding of events, an entire memory of them, which has little to do with what their parents have told them; in fact, part of the problem for many children was just this want of actual telling by the parents, an overload of behavioral and nonverbal signs that are so difficult to interpret. Part of their parents' testimony has come in feelings of permanent dislocation, overprotectiveness, an implicit diminishing of adolescent problems (in light of Auschwitz), or just plain guilt at having survived. None of these responses may have been articulated or narrated as such but have been conveyed in a thousand daily ways to the children as memory. And as the parents' body language, silences, and other nonverbal behavior communicate something to their children, the survivors in video testimony convey particular nonverbal messages and kinds of memory to its viewers as well.

In watching *Breaking the Silence*, *Shoah*, or the video testimonies, we thus find transmitted a universe of nonverbal memory—signs no less than language to be interpreted and decoded. Though images work often to reinforce verbal testimony, to authenticate both the speaker and what the speaker says, they also work to undercut and complicate this testimony. This is apparent especially in *Shoah*, where words alone often seem to tell very little of the story. Among other instances, we recall the Polish villager who is asked if he remembers the Jews' deportation from Grabow. At that time, he answers, he worked in the mill, there, opposite, and they saw it all. "What did you think of it? Was it a sad sight?" Lanzmann asks. "Yes," comes the answer, "it was sad to watch. Nothing to be cheery about."[9]

"Nothing to be cheery about," comes the reply. Yet, our speaker smiles. Is he embarrassed, or proud, or pleased, or merely self-conscious in front of a camera? Is he trying to be ironic here, attempting to give both the answer Lanzmann would like to hear and the one he would like to give? These are all possible interpretations, but they are only possible because we have both the image and the words before us. Yet the smiles remain, which combine with his testimony to create an irony, a message far more profound than those five words, "Nothing to be cheery about." Meaning here is dependent on the entire text, including glances, averted gazes— and smiles.

The visual images in video testimony carry other significance as well. Of all the obscenities inflicted upon the Jews during the period of the Holocaust, one of the most perverse may have been the calculated displacement of a millennium-old civilization by what David Roskies has called "an enormous freak show of atrocity victims." Unfortunately, the unassimilable images of the wretched dead and survivors have become for many in America not only the sum of European Jewish civilization but also the sum of knowledge about the Holocaust and its survivors. Too often the point of departure for the "popular study" of the Holocaust begins and ends with these images alone, the unmitigated horror at the end of Jewish history in continental Europe, not the conditions of history, politics, culture, and mind—or the rich history of European Jewry—that preceded it.

But as thriving Jewish communities were reduced to—and displaced by—images of corpses and skeletal prisoners, these pictures of survivors might now be displaced by the well-groomed, outwardly mended survivors on the video tapes. By showing us whole human beings, however inwardly scarred they are, the video tapes rehumanize the survivors, and in so doing, rehumanize the murdered victims as well. Instead of static black-and-white images of hollow-eyed victims, we find the survivors as they are now, which suggests to us the humanity of all the victims before the war. Both victims and survivors are thus relocated in the human community, which simultaneously rehumanizes and reindividuates them. In this way, the tapes might return just a fraction of the dignity and humanity the Nazis attempted to destroy; and as this dignity is returned to the survivors in their testimonies, it is also returned to those still stripped of it in the footage of the camps' liberation.

III. VIDEO TESTIMONY AND THE HISTORIANS

Unfortunately, it seems to be precisely these images in Holocaust video testimony—and the essential reflexivity thus captured—that undercut these testimonies' value for historians. Even though historians are dependent on just this kind of reconstructed source material, they often tend to distrust "documents" too heavily laden with pathos, which seem so clearly constructed and so dependent on individual memory alone. For it is true that images and pictures of faces, in particular, affect us viscerally, evoking emotional, parasympathetic responses over which viewers have little control: that is, we respond to pictures of people as if they actually were people. When the teller and his story remain united in video testimony, we may therefore respond emotionally to it. But the more emotive the video text, the more melodramatic it seems to be; and as drama of any sort, it loses its credibility in the historians' eyes as unconstructed evidence.

In addition to problems of evidence, other aspects of video make it difficult for some historians to find an appropriate use for these testimonies. Like music or film, for example, the videos move laterally away from any given point or moment in their narrative, are in fact dependent on this movement, which discourages contemplating a particular moment or detail, now embedded in new ones. When we stop the tape, there is no more story, no sound, only the image of the survivor, but now without caption or commentary. The viewer thus tends to ride the movement of the tape, to become absorbed in the medium and picture, without opportunity to stop and reflect on what is being said. There is an accumulation of impressions, unfinished thoughts, responses, and emotions running together in the video stream, which don't allow for pauses and reflection.

In fact, between the content of the speaker's story, the medium itself (and its associations with pseudohistory and docu-drama), and the sheer pathos of the images on the screen, many historians find an anticognitive bias built into the very essence of video tapes that seems to them irreconcilable with traditional notions of objectivity and reliability. As we have already noted, the more dispassionate a text seems, the more rhetorically veracious or authentic it becomes. But this ignores the more contemporary truism that even style-less narrative is a style in itself, a way of masking the seams of a text's construction precisely to make it appear objective, natural, and true—all of which makes the traditional historians' objections to Holocaust video testimonies so problematic. For it seems that by preferring to rely instead on sources that are rhetorically objective—like photographs, train schedules, or eyewitness accounts from the era—which are just as constructed, just as provisional as video testimony, many historians neglect the constructed nature of all evidence.

Rather than becoming entangled in the historian's rules regarding evidence and factuality, however, it may be prudent here to shift the discussion of Holocaust video testimony away from questions of proof and evidence altogether. Instead of asking to what extent video testimony is to be construed as proof that particular events happened or to what extent they compel belief in a particular construction of events, we might look at that to which witness is actually being made: the manner in which survivor-witnesses have understood and expressed their experiences, the kind of understanding they now bring to such disaster, and the ways in which they now understand the world in light of the Holocaust. For the challenge of memory and recall in the video tapes is not a challenge of accuracy. The problem with video testimony is not that survivors get the facts wrong (which they occasionally do), but that we come to these tapes for verifiable facts. For as I have already suggested, it was not the facts in and of themselves that motivated the killers or disoriented the victims, but a particular apprehension of facts that led to actions taken on their behalf. Keeping this in mind, we acknowledge the understanding that shapes facts—the hope, the wishes, the dreams—all of which are important in understanding the victims and their responses to experiences.

Once historians recognize their own activity as meaning-makers, they might be more comfortable with the meanings created in the survivors' testimonies. Numbers, places, names, dates, and sequence of events are all important here: one of the historical tasks is to assemble these data as clearly and as self-consciously as possible. But how these events have been grasped by both victims and perpetrators, explained by them, contextualized by them—even at the expense of historical accuracy—must remain as important in historical inquiry as the collection of "raw data." For these understandings, misunderstandings, figures of understanding, and perversions of understanding all played a role in the events themselves, all as agents in the events as they unfolded. In this way, contemporaneous historical interpretations actually contributed to the events themselves—an aspect of the data that should interest historians greatly.

The historical value of these tapes thus lies not in their supposed neutrality as source material but in their record of "telling history." The faculty advisor to the Yale Video Archives, Geoffrey Hartman, explicitly states that "The primary purpose of our interviews . . . is not to augment the already considerable detailing of these terrible years. Oral history is a matter of memory, reconstruction and imagination."[10] Though written history is also largely a matter of memory, reconstruction, and imagination, unlike narratives that tend to hide their lines of construction, these audio-visual testimonies retain the process of construction, the activity of witness. The kind of knowledge they bring us is not purely historical, but metahistorical: the activity of telling history, of organizing it, of being affected by both events and their pathos. Viewed with these conditions of history and history-telling in mind, Holocaust video testimonies might even be considered examples of postmodern history: events told with pathos, indirection, confusion, and activity of telling intact. Though the medium itself—like other photographic media—is a naturalizing one, both the video's and the speaker's narrative-making process can remain visible by keeping these qualifications in mind.

This may be why Hartman has also written that instead of adding to the body of historical knowledge, the Yale Testimonies "focus on the individual rather than the mass, on each person's embodied and ongoing story, on the mind as it struggles with its memories, making sense of or simply facing them, on transmitting in oral form each version of survival."[11] By examining the process of making testimony, we are able to shift our emphasis away from a putatively normative product of testimony to the activity itself of witness. This is making witness, reminding us that it is made, not just transmitted, and that we as viewers are part of its making. The aim here becomes to document the witness, the witnesses' memory of events, and the transmission of this memory—not the events.

IV. THE LISTENERS AND INTERVIEWERS

What then is the role of the listener and interviewer in Holocaust video testimony? Elie Wiesel has suggested that the listener is an inspiration to the Holocaust survivor with a story to tell. But in this case, we find that the listener-inteviewer is much more than just an inspiration: the interviewers' questions do not merely elicit testimony but quite literally determine the kind, shape, and direction survivors' stories take. Depending on the training and knowledge of the interviewers, their own experiences and memory of the Holocaust, their preoccupations, and their own perceptions of their task, interviewers may be as much a part of the survivors' testimony as the survivors themselves.

In fact, little attempt has been made in either cinemagraphic testimony like *Shoah* or in video testimony to hide the interviewers' role in making Holocaust witness, which points to the extraordinary critical awareness most of these projects' directors bring to their task. Even though the aim at Yale "is to gain as free-flowing a testimony as possible," Hartman tells us, "the interviewers should not fade out entirely or pretend they are not present."[12] To a great extent, this balance is accomplished in the Yale tapes, though by dint of camera and sound arrangement, the interviewers are almost always completely out of the viewers' sight. In this way, the interviewers at Yale, most of whom are trained psychotherapists, seem not to intrude into the testimony, even as they continue to direct it.

Of all possible kinds of interviewers, trained psychoanalysts and therapists may well be the best qualified to elicit testimony. Trained to encourage narrative telling and interpretation, and through them insight into traumatic events, with a minimum of new psychic damage or further trauma, the psychiatrists who interview at Yale attempt as low a profile as possible. Psychoanalytic dialogue is thus one of several implicit models for interviewing survivors at the Yale Video Archives. Occasionally, however, the interviewer who is also a therapist cannot avoid crossing over into the reflexively therapeutic question.

In one tape, for example, a particularly sensitive survivor describes how his grandmother had asked a German soldier for help getting onto a cart during a deportation, only to receive instead a blow to the head that killed her. The narrator stops at this point, seeming to look inward and begins to cry silently. After a few minutes, the survivor regains his composure and tries to continue, when he is gently interrupted by the interviewer-psychiatrist. "May I ask you," the interviewer begins softly, "I understand you are in emotional upheaval, remembering, but what [are] you now moved by? The memory then? Did you then cry?"[13] At the same time, the camera zooms in on the survivor's face for a close study of his eyes and pain. Depending on how we interpret this scene, the text of this testimony either expands here to include the emotional effect a witness's testimony has on himself, or narrows to focus on the pathos of the moment in order to elicit a similar response in the viewer. Given the interviewer's impulse to find and relieve the source of a "client's" trauma, to encourage fuller understanding of memory, it may have been natural to ask why the survivor broke down and cried. But whether or not this impulse leads to further testimony, or even helps a survivor understand his story, may depend on what role the interviewer perceives himself to be playing in the taping session. In either case, the interviewer helps create testimony not just to memory but to the survivor's own capacity to assimilate it.

In a similar instance, the interviewer of a priest who saw but did not participate in a deportation, decides at one point to pinpoint what she perceives as a significant omission. After describing his own witness-act at the time, how he spied through a fence hole a trainload of Jews after their roundup, the priest turns to a forty-minute discussion of Hungarians' and Germans' behavior and the moral issues underlying it. After hearing him out, the interviewer then asks whether the priest told anybody what he had seen. "That's a good question. You know . . . [long pause], I really don't think so. I don't think that I did." "Where did you think they were going?" asks the interviewer. "I just couldn't tell you now," the priest replies.[14] The interviewer here is attempting to reveal something to the witness himself, gently but firmly insisting that the speaker return to a moment he seemed to be avoiding. It is not to relieve the trauma of the moment, however, but to intensify it, to confront the speaker with his own actions—or in this case, with his inaction as a bystander. In this way, the interviewer is not only directing the narrative but creating significance in it as well. The speaker realizes what the interviewer is after and finally submits to it: "I never saw anything like this in my life, I simply ran away." Satisfied at having gained this insight for both the speaker's and, one feels, the viewers' benefit, the interviewer allows the priest to continue without further interruption.

Where the inteviewers' questions come largely from behind the camera in the video tapes, those in *Shoah* come from the central character in the film: Lanzmann himself. Though the sheer weight of this film's 9 1/2-hour length combines with the rhetorically factual nature of the medium to imply a certain definitiveness in *Shoah*'s testimony, the one-on-one encounters between Lanzmann and his witnesses hold in constant view the process of making testimony through dialogue. Lanzmann as interviewer not only interrupts and even baits his subjects but eventually shares the screen frame with them much of the time. In addition, elaborate attention is paid to filming of the filming, especially when it is being done surreptitiously. In his own remarks on the essential constructedness of *Shoah*, Lanzmann is thus explicit in his role not just as participant in this testimony but as choreographer and even writer of it, which he compares freely to a play, a drama, a "fiction of reality."[15] When asked how he selected which survivors to use, which segments of the 350 hours of film to incorporate, Lanzmann's answer is simple: "The film is made around my own obsessions" (p. 30).

In one of Lanzmann's most strikingly choreographed scenes, he puts survivor Abraham Bomba back to work in a Tel Aviv barbershop where he queries the retired barber about his task as haircutter at Treblinka. As Bomba cuts a customer's hair in Tel Aviv, Lanzmann asks him to tell how he cut the victims' hair at Treblinka before they were gassed. Lanzmann created this long haircutting scene solely in order to frame his questions to Bomba about his experiences as haircutter in Treblinka, and the effect is undeniably fierce: cutting hair in the Jewish state in a normal Tel Aviv barbershop heightens the grotesqueness of his being forced to cut the hair of Jews—including his own family—on their way to death. It suggests visually that which he narrates, heightening the impact through irony. This kind of visual play is entirely effective in chilling the viewer, and in ironic ways lends further weight to Bomba's testimony, but it also raises questions about the interviewer's treatment of his witnesses.

In a different context, Susan Sontag reminds us that shooting a camera and a gun entail parallels beyond the figures we use to describe these acts: we sight and frame the target, squeeze the trigger, and thereby capture the life of our object.[16] Nora Levin has questioned whether we do the same in Holocaust video testimony: in some sense, do we revictimize the survivors by forcing them to re-create experiences, to suffer them once literally and then again imaginatively now before our eyes?[17] She refers specifically to Lanzmann's relentless questioning of Bomba, in which the survivor is asked to tell us not just what the experiences were like, but how he felt on seeing "all those naked women" going into the gas chamber. Bomba avoids this part of the question, and Lanzmann comes back to it. "But I asked you and you didn't answer: What was your impression the first time you saw these naked women arriving with children? What did you feel?" Bomba tries to reply and then stops, "I can't. It's too horrible. Please." "We have to do it. You know it," insists Lanzmann. "I won't be able to do it," Bomba says. "Please. We must go on."[18] Until finally, Bomba reinflicts on himself through description what he felt like. He cries here, obviously feeling like hell. Lanzmann intended that we witness not just the testimony but some of the pain elicited by testimony: as a model for our own response or for the sake of effect only?

In another part of Shoah, the relationship between Lanzmann, the survivor, cameraman, and onlookers grows unnervingly complex. Simon Srebnik, the lone Jewish survivor of a village near Chelmno, returns to his hometown, to the initially warm embrace of his former townspeople. Under pointed questioning by Lanzmann, the villagers offer their candid opinions as to why the Jews were rounded up in the church and killed. Supposedly quoting the town rabbi's own explanation to his people, the village scholar explains that because Christ was innocent, "the Jews cried out 'Let his blood fall on our heads!' " (p. 100). All the while, survivor Srebnik stands silently in their midst, increasingly uncomfortable, a tight smile fixed on his lips. His eyes seek assurance from those who brought him back here, flitting from the camera and back to Lanzmann, almost as if to establish the route of his next escape. His eyes show that he has heard it before, here in the same town, from the mouths of the same people, in front of the same church, whence his family was deported. He tells us and Lanzmann what happened that day, but his eyes and ironic grimace tell us much more.

"Will members of the audience grow more conscious of their own agendas by recognizing the interviewers' [agenda]?" Langer asks at one point.[19] It is an excellent question, for once we recognize which part the interviewers play in video testimony, we might better understand our own preoccupations as well. In examining the role of the interviewers, the aim is not to discredit their line of questioning or the answers they might "lead the witness" toward, but merely to *credit* the interviewers for some of the shape this testimony takes. It is to recognize that among other factors mediating— i.e., generating—testimony, the interviewers' questions play a crucial part; it is to recognize that testimony exists in the exchange between the witness's and the interviewer's—and ultimately our own—preoccupations and obsessions.

V. VIDEO TESTIMONY AND THE CRITICS

Geoffrey Hartman has observed that audio testimony alone tends not to embody witness so much as to disembody it, to separate the speaker from his voice.[20] Like the literary witness, the speaker in audio tends to be displaced by the words themselves. Even if the speaker's presence cannot affirm every detail in his testimony, we are witness to his existence, which concretizes testimony in ways written texts cannot. Unlike the case in audio or literary testimony, however, in video testimony the speaker remains united with his story. Because we watch the speaker as he tells his story, his words continue to draw their life from the narrator's very breath; they remain animate in the speaker's presence. Rather than becoming separated from his words, the speaker reinvests them with his presence, his authority, and the link between a survivor and his story is sustained in video as it cannot be in literary narrative. Where literary testimony can ultimately leave only a trace of the story itself and perhaps the writing activity that produced it, video testimony appears to leave behind a trace of the survivor as well. Where the survivor and his narrative are separated in the literary act, with detached signs coming to stand for narrator and experiences, the speaker and his narrative seem literally to embody each other in video testimony.

This is one of the principal characteristics of video testimony that make it so difficult to approach critically: by interpreting a survivor's video testimony, one seems to offer a critique of the survivor himself. As one of the first scholars to subject Holocaust literature to a new-critical analysis, Lawrence Langer seemed a natural candidate as the first to treat Holocaust video testimony as literary text. But after taking hundreds of these tapes home and watching them night after night, he found that they seemed to exempt themselves from critical analysis. He could not separate the survivor from his story, as he could in literature. Unlike words on a page, the animate faces, voices, and images represented in the tapes all seemed so *im*mediate that they knocked the critic off balance. "Trained though I am in the interpretation of narrative," Langer writes, "I am unable to touch [these video testimonies] with my imagination."[21] As long as the survivor and his story remain one, united in the video image, the tape and narrative become as inviolable as the teller himself. As many other critics have felt about Holocaust literature, Langer is so reluctant to reduce these testimonies to mere text, to so much more grist for the critical mills, that he is tempted to let them speak for themselves, with little intrusive commentary.

For these texts are indeed "privileged" in that they represent authentic eyewitness accounts and understanding of the Holocaust. But just as other privileged—even sacred—testimony requires exegesis as part of that which vivifies and sustains it within Jewish tradition, these video texts also demand our careful interpretation. Again, Geoffrey Hartman has put the critical dilemma most succinctly: "These testimonies are texts, not because we wish to study them as literature—that would be another way of profaning them—but because they are unintegrated, exposed, fallible memories that need interpretation."[22] For like holy scripture—which refers to itself as *edut*, or testimony—video testimonies inevitably construct experience even as they ask us to interpret it further; like other privileged texts, Holocaust video testimonies create meaning and understanding in events, even as they invite viewers to find further meaning and understanding in them.

In fact, by removing these testimonies from the realm of critical response, we may force them outside knowledge and consciousness altogether, to exist only on the visceral, emotional level; instead of being moved toward understanding, we are only moved—and these testimonies are reduced to so much entertainment at the survivors' expense. It may indeed be more difficult to interpret and to critically examine such animate texts without destroying some of their very life, but the alternative is much more cruel—and ultimately inadmissible in a tradition that guards its sacred texts through interpretation. Our aim here then is to sustain both the privileged status of these testimonies and their invitation to critical interpretation. As privileged texts, these testimonies ask only that we are that much more careful and gentle in our speculations, not that we place them outside interpretation altogether.

Even though writers and speakers of testimony often desire acutely to share their experiences as well as their telling with us, all we can actually share with them is their special knowledge and memory of the Holocaust— the experiences are theirs alone. For survivors, the historical imperative to remember—*zakhor*—means not merely to remember as a self-contained activity but to tell their remembrances, to remember to others what happened. If to testify means literally to make witness, then perhaps it also means to make others into witnesses. In viewing these testimonies, however, we become witness not to the survivors' experiences but to the making of testimony and its unique understanding of events. For it is not the experiences that are being transmitted in testimony but the special understanding of them that only a survivor can have, the particular understanding of one who was subject to both events and his interpretation of events as they occurred. This understanding becomes particularly valuable for our current understanding of events in their context, how one led to another, given the particular interpretations of events at the time. This special memory of events will be lost when the survivors are gone, which is why we must guard so vigilantly both the testimonies and their interpretations.

TEN

The Texture of Memory

Holocaust Memorials and Meaning

Give us a blank wall that we might see ourselves more truly
and more strange. Now give us the paper on which to write.
Now give us the day, this day. Take it away. The space that
is left is The Monument.

—Mark Strand

No one knows where Moses was buried, but we know where
he lived and we still know all about his life. Nowadays everything is the other way around. We know only where the
burial places are. Where we live is unfixed and unknown.
We roam about, we change, we shift. Only the burial place
is known.

—Yehuda Amichai

I

While I was carrying out archival research for this study of Holocaust literature, my eyes would occasionally wander from the pages of diaries, memoirs, and documents in front of me to the surrounding museum and exhibition halls. At these moments, the texts before me suddenly opened to encompass the very buildings and repositories—the times and places—in which I studied past events. Over the course of my research, it became impossible to ignore the extraordinary range of Holocaust memory I found in Europe, Israel, and America. The stacks at YIVO in New York, the archives at Dachau and Neuengamme in Germany, the study room at the Jewish Historical Institute in Warsaw, the library and museum at Auschwitz, the State Jewish Museum in Prague, and the archives and museum at Yad Vashem in Jerusalem: each place fostered its own texture of memory. In every country's memorials, in every national museum and archive, I found a different Holocaust; and at times, I found no Holocaust at all.

In an age that tends to probe the significance of every message and text, it was surprising to me how little critical attention was being devoted to the forms and meanings of remembrance engendered by memorials and museums constructed expressly to deepen the memory of the Holocaust. Though a sophisticated critical literature now attends the memory of the Holocaust in its literary, historical, and religious texts, no single work has explored the literal process—the construction—of memory in its memorials. In their iconographic, architectonic, and textual organization, Holocaust monuments reflect particular kinds of political and cultural knowledge even as they determine the understanding future generations will have of this time.[1]

The aim of this particular inquiry into the "texts" created in Holocaust memorials and museums is neither merely to expose the various ideological transformations of events nor to evaluate these monuments as high or low art—though both kinds of critiques are implied. Rather, it is to examine the activity itself of Holocaust memorialization: the simultaneous preservation and limiting of memory, the types of meaning and knowledge of events that are generated, the evolution of these meanings in time, the manner in which viewers respond to memorial reifications of memory, and the possible social and political consequences of Holocaust memorials. If the raison d'être for Holocaust monuments is "never to forget," this chapter asks precisely what is not forgotten at Bergen Belsen, Dachau, Auschwitz, Babi Yar, Yad Vashem, or Liberty State Park in Jersey City. For what is remembered here necessarily depends on how it is remembered; and how these events are remembered depends in turn on the shape memorial icons now lend them.

"All art is an abstraction to some degree," the sculptor Henry Moore has written; "(in sculpture the material alone forces one away from pure representation and toward abstraction)."[2] To this we might add that as his material forces the monument-maker away from pure representation, it also forces his vision into particular shapes and sizes—all of which determine the texture of memory. Available memorial settings, source of funds, size of the artist's studio, kinds of stone, even the casting and pouring of metal works all contribute to a final version of monumentalized memory. Through a critical telling of these memorials' construction, this chapter will bring into view the activity of Holocaust memorialization that takes place both between events and memorials and then again between memorials and viewers.

By drawing on the interpretive methods I have already applied to other texts of the Holocaust, I would like to pursue the lines of these memorials' construction without threatening the integrity of the memorial-makers themselves. Though I inevitably compare national reconstructions of events, isolating at times specific ideological premises underpinning a nation's official memory of the Holocaust, the primary aim here is not to discredit these memorials but to make visible as many of their governing paradigms and preassumptions as possible. At issue is not so much the conscious or unconscious manipulation of history, which is intrinsic to all memory and representation, but the automatic transformations of Holocaust memory created in its spatial, plastic, and iconographic representations. As in my study of Holocaust narrative, the twin objects of this inquiry will thus be both Holocaust memory and a critical awareness of how this memory is gained.

I I

A rosebush at Dachau designates the plot of ground where thousands of prisoners were lined up and shot. One hundred crab-apple trees in the "Babi Yar Park" in Denver, Colorado, signify thousands of Jews cut down in a ravine outside of Kiev, Russia. A solitary concrete obelisk amid dozens of mass graves condenses Jewish memory at Bergen-Belsen. Mountains of hair, eyeglasses, and toothbrushes at Auschwitz refer metonymically to the lives that once animated them. In coming to stand for past realities, each of these icons displaces them and creates new ones in their stead: hence, an inescapable potential for "historical revision" in the memorialization process.

By identifying 100,000 victims massacred at Babi Yar only as "citizens of Kiev and prisoners of war," for example, the memorial there not only inflates the actual number of victims but also forgets that almost all were killed for having been Jews.[3] By juxtaposing in a photographic montage images of *Wehrmacht* soldiers killed in battle, bombed German cities, and liberated Jewish *KZ-Häftlinge*, the museum at Neuengamme recalls collectively the "victims of war" as it forgets who the specific makers of that war were. In this way, a nation's monuments efface as much history from memory as they inscribe in it.

Once again, however, the danger in these "forgetful monuments" lies in the viewer's mistaking the rhetoric of a monument for the nature of the events it commemorates. In contrast to literature, for example, which calls attention to itself as a medium, these more monumental and putatively documentary representations of the Holocaust often cause a confusion between memorial texts and remembered events. This confusion is most striking in the case of monuments located at the sites of the original concentration camps, where a sense of authentic place tends to literalize the particular meanings assigned.

In the "memorial camps" (as I will call them), the icons of destruction seem to appropriate the very authority of original events themselves. Operating on the same rhetorical principle as the photograph, in which representation and object appear to be one, the memorials at Majdanek and Auschwitz are devastating in their impact—not just for what they remember but because they compel the visitor to accept the horrible fact that what they show is "real." In both cases, the camps have been preserved almost exactly as the Russians found them forty years ago. Guard towers, barbed wire, barracks, and crematoria—abstracted elsewhere, even mythologized—here stand palpably intact. Nothing but airy time seems to mediate between the visitor and past realities, which are not merely *re*-presented by these artifacts but present in them. As literal fragments and remnants of events, these artifacts of catastrophe collapse the distinction between themselves and what they evoke. Claiming the authority of *un*reconstructed realities, the memorial camps invite us not only to mistake their reality for the actual death-camps' reality but also to confuse an implicit, monumentalized vision for unmediated history.

Like photographs without captions, however, the memorial camps remain essentially meaningless: their significance derives both from the knowledge we bring to them and from their explanatory inscriptions. But just as the silent ruins of the camps are "completed" by inscriptions, their simple reality as ruins unfortunately works to corroborate all historical explanation—no matter now insidious or farfetched. Entire barracks at Majdanek now function as exhibition storerooms of the victims' shoes and hats—proof of the economic plundering and exploitation of victims by the German Nazi Industrialists, according to explanatory notes inside. In this way, the commentary that accompanies the "black wall" at Auschwitz appears to find its material testimony in the wall itself. If it is written that the killings here were primarily political, or that these barracks housed prisoners-of-war identified only as Polish, then this is what these memorial icons remember.

On the death ramp at Auschwitz-Birkenau, surrounded on all sides by crumbling barracks, rusty electric fences, bombed-out crematoria, and ash-filled ponds, four blocklike sarcophagi mark the end of the rail line, the beginning of the "death zone." Behind them stands a tower of stone blocks, resembling a giant tombstone, bearing in its center a single triangle recalling the patch all prisoners wore on their camp clothing. In concert with the artifacts all around them, these monuments thus remember and provide evidence for the simple message inscribed on twenty stone tablets in twenty different languages, including Yiddish and Hebrew: "Four million people suffered and died here at the hands of the Nazi murderers between the years 1940 and 1945." Within the context of the remembering icons, the religious identity of these people and why they suffered is elided.

The inside of the barracks at Auschwitz-I have been converted into national pavilions, including one devoted solely to an exposition of the Jewish experience at Auschwitz, which was dedicated in 1978. The massacre of Polish Jewry is not only contextualized here in the midst of other nations' suffering, but it is also linked specifically to Poland's own overwhelming destruction. In his 1978 address delivered at the opening of the Jewish Pavilion in Auschwitz, Janusz Wieczorek thus articulated the contemporary Polish understanding of Auschwitz now reflected in its memorial:

Distinguished Guests, here at the graveyard of Europe, at this necropolis of human hopes and inconceivable drama, one should keep silent . . .
But to keep silent also means to resign, yet our presence today proves we have not given up.
We are richer with true facts discovered in the laboratories of scientists

and statisticians examining the history of World War Two, martyrology of states and nations condemned by Nazi Germany to political and biological extermination. Among those doomed, Jews and Poles rank the first place . . .

In their studies scientists and statisticians have almost completed calculating the millions of Jews and Poles who perished in that holocaust. Oświęcim, Treblinka, Chelmno, Płaszow, Bełzec, Sobibor, Lodz, Bialystok and the Warsaw Ghetto, and dozens of other places of "the Warta district" and "the General Gubernyia"—they are all stages of extermination, stations of the Cross of Polish Jews and Jews treacherously brought from other countries of Europe. We know nearly everything about their gehenna, the misery of Poles.[4]

In this address, Jews and Poles not only come to share first place in a hierarchy of victims, but in equating political and biological extermination, the speaker suggests that they were to have shared the same fate as well. The overwhelming number of specifically Jewish victims at the camps and ghettos enumerated here notwithstanding, the Polish names of these places automatically figure their memory in Polish ways, creating distinctly Polish significance in the Jewish landscape of martryology. In coming to know "nearly everything about their [i.e., the Jews'] gehenna," the Poles come increasingly to know their own misery.

As widespread as is the tendency to make Jews and Poles apposite in the Polish memorial texts of the camps, however, the reasons are more complex than mere appropriation of the Jews' experience—or effacement of it altogether. In fact, given the Poles' own experiences during the war and their general self-recollection as the Germans' first—even principal— victims, these shared monuments to Jewish-Polish martyrdom are almost to be expected. That the death camps were located on Polish soil is viewed by the Poles not as evidence of local antisemitism or collaboration but as a sign of the Germans' ultimate plans for the Polish people. In this view, the killing centers in Poland were to have begun with the Jews and ended with the Poles. The mass murder of Jews becomes significant in Polish memory only insofar as it is perceived as precursor to the Poles' own, unfulfilled genocide.

Liberated by the Red Army in July 1944, the concentration camp at Majdanek, on the outskirts of Lublin, was thus turned immediately into the first monument and museum of its kind. What kind of "Holocaust museum" is specifically decreed by the Parliament of the Polish People's Republic on 2 July 1947: "The territory of the former Nazi concentration camp Majdanek is to be forever preserved as a monument to the martrydom of the Polish nation and of other peoples."[5] Like the barracks at Auschwitz, those at Majdanek were converted to house individual exhibitions, not on the fate of separate nationals, but on the entire operation of the camp itself: its planning and construction, the transports and kinds of prisoners interned there, living conditions, economic theft and plunder, resistance, extermination, and liberation.

The exhibition on mass killing at Majdanek begins with several panels devoted to the Jews' fate at Majdanek and the other camps, describing the Jews as the first of many victims in the Nazis' genocidal policies. At the back of the hall, empty canisters of Zyklon-B are stacked grocery-style to the ceiling, surrounded by wall-sized enlargements of German lists of murdered prisoners. Though the prisoners on these rolls are almost all designated by the Germans as "Polish Jews," each exhibit wall-panel is punctuated by a red triangle, denoting political—not racial—victims. Having introduced the extermination process at Majdanek with its first victims, the Jews, the exhibition ends with a panel illustrating the potential political extermination of the Poles. The Poles' averted extermination is thus framed here by the actual massacre of Jews; as such, it is grasped as an extension of the Jewish Holocaust, even its last stage.

To some extent, the state's current interest in preserving Jewish monuments reinstates Poland's lost Jews as an integral part of the Polish national heritage, even as it creates a kind of metonymy whereby the fate of the entire Polish nation during World War Two is grasped through the fate of its Jewish part. In this view, not only were the Jews murdered as both Jews and Poles, but the Poles' own destruction is recalled in Jewish terms: one set of victims comes to represent the other. In the figural exchange between Jews and Poles in the official memorial iconography of this period, Jews and Poles thus come to share the same, reciprocal fate. Through their monuments to what they call the Hitlerite Era, the Poles have thus come to see and represent the genocide of the Jews as both paradigm and figure for their own averted catastrophe.[6]

While references to Jewish victims are for the most part submerged in the political character of Eastern Bloc memorials, the issue of historical distortion and effacement grows extremely complex upon closer examination. At Treblinka, for example, references to the Jews murdered there are simultaneously direct and oblique. Large inscriptions at the entrance to the memorial inform visitors in several languages that of the 800,000 people murdered there, almost all were Jews. From here, the visitor walks for two hundred meters through dense woods along a path of railroad ties laid to symbolize the tracks that used to feed this death camp. These tracks once led to barracks, mass graves, and gas chambers, but all traces of the camp itself were destroyed, plowed under, and planted over by the Germans. At the end of the line now, the visitor steps into a huge expanse of open land, enclosed by trees. A great obelisk stands in its center, surrounded by a symbolic graveyard of over 17,000 jagged granite stones set in concrete, several thousand of them bearing the names of Jewish communities in Poland destroyed during the Holocaust.

Like sentries to the memorial area, a separate row of granite stones two to three meters high stands before the clearing. On each of these the name of a country is inscribed, the national homes of Jews who perished at Treblinka. By breaking the identity of victims into their states of origin, however, national martyrs displace Jewish victims. Though they were killed as Jews, the victims here are remembered on these sentinel stones as Yugoslavs, Poles, Frenchmen, Russians, and Germans—descriptions that fragment the martyrdom of a people into that of so many nations.

The Jewish identity of victims at Treblinka is not displaced altogether, however. After direct narrative reference to Jewish victims at the entrance, the Jewish character of this memorial only grows more subtly iconographic: a menorah is carved into the cap of the obelisk on its reverse side; jumbled together and protruding in all directions, the densely packed stones bear striking resemblance to the ancient Jewish cemeteries in Eastern Europe. Additional Jewish reference here comes in the languages used to inscribe the memorial message. At the base of the obelisk, a stone plaque reads from top to bottom in Yiddish, Russian, English, French, German, and Polish: "Never again." What must not happen again is left to the visitor's imagination or prior knowledge of events.

In addition to being subsumed in the larger Polish consciousness of this time, memorials to the death camps are often swallowed up more literally by the vast Polish landscape. By deliberately hiding the extermination centers in the most remote regions of Poland, the Nazis effectively obscured both their deeds and the monuments to their deeds. As it turns out, hidden death camps lead to hidden Holocaust memorials. In the cases of monuments located at Treblinka and Sobibor, in particular, memory must be sought as deliberately as the camps were hidden—or it is not found at all.

To some extent, the relative absence in Poland of specific iconographic reference to its murdered Jews thus becomes emblematic in itself, recalling the way in which two holes in a doorjamb might signify the *mezuzah* that is no longer there. Upon inquiring at the State Museum in Kielce, for example, one learns that there is no record of the pogrom that occurred there 4 July 1946, which left forty-six returning Jewish survivors dead and hundreds injured. At first, the archivist feigns ignorance of the entire matter; but on being pressed further, she admits that there are actually many detailed photographs and eyewitness accounts—the result of an official investigation. But they have been sealed for one hundred years to allow "memory to heal itself." Why no plaque, no sign at all? It is not necessary, for there are no Jews left here anyway. "Besides," she says, "this is a political matter, and I am only an archivist."

In spite of the government's recent efforts to restore Poland's Jewish monuments, absence and brokenness remain the most dominant of Jewish memorial motifs here. Since many of the Jewish cemeteries in Poland were vandalized by the Nazis, the ones that have not been plowed under for soccer fields or paved over for highways are now simply ruins of ruins. In Lukow and Sandomiercz, camp survivors have gathered their communities' broken and scattered tombstones and piled them—pyramidlike—into memorial obelisks. The only sign of a Jewish presence in Lukow, which was half Jewish before the war, is now this monument to the Jewish cemetery. Even more striking, iconographically, are the "tombstone walls" in the Warsaw and Krakow Jewish cemeteries: retaining walls built from the broken fragments of tombstones smashed by the Nazis. Arranged into a pastiche and set in mortar, angular chunks of Hebrew-inscribed marble and granite, variously smooth and time-eaten, now recall not only the broken Jewish communities of Warsaw and Krakow but also the "pogrom" of headstones itself.

As an icongraphic echo of both the broken tablets (round-topped tombstones shaped to recall Moses' tablets) and destroyed communities, this motif has even been adopted by a new generation of Holocaust memorialmakers in Poland. The founders of "the citizens' committee for the protection of Jewish cemeteries and cultural monuments in Poland," Monika and Stanislaw Krajewski, have thus preserved the literal remnants of Jewish memory in Przasnysz and Kazimierz by incorporating them into Holocaust memorials. Attempting unsuccessfully to return headstones to their former places in the Kazimierz cemetery, townpeople commissioned the architect Tadeusz Augustynek to design a memorial that might simultaneously reconstruct the memory of a lost community and commemorate the tremendum in Jewish memory. The result is a freestanding tombstone-wall, twenty-five meters long and six meters high, assembled out of the shards of shattered headstones—with a small cluster of broken headstones still standing before it. Rather than attempting to mend Jewish memory, however, the makers of this wall have built into it—and thereby preserved— the irreparable break in the continuity of both Jewish life and memory in Poland: the wall itself is torn by a jagged and gaping crack.

History, memory, and state policy intersect in even more complicated ways in Warsaw, where the Jewish ghetto uprising preceded by months the Poles' own revolt against the Nazis—the latter rebellion crushed by the Germans while the Red Army watched from across the Vistula. That the state has chosen to commemorate these uprisings at all may thus be as significant as the differences between Jewish and Polish monuments. Without reference to the Jewish revolt, the memorial to the Polish uprising is modeled after the open-air memorial camps: one block of reconstructed rubble and burned-out armored personnel carriers is supported by an indoor exhibition detailing the histories of rebel brigades, battles, and strategies. Of the Jewish ghetto, on the other hand, there is nary an artifact left: torched and demolished a block at a time by the Germans, it was eventually bulldozed altogether for new apartment buildings. All memory of the rebellion and destruction is thus compressed into Nathan Rapoport's Warsaw Ghetto Monument, which stands strikingly alone in an otherwise clear— and well-maintained—memorial square.

Designed by the Warsaw-born sculptor within months of the uprising in 1943 during his exile in Novosibersk, this monument was initially submitted by Rapoport to the Party Art Committee in Moscow, who rejected it straightaway as too nationalistic—i.e., too Jewish—in its conception.

When Rapoport returned to Warsaw in late 1946 with a clay maquette of the monument, the Warsaw City Arts Committee accepted it immediately— but only on the condition that it be unveiled on the fifth anniversary of the Warsaw ghetto uprising, 19 April 1948. Although the City Arts Committee was not even certain that the city itself would be rebuilt on the site of its destruction, Rapoport insisted that the monument be located at the site of Mordechai Anielewicz's bunker. To some extent, the city itself was thus rebuilt around the Warsaw Ghetto Monument.

Cast and poured in Paris because no foundry stood in Warsaw after the war, this bronze statue of seven mythically proportioned fighters is set in granite blocks intended to recall the Western Wall in Jerusalem.[7] Thus framed by the *kotel*, a muscular and bare-chested Mordechai Anielewicz emerges heroically amid flame and ruin. Clenching a homemade grenade hammerlike, in his tattered trousers and rolled-up sleeves, this Anielewicz has risen against the Nazis as both partisan-worker and Jew: each kind of hero now figuring the other. At its base, the monument is dedicated in Hebrew, Yiddish, and Polish to "The Jewish People, its heroes and its martyrs."

For the martyrs, however, we must walk around to the stone bas-relief on the dark side of the monument, where they are remembered separately and just as archetypally as the heroes. As surely as Anielewicz is a worker, the huddled and stooped figures on the reverse are archetypal Jews in exile, with only three Nazi helmets and two bayonets barely visible in the background to distinguish this expulsion from any other.[8] Eyes to the ground, all trudge resignedly and passively to their fate—except for a rabbi holding a Torah scroll in one arm, who looks up and reaches to heaven with his free hand, as if to beseech God. The result is a two-sided monument, each side to be viewed separately, each preserving an archetype as much as a historical event.

Like the lives of other memorials, that of the Warsaw Ghetto Monument consists in three parts: its literal conceiving and construction;[9] its finished form as public memorial; and its life in the mind of its community and people over time. For meaning and memory here depend not just on the forms and figures in the monument itself, but on the viewers' responses to the monument, how it is used politically and religiously in the community, who sees it under what circumstances, how its figures are used and recast in new places, in foreign contexts. Initially conceived as a Jewish monument, but in anticipation of the Moscow authorities' response, this monument has subsequently been criticized as not Jewish enough: in its panoply of figures drawn from both socialist and Jewish traditions, it lends itself now to both specific and universal interpretations. It has thus provided an iconographic context for everyone who visits it: from Willy Brandt to Nehru, from Jimmy Carter to Lech Walesa, and from Pope John Paul to Yasir Arafat. On each occasion, this Jewish icon functions as a monumental figure for someone else's cause: whether it is adopted by Solidarity as a symbol of resistance, or by the Palestinians as their own fighting icon, it lends a Jewish cast to all who gather in its square, even as its own monumental vision is redefined by every new commemoration.

I I I

In Germany, two factors mitigate against the iconographic memory of mass murder: there were no killing centers per se in Germany, and because so few non-Jewish Germans were interned in the death camps, they seem to have entered German memory only in an abstract sense. For what was a period of "Holocaust," "*Sho'ah*," or "*dritte Churbm*" in the victims' eyes is to this day "*Hitlerzeit*," "*Weltkrieg*," or increasingly "*KZ-Zeit*" for the Germans themselves. Though these terms—like the monuments—refer generically to the same era and occasionally to the same events, they cannot be considered synonymous; for what is signified in each instance depends profoundly on the manner in which each term organizes, locates, and even explains these events for its users. As a result, what we would call Holocaust memorials in Germany tend to be highly stylized when remembering the Jews and oriented largely toward all victims of Fascism when remembering the Germans.

In a shaded clearing at the end of a farm road near Timmendorf, West Germany, an inscribed plaque and large wooden cross commemorate the "Catastrophe of the *SS-Cap Arcona*," a German luxury liner with 4600 people aboard that was sunk by the R.A.F. in the first days of May 1945. From the narrative of events and diagrams inscribed on this plaque, we learn that the *SS-Cap Arcona* was one of three converted cruise liners carrying thousands of *Häftlinge* (i.e., concentration-camp prisoners) from Concentration Camp Neuengamme into the Baltic Sea, where, we are told, it was strafed and bombed by R.A.F. warplanes. According to local villagers, *Nacht und Nebel*–clad bodies washed onto their meticulously groomed beaches near Neustadt and Timmendorf for months afterwards and were immediately buried by the townspeople to prevent the spread of disease.

From the plaque, however, it is not clear whether the "catastrophe" of the *SS-Cap Arcona* lay in the massacre of so many innocents by the R.A.F. or in the horrible irony of these camp survivors' ultimate fate. For even though the attack on this ship is recorded here in detail, there is no mention of where these *Häftlinge* had been before Neuengamme (one of the political camps), or how they came to be gathered in Lübeck Bay, or where they were going, or why the R.A.F. bombed the ships. That it was a catastrophe of some sort demanding memorialization seemed clear enough. But what kind of catastrophe came into view only within the context of its memorialization: the result is a monument to 7,000 defenseless prisoners killed by the British. That many of these prisoners had survived the death marches from Auschwitz, that most were Jews, and that all were being hastily evacuated from concentration camps in northern Germany to somewhere—anywhere—away from German soil is not recalled in this memorial.[10]

At issue here, however, is not that this plaque in Timmendorf deliberately manipulates the events surrounding "the catastrophe of the *Cap Arcona*," but that the creators of memorial texts necessarily reconstruct these events, and so reflect as much their own understanding and experience as the actual events they would preserve. Self-interest and selective memory may indeed have played some role in the creation of the memorial plaque at Timmendorf. But as should become clear, such distortion is inevitable. The problem may not be so much the conscious or unconscious manipulation of history, which is intrinsic to all memory and representation. Rather, as we have seen in the Bitburg affair, the real danger may lie in an uncritical approach to monuments, so that a constructed and reified memory is accepted as normative history—and then acted upon as if it were pure, unmediated meaning.

President Reagan thus drew what seemed to be "natural" conclusions from the memorials to the German war dead at Bitburg. Because both *Waffen S.S.* and *Wehrmacht* soldiers lie together in a patch of land designated to commemorate Germany's war dead, the different roles they may have played in the war are subsumed in the larger, more general memory of their common fate. United now with countrymen they may have spurned during the war and with forebears from the First World War, some of whom—if Jews—would have been considered their enemies, the S.S. soldiers buried here have not only been absorbed into the greater continuum of all Germans who ever fell for their *Vaterland* but have also become the universal victims of war itself. On the strength of this particular configuration of memory at Bitburg and its "self-evident" truths, both Ronald Reagan and Helmut Kohl ignored many other historical perspectives on the war, and even encouraged their loss.

As the first concentration camp in Germany, Dachau epitomizes now the German memorialization of their "*KZ-Zeit*." Built in 1933 for political enemies of the Reich, Dachau housed and thereby created *German* victims, many of whom were also Jews. As horrifying as the conditions were at Dachau, its gas chamber was never used, so the crematoria burned "only" the remains of those who died of shootings, beatings, or most often, disease. Of the Dachau survivors still living in Germany, most are Christians, many of them clergymen and Social Democrats, whose own memories constitute the core of these memorial projects. There are, therefore, three religious memorials in the camp: one each for the Catholic church, the Protestant church, and the Jewish community.

As the name "The Trustees for the Monument of Atonement at the Concentration Camp Dachau" suggests, however, the very reasons for the memorials at Dachau differ for each group of victims. It was not to mourn the loss of a Jewish population that either of the Christian memorials was established, but rather to atone for Nazi sins against humanity. Stylized and cerebralized, all of the monuments within the grounds of the camp tend to emphasize the great gulf between past and present. From well-scrubbed barracks floors, to the swept gravel walks outside, to the crematorium (open, a sign tells us, from 9:00 to 5:00), cleanliness and order now govern the "remembrance" of filth and chaos. Given the almost antiseptic cleanliness of the grounds and of the two replicated barracks, the tasteful symbolism of the other barracks' foundations, and the excellent museum, it is not so surprising to hear visitors complain that this memorial aesthetizes the past as if to vanquish it rather than to recall it. Where the seemingly unadorned ruins of memorial camps in the East compel visitors to take them literally as the physical artifacts of the Nazi era, the freshly painted, efficiently organized icons at Dachau openly invite *meta*physical speculation.

The memorial at Bergen-Belsen, on the other hand, is conceived of and approached by visitors as a cemetery, a great burial ground. Except for an exhibition that briefly chronicles Nazism and the concentration camps in a one-room stone and glass museum here, little of what transpired specifically at Bergen-Belsen until the liberation is represented. The principal theme here instead is the prisoners' deaths and their mass graves. Signified now by rows of burial mounds, each grave is marked by a small stone and mortar façade, inscribed with the number of dead buried: "Here rest 5,000 dead," or 2,000 dead, or 1,000 dead. Amid burial mounds and scattered individual tombstones inscribed in Hebrew, a four-meter stone-block marker inscribed in English and Hebrew condenses Jewish memory. More general memory of anonymous victims is represented in a thirty-meter-high, all-white marble and granite obelisk standing in front of a free-standing wall 100 meters removed. Deathly quiet now except for the song of birds and roar of planes landing at the British military camp adjacent, the land now has covered itself modestly with shrubs and flowers; the surrounding forest acts as a kind of natural barrier between this place and the outer world, again a result of the Nazis' own efforts to keep the camp hidden.

Taking a lesson from the Allied efforts at reeducation in Germany after the war, museums to the Second World War era in Germany now make memory and pedagogy their twin aims: one comes automatically with the other. The directors of the memorial and museum in Neuengamme, just outside Hamburg, have thus instituted a summer work camp for international students on the grounds of the former concentration camp there. According to Wilfried Meiller, a lecturer in the document center here, the two objectives of the program are to teach today's youth about Germany's Nazi past and to foster greater understanding among the youth of different nations. Both aims are accomplished within the context of memorialization, which literally becomes a kind of "Denkmal-Arbeit"—or "memorial-work." Mindful of the pernicious echo in the German phrase "*Arbeitslager*," the project refers to itself instead by the more innocent and international English term, "workcamp."

Where prisoners of the camp were once worked to death in the brick factory as slaves to build Hitler's Reich, volunteers at "Workcamp Neuengamme" now work as excavators of remembrance. The concentration camp is now treated as an archeological dig, where remnants of a Holocaust past are excavated and catalogued as evidence of Nazi atrocities. In this archeology of the Holocaust, students dig up artifacts of the era—e.g., nails, tools, old shoes—around which the instructors reassemble, teach, and memorialize events. On one level, the archeological approach at Neuengamme threatens to turn the Holocaust and the camps into ancient and inaccessible history. But at a deeper level, this may be a consequence of all museums. For as T. W. Adorno has warned, "The German word *museal* [museumlike] has unpleasant overtones. It describes objects to which the observer no longer has a vital relationship and which are in the process of dying."[11] By bringing the past into the present one rusty artifact at a time, archeologists of the Holocaust necessarily atomize events in order to reconstruct them.

I V

In light of Adorno's warning, the very existence of a museum—*Beit Hatfutsot*—in Tel Aviv dedicated to the diaspora may reflect aptly the official view in Israel of dispersed Jewry as a dead and withered civilization. In its representation as museum object, life in the diaspora is addressed in the past tense; as its last and most significant manifestation, the Holocaust is proof of the untenability of life in exile, the ultimate justification for a Jewish state to ensure Jewish life after the catastrophe. It is precisely this emphasis on Jewish life before and after the Holocaust, however, that distinguishes Israeli Holocaust museums and memorials from those in Europe. Where monuments and museums in Europe focus relentlessly on the annihilation of Jews and almost totally neglect the millennium of Jewish life in Europe before the war, those in Israel locate events in a historical continuum that includes Jewish life before and after the destruction.

Outside of their destruction, the Jews barely exist now in European museums: neither their rich life before the war, nor their life in Israel and America after the war bear much consideration. In Israeli museums at kibbutzim like Lohamei Hageta'ot, Tel Yitzchak, Givat Chaim, and Yad Mordechai, and at Yad Vashem Martyrs' and Heroes' Memorial Authority in Jerusalem, Jewish life is given first priority. In Israel, the Holocaust marks not so much the end of Jewish life as it does the end of viable life in exile. It is thus integrated into Jewish history: it may be a turning point, a confirmation of Zionist ideology, but it is linked nevertheless to Jewish life before in Europe and to Jewish life after in Israel. Kibbutz Lohamei Hageta'ot (literally Fighters of the Ghettos) was thus founded by survivors of the camps and ghettos, many of them partisans and members of *He-*

halutz and the Jewish Fighting Organization, as a living monument to what they had seen. Although the museum there is now dedicated to the memory of poet Yitzhak Katzenelson, in both its name and memorial configuration, the kibbutz commemorates less the dying and more the fighting of Jews during the war and their surviving after the war. Of the twelve halls of the museum there, only two are devoted to the ghettos, concentration camps, and exterminations. In the narrative constructed in this museum, one arrives at these halls only after visiting graphic reconstructions of Vilna, "the Jerusalem of Lithuania," and "The Shtetl, Olkieniki." If, in this layout, the path to Holocaust lay through the centers and *shtetlach* of diaspora life, then the road from Holocaust leads through resistance to survival, to the kibbutz itself and to the vibrant new self-sufficiency of Jews in their own land. In this way, the Holocaust is contextualized not only to include aspects of life in exile but also to remind us that Jewish life preceded and will now follow it. In its conception and design, the theme at Holocaust Remembrance Day ceremonies at Lohamei Hageta'ot is always the same: "From Destruction to Redemption."

In fact, Holocaust memory is performed throughout Israel on a number of different levels on Holocaust Remembrance Day—*Yom Hasho'ah Vehagvurah*. Initially established by a law of Knesset in 1953 as part of the mandate for a Holocaust Martyrs' and Heroes' Remembrance Authority (Yad Vashem), *Yom Hasho'ah* was not officially activated until 1959. In many ways, it is significant that a separate day for remembering the Holocaust was decreed at all—and that it was to denote both Holocaust *and* heroism (*gvurah*). For this is a national, not religious, day of remembrance. While most orthodox congregations have incorporated the Holocaust into the liturgy of lamentations recited on *Tesha B'av* to recall the destructions of the First and Second temples, the orthodox rabbinate in Israel officially mourns Holocaust victims on the Tenth of Tevet—*Yom Hakaddish*. By giving the *Sho'ah* its own day and linking it to heroism—i.e., the Jews' (not God's) attempted deliverance of themselves—the government has effectively pulled it out of the religious continuum altogether in order to nationalize remembrance. Neither a day of fasting nor of lamenting in Israel, the date chosen for *Yom Hasho'ah* was not a day of destruction at all: the twenty-seventh day of Nissan comes from the middle of the six-week Warsaw Ghetto Uprising, which began on 19 April 1943—*Erev Pesach*—itself a commemoration of deliverance and freedom. Now falling on the Hebrew calendar in the same month as Passover, seven days before *Yom Hazikkaron* (remembrance day for Israel's war dead) and eight days before *Yom Hatzma'ut* (Israeli Independence Day), Holocaust Remembrance Day in Israel simultaneously recalls—and thereby links—biblical and recent historical liberation, modern resistance and national independence.

This notion of the Holocaust as part of a long view of Jewish history is exemplified in Nathan Rapoport's "*Megilat-esh*" (Scroll of Fire), set high in the Judean hills between Jerusalem and Tel Aviv. Originally conceived as a memorial for Riverside Park in New York City, this scroll of Jewish history was rejected by the City Arts Commission as "too heavy and depressing." It was adopted eagerly, however, by B'nai B'rith, who perceived that its natural home was Israel. Scenes from the Holocaust are thus integrated here in Israel's history, as part of an unfurling narrative, each event linked to the one before and after it. On any given day at the "Scroll of Fire," large groups of Israeli schoolchildren can be found studying this monument to all parts of Jewish history.

Of all memorials to the Holocaust, the vast complex of monuments, shrines, archives, and exhibitions at the Yad Vashem Martyrs' and Heroes' Memorial Authority in Jerusalem represents the most sophisticated and multilayered commemoration of events. Established by an act of the Israeli parliament on 19 August 1953 partly as a response to the unveiling of "the memorial to the unknown Jewish martyr" in Paris the day before, Yad Vashem was authorized expressly to "gather in to the homeland material regarding all those members of the Jewish people who laid down their lives, who fought and rebelled against the Nazi enemy and his collaborators, and to perpetuate their memory and that of the communities, organizations, and institutions which were destroyed because they were Jewish."[12] Among additional tasks as defined in Article 2 are "to collect, examine, and publish testimony of the Holocaust and the heroism it called forth and to bring home its lesson to the people" and "to promote a custom of joint remembrance of the heroes and victims" (p. 5). Yad Vashem (literally a "Monument and a Name," from Isa. 56:5) would thus institutionalize—even codify—the perpetual activity of Holocaust memorialization in Israel.

Though diverse and complicated, Yad Vashem's icons also locate events in several distinct traditions, thus conferring specific national and historical meaning onto them. By preserving the memory of the *heroes* as well as the *martyrs* of the destruction, Yad Vashem would actively oppose what Israelis view as an exaggerated fascination with the Jews as victims—and victims only. This is one of the reasons why a reproduction of Rapoport's Warsaw Ghetto Monument has a home at Yad Vashem; yet instead of allowing these particular archetypes to stagnate, Zionist ideology requires that the contrast between the passive "old Jews" and the fighting "new Jews" be heightened. For in Israel there exists an acute sensitivity to the historical consequences of these competing images. Since the historians in Israel find that commonly held stereotypes of the Jews in Christian Europe may have underpinned traditional antisemitism, and that the Jews' own limited perception of themselves as victims may have contributed to their vulnerability, current Israeli memorial-makers ensure that alternative icons are provided for subsequent generations. Thus, the traditional vulnerability and weakness of diaspora Jewry (central tenets of Zionism) are recalled side by side with iconographic images of the new, fighting Jews, in order both to explain past events and to provide viable models for the young.

Divided into three principal sections, the powerful historical exhibition at Yad Vashem also reflects a characteristically Israeli grasp of events. In the first section, the rise of anti-Jewish laws and actions between 1933 and 1939 is traced through a mixture of photographs, leaflets, Nazi propaganda, and historical narrative. The harassment, deportations, and even the pogroms of *Kristallnacht* are all presented here as being consistent with the European antisemitic tradition. From this room, one goes around the corner into a section entitled "The Struggle to Survive: 1939–41"—an extension of the first phase.

But then there is a break in the exhibition, and we must move physically from one hall—i.e., one era—to another. After walking out of this section and back through the museum lobby, we enter the next room. This hall is devoted solely to the killing process itself between 1941 and 1945, the proportions and methods of which were so unlike anything before, that— as the layout suggests—it cannot be located iconographically within the context of traditional anti-Jewish persecution. A section on the world's silence and sealed ports of refuge is included in this hall. But finally, unlike other memorial expositions of the Holocaust, the history traced at Yad Vashem does not end with the liberation of the camps, but continues: in another break from the past, the next hall represents armed Jewish resistance and the Aftermath. In adjoining exhibits, the Warsaw Ghetto Revolt and Jewish Partisans are both linked spatially to the current historical moment: the State of Israel itself. For as the photographs of survivors coming ashore at Haifa and Caesarea illustrate, the "end of the Holocaust" comes only with the survivors' return to and redemption in Eretz Israel.

As we enter the great memorial hall at Yad Vashem—a huge megalithic tomb sunk into the earth—we also pass beneath the words of the Baal Shem Tov, which distill the *raison d'être* of this memorial in Israel: "Forgetting lengthens the period of exile! In remembrance lies the secret of deliverance." In the dim light, our eyes are drawn downward to the eternal flame and to the names of the death camps inscribed on the stone floor. Invited to remember and then to contemplate remembrance in this great dark space—itself an objectification of absence—we do so within an ever-vigilant context: exile, memory, and redemption.

I V

While the Holocaust is studied and taught in Israel as one event—even of watershed proportions—among others in a long Jewish history, it has already begun to dominate all Jewish past and present in America. Instead of learning about the Holocaust through the study of Jewish history, too many students in America are learning the whole of Jewish history through the lens of the Holocaust. Without other kinds of museums to a Jewish past, even to current life in the diaspora, Holocaust museums in America tend to organize Jewish culture and identity around this one era alone, rather than representing events as part of a greater Jewish continuum.

Thus, even as the Holocaust museum proposed for New York State locates events in a Jewish continuum that includes life before and after the destruction, its designated name—"Museum of Jewish Heritage—A Living Memorial to the Holocaust"—still conflates Jewish culture and the Holocaust, wherein one becomes a permutation of the other.

If the monuments in Europe and Israel are inevitably constrained by political and ideological coordinates, those in the United States are equally limited by our own experience of the Holocaust. For the young American G.I.'s who liberated Dachau and Buchenwald, for example, a history of the Holocaust necessarily excludes the conditions in Europe before the war, the wrenching break-up of families, deportations to the ghettos and camps, and even the killing process itself. They were not witnesses to the process of destruction, only to its effects. Inasmuch as the "American experience" of the Holocaust in 1945 was thus confined to the *liberation* of the camps, it is appropriate that the monument entitled "Liberation" should be located in Liberty State Park, New Jersey, within sight of our greatest ideological icon, the Statue of Liberty. In this work by Nathan Rapoport, a young, solemn-looking G.I. walks forward, his eyes on the ground, cradling—almost pietà-like—a concentration-camp victim. With skeletal chest showing through tattered prison-garb, his arms spread, and his eyes staring vacantly into the sky, the victim exemplifies helplessness. This monument is thus consonant with both the specific experiences of Americans in the war and with traditional self-perceptions and idealizations of our role as rescuers in war and as sanctuary for the world's "huddled masses."

Given America's pluralistic concept of itself, it is not surprising that ideals like liberty and pluralism would constitute central memorial motifs in both current and projected museums to the Holocaust in this country. The Holocaust museum at the Simon Wiesenthal Center in Los Angeles is thus renamed "The Museum of Tolerance," to reflect both its pedagogical aim (tolerance) and the plural audience it hopes to attract. After falling short of funds, the Babi Yar Memorial Committee in Denver was able to complete its memorial there only with assistance from the local Ukrainian community: the Babi Yar Memorial there now commemorates "The Two Hundred Thousand Victims who died [at] Babi Yar, Kiev, Ukraine, USSR, September 29, 1941–November 6, 1943. The Majority Jews with Ukrainians and Others." From the steps of the new museum in New York, one will be able to hold in view the Holocaust, Ellis Island, and the Statue of Liberty. Having defined the Holocaust as the murder of eleven million innocents by the Nazis, Jimmy Carter established a Holocaust Memorial Commission in Washington: will the proposed museum recall the six million Jews slaughtered for having been born Jews, or the eleven million who were murdered in all the camps, for all different reasons? Or will it become a generic museum of all holocausts, including the massacres of Armenians, Cambodians, and Russians? Given American egalitarian ideals, it may not be possible for an American national museum of the Holocaust to define its aims otherwise.

The Nazis had intended the destruction of the Jews to be total: they were to have been removed from history and memory. Any record of the Holocaust thus appears in principle to defeat Nazi plans. But beginning with an ordinance in 1936 forbidding German stonemasons to carve gravestones for Jews, continuing through the Nazis' methodical destruction of documents in Vilna recording past persecutions, and ending with Hitler's plans for a museum in Prague to the extinct Jewish race, it grows clear that if the first step toward the destruction of a people lay in the blotting out of its memory, then the last step would lie in its calculated resurrection. Through the Prague museum and other monuments to his victory over the Jews, Hitler never planned to "forget" the Jews, but rather to supplant their memory of events with his own.[13] Total liquidation would not have come through the Jews' physical annihilation only, or in the expunction of all reference to them afterward. But by eradicating the Jewish *type* of memory, the Nazis would also have destroyed the possibility of regeneration through memory that has marked Jewish existence.

The usual aim in any nation's monuments, however, is not solely to displace memory or to remake it in one's own image: it is also to invite the collaboration of the community in acts of remembrance. To the extent that the myths or ideals embodied in a nation's monuments are the people's own, they are given substance and weight by such reification and will appear natural and true; hence, an inescapable partnership grows between a people and its monuments. It is at precisely this point, however, that a critical approach to memorials might rescue us from a complicity that allows our icons of remembrance to harden into idols of remembrance. For memorialization occurs not merely within these icons, but between the events and icons, and then again between the icons and ourselves. By recalling this movement between events, icons, and ourselves, we accept more than a ritual responsibility for the images that lie enshrined in our monuments. It is not to Holocaust monuments as such that we turn for remembrance, but to ourselves within the reflective space they both occupy and open up. In effect, there can be no self-critical monuments, but only critical viewers.

Conclusion

Implicit in a critical study of any literary genre is both a definition of the genre and an assumption of bibliographical completeness. Like other histories, literary history functions as a discreet arbiter of existence: events, writers, and their works, in this case, all come to exist in critical consciousness because they also exist (in determined ways) in "the book." And like other histories, Holocaust literary history is constructed in such a way as inevitably to select and omit particular authors and works: this study is no exception. Depending on whether Holocaust literature is perceived as only that written during the events (as opposed to after), as part of a general "literature of atrocity," as part of Jewish responses to catastrophe in particular, or as part of no continuum at all, the shape, size, and definition of this literature will necessarily vary. But as responsible history must, literary history must also account for the manner in which its critical assumptions have both shaped the canon and led critics to their conclusions regarding it. The next step, therefore, is to cultivate an awareness of the critical language and models by which we interpret events as they have existed both in historical time and in their texts.

In his landmark essay "White Mythology," Derrida warns against the "metaphysical naivety of the wretched peripetic" who does not recognize the figure of his own culture, a "white mythology" that has effaced itself from view even as it continues to structure reality and lead us to our philosophical conclusions about reality.[1] The fundamental problem now facing writers, historians, philosophers, and literary critics becomes how to pull themselves far enough out of their critical language, metaphors, and metaphysical assumptions to distinguish between meanings and conclusions they have projected onto texts and realities, and those which they seem to have extracted from them. Just as these figures of culture have "whitened themselves out" in the course of history, leaving behind victims of both history and their apprehensions of it, so too do the figures of critical interpretation tend to whiten themselves out, leaving behind a palimpsest of naturalized historical and critical conclusions.

Instead of perceiving without knowing it the shapes of mind superimposed onto events of the Holocaust, therefore, the critical writer might now aspire to perceive these shapes of mind with knowing it. For the hidden structures and biases of our minds may be as inimical to our critical understanding of the Holocaust as the victims' and writers' assumptions have been to theirs. In attempting to formulate a critical metalanguage with which to interpret both events of the Holocaust and the literature in which events are subsumed, perhaps the only aspect of our inquiry to transcend our projections of mind onto events is the awareness of these projections. As difficult as it is to distinguish between historical facts of the Holocaust and the ways we write them, a "critically thinking" approach to the Holocaust and its literature ultimately presumes a qualitative difference between actions and conclusions on the parts of critics, readers, and participants in history deriving from the self-reflecting construction of reality and those deriving from the unreflecting projection of mind onto reality. This would not be to discourage critics, writers, and readers from making judgments, drawing conclusions, or taking actions based on any particular knowledge of the Holocaust—all of which could be said to constitute scholarly praxis. But rather, it is to insist that we never again submit unquestioningly to our respective patterns of mind: the difference is between intemperate action and circumspect action, the latter claiming no higher authority than any given pattern of mind.

This is to suggest that by remaining aware of both the ideational character of interpretation and the potential in this knowledge for its utility as agency in the world, writers and critics of Holocaust texts remain able to produce further knowledge of the Holocaust, even as they regulate the practical consequences of this knowledge. Even though any critical interpretation may be limited by its own preassumptions, there is a sense in which, by remaining aware of its construction, it might temper action taken on its behalf. For self-critical interpretation can call attention both to its relative truth and to the relative authority by which it suggests itself as agency. What makes such self-critical thinking so helpful here is that it takes into account *all* possible conditions of agency, including religious, tropic, and literary frames of reference. In this approach, the self-interpretation of actions becomes regulatory of these same actions and might thus function as part of the conditions we evaluate before acting.

Rather than allowing self-reflexive knowledge of the Holocaust to neutralize or paralyze all potential action issuing from this knowledge, however, we still need to consider further criteria by which to decide when to act on a particular knowledge and when not to act on it. That is, even if we recognize the shapes we have conferred on worldly phenomena, what then determines the "appropriateness" or "inappropriateness" of a given interpretation? After Nietzsche, we might regard as one criterion the extent to which our interpretations are "life-providing, life-preserving, and perhaps even species-cultivating."[2]

As Mark Warren notes in his revealing essay on "Nietzsche and the Concept of Ideology," even as Nietzsche attempts on the one hand to undermine absolute truth claims of any given idea by denying its universal truth, he *does* accept their relative, pragmatic truth, but only in terms of their value for particular forms of life.[3] As criteria with which to evaluate interpretations of the Holocaust, these seem especially appropriate to our study of its narrative; for they allow both a plurality of meaning *and* a basis for evaluating these meanings. What makes an interpretation of a particular event appropriate or inappropriate is not some intrinsic quality of the interpretation but, as Warren concludes, "Forms of consciousness . . . are ulti-

mately to be assessed in terms of their functions in enabling forms of 'life' "
(p. 549). In this view, it is not a question of veracity in interpretation or its
intrinsic correctness that determines appropriateness, but its capacity to
sustain and enable life itself. Whether or not we can ever achieve this critical
awareness may be debatable. But I propose that an attempt at this kind of
self-reflexivity now become part of the critical methodology by which we
approach Holocaust narrative.

"Today Jewry lives a bifurcated life," Yerushalmi writes. "As a result of
emancipation in the diaspora and national sovereignty in Israel, Jews have
fully re-entered the mainstream of history, and yet their perception of how
they got there and where they are is most often more mythical than real.
Myth and memory condition action. There are myths that are life-sustaining
and deserve to be reinterpreted for our age. There are some that lead
astray and must be redefined. Others are dangerous and must be exposed."[4]
Though it may be difficult to distinguish between mythical and real perceptions, through critical thinking we may be better able to recognize the
difference between the life-sustaining and the life-threatening myths by
which we interpret the world. For the choice here is not whether or not to
have a mythical past but, as Yerushalmi makes clear, what kind of past we
have. By recognizing the past in the present, its force over our perceptions
and our understanding of the present, we sanction the ways it makes sense
of our world and leads us to our actions, rather than submit to it altogether.

As I hope to have shown in this study, so long as we are dependent on
the "vocabulary" of our culture and its sustaining archetypes, it may not
be possible to generate entirely new responses to catastrophe. It may now
be possible, however, to respond from within our traditional critical paradigms with self-critical awareness of where traditionally conditioned responses lead us in the world. For if modern responses to catastrophe have
included the breakdown and repudiation of traditional forms and archetypes, then one postmodern response might be to recognize that even as
we reject the absolute meanings and answers these "archaic" forms provide,
we are still unavoidably beholden to these same forms for both our expression and our understanding of the Holocaust. With this in mind, critical
reading can lead not only to further understanding of sacred and modern
literary texts, but also to new understanding of the ways our lives and these
texts are inextricably bound together. It seems only fitting that this insight
in itself might now become part of the tradition.

Notes

INTRODUCTION

1. Quoted from Yosef Hayim Yerushalmi, *Zakhor: Jewish History and Jewish Memory* (Seattle: University of Washington Press, 1982), p. 70.

2. Robert Alter, "Deformations of the Holocaust," *Commentary*, February 1981, p. 49.

3. For insight into the ways Sholem Alcichem's literary and historical worlds interpenetrated, see David Roskies, "Laughing Off the Trauma of History," in *Against the Apocalypse: Responses to Catastrophe in Modern Jewish Culture* (Cambridge, Mass., and London: Harvard University Press, 1984), pp. 163–95.

4. Hayden White, *Tropics of Discourse: Essays in Cultural Criticism* (Baltimore and London: Johns Hopkins University Press, 1978), p. 126.

5. Edouard Roditi, "Post-Holocaust Prophets," *European Judaism* 5, no. 2 (Summer 1971): 51, a review of Irving Halperin, *Messengers of the Dead: Literature of the Holocaust* (Philadelphia: The Westminster Press, 1970).

6. This point is made very well by David G. Roskies in *Against the Apocalypse: Responses to Catastrophe in Modern Jewish Culture*, p. 35.

7. See Hayden White, "The Burden of History," *History and Theory* 5, no. 2 (1966): 127.

8. Yehuda Bauer, *The Holocaust in Historical Perspective* (Seattle: University of Washington Press, 1978), p. 46.

9. Ironically, as J. Hillis Miller has suggested, it may not even be the narratological principle of "constructed history" that undermines the possibility of "historical facts" in fiction, but rather the questioning of novelists like Anthony Trollope and their constant awareness of the fabulative nature of their constructions—even those with historical claims—that ultimately called into question the possibility of unvitiated facts in narrative:

> Insofar as a novel raises questions about the key assumptions of story-telling, for example, about the notions of origin and end, about consciousness or selfhood, about causality, or about gradually emerging unified meaning, then this putting in question of narrative form becomes also obliquely a putting in question of history or of the writing of history. What seemed to be the *locus standi* by analogy with which the novel was written turns out to be itself undermined by the activity of story-telling. Insofar as a novel "deconstructs" the assumptions of "realism" in fiction, it also turns out to "deconstruct" naïve notions about history or about the writing of history.

See J. Hillis Miller, "Narrative and History," *English Literary History* 41 (1974): 462.

10. Hayden White, "The Fictions of Factual Representation," in *Tropics of Discourse: Essays in Cultural Criticism* (Baltimore and London: Johns Hopkins University Press, 1978), p. 121.

11. At this late stage, it would be difficult to cite all of the contemporary theorists at work on the literary construction of history; it is important here, however, to mention some of the books and essays that have most influenced the course of this particular inquiry: Roland Barthes, "Historical Discourse," in Michael Lane, ed., *Introduction to Structuralism* (New York: Basic Books, 1970), pp. 145–55; J. Hillis Miller, "Narrative and History," *ELH* 41 (1974): 455–73; Lionel Gossman, "History and Literature: Reproduction or Signification," Louis O. Mink, "Narrative Form as

a Cognitive Instrument," in Robert H. Canary and Henry Kozicki, eds., *The Writing of History: Literary Form and Historical Understanding* (Madison: The University of Wisconsin Press, 1978), pps. 3–39, pps. 129–49; Paul Veyne, *Writing History* (Middletown, Conn.: Wesleyan University Press, 1984); Paul Ricoeur, *Time and Narrative*, vol. 1 (Chicago and London: University of Chicago Press, 1984).

As will become clear, I owe a great debt to Hayden White's work, particularly, "The Burden of History," *History and Theory* 5, no. 2 (1966); "Interpretation in History," *New Literary History* 4 (1972–73); "The Historical Text as Literary Artifact," *Clio* 3, no. 3 (1974); "Historicism, History, and the Figurative Imagination," *History and Theory* 14 (1975); "The Fictions of Factual Representation," in *The Literature of Fact*, ed. Angus Fletcher (New York: Columbia University Press, 1976), all of which are collected in Hayden White, *Tropics of Discourse: Essays in Cultural Criticism* (Baltimore and London: Johns Hopkins University Press, 1978); "The Value of Narrativity in the Representation of Reality," *Critical Inquiry* 7 (Autumn 1980); "The Politics of Historical Interpretation: Discipline and De-Sublimation," *Critical Inquiry* 9 (1982). Also see *The Content of the Form: Narrative Discourse and Historical Representation* (Baltimore and London: The Johns Hopkins University Press, 1987).

In addition to these works on the theory of historical narrative, two recent studies on the "literature of fact" have added invaluably to the present work: Barbara Foley, *Telling the Truth: Theory and Practice of Documentary Literature* (Ithaca and London: Cornell University Press, 1986); and Shelley Fisher Fishkin, *From Fact to Fiction: Journalism and Imaginative Writing in America* (Baltimore and London: Johns Hopkins University Press, 1985). Other contributing works will be cited in the text and notes.

12. White, "The Politics of Interpretation," p. 124n.

13. Barthes, "Historical Discourse," pp. 148–49.

1. ON REREADING HOLOCAUST DIARIES AND MEMOIRS

1. Yosef Hayim Yerushalmi, *Zakhor: Jewish History and Jewish Memory* (Seattle and London: University of Washington Press, 1982), p. 69.

2. Frederick Hoffman, *The Mortal No: Death and the Modern Imagination* (Princeton: Princeton University Press, 1964), p. 159.

3. Terrence Des Pres, *The Survivor: An Anatomy of Life in the Death Camps* (New York: Oxford University Press, 1976), p. 29. For an excellent discussion of the "will to bear witness," see pp. 27–50.

4. Lawrence Langer has written, for example, that "[B]efore 1939 imagination was always in advance of reality, but after 1945 reality had outdistanced the imagination so that nothing the artist conjured could equal in intensity or scope the improbability of *l'univers concentrationaire*" (*The Holocaust and the Literary Imagination* [New Haven and London: Yale University Press, 1976], p. 35).

In a parallel vein, Edward Alexander has written, "What we complacently call 'reality' has become more incredible than anything previously dreamt of by the most imaginative writer of fiction" (*The Resonance of Dust: Essays on Holocaust Literature and Jewish Fate* [Columbus: Ohio State University Press, 1980], p. 19).

5. Saul Friedländer, *Reflections of Nazism: An Essay on Kitsch and Death* (New York and London: Harper and Row, 1984), pp. 94–95.

6. Robert Scholes, *Structural Fabulation* (Notre Dame: University of Notre Dame Press, 1975), p. 7.

7. See Janet Blatter, "Art from the Whirlwind," in *Art of the Holocaust*, by Janet Blatter and Sybil Milton (London: Pan Books, 1982), pp. 22–35.

8. See Abraham Katsh, ed., *The Warsaw Diary of Chaim A. Kaplan* (New York: Collier Books, 1965), p. 104.

9. Lionel Gossman, "History and Literature: Reproduction or Signification," in Robert H. Canary and Henry Kozicki, eds., *The Writing of History: Literary Form and Historical Understanding* (Madison: University of Wisconsin Press, 1978), p. 32.

10. David Roskies, *Against the Apocalypse: Responses to Catastrophe in Modern Jewish Culture* (Cambridge, Mass., and London: Harvard University Press, 1984), p. 35. Also see Yerushalmi, *Zakhor: Jewish History and Jewish Memory,* pp. 10–15.

11. Elie Wiesel, "The Holocaust as Literary Inspiration," in *Dimensions of the Holocaust* (Northwestern University, 1977), p. 9.

12. Lily Edelman, "A Conversation with Elie Wiesel," in Harry J. Cargas, ed., *Responses to Elie Wiesel: Critical Essays by Major Jewish and Christian Scholars* (New York: Persea Books, 1978), p. 14 (emphasis mine).

13. Primo Levi, *If This Is Man and The Truce* (London: Penguin Books, 1979), p. 72.

14. For more on the self-interpreting quality of scripture, see Michael Fishbane, "Revelation and Tradition: Aspects of Inner-Biblical Exegesis," *Journal of Biblical Literature* 99, no. 3 (1980): 343–61.

15. See Emil Fackenheim, "Midrashic Existence after the Holocaust: Reflections Occasioned by the Work of Elie Wiesel," and Byron L. Sherwin, "Wiesel's Midrash: The Writings of Elie Wiesel and Their Relationship to Jewish Tradition," in Alvin H. Rosenfeld and Irving Greenberg, eds., *Confronting the Holocaust: The Impact of Elie Wiesel* (Bloomington and London: Indiana University Press, 1978), pp. 99–116, pp. 117–132.

16. For the details of a similar discussion in a more strictly theological context, see "Controversy: Fragments of the Rock: Contemporary Literary Theory and the Study of Rabbinic Texts—A Response to David Stern," by Susan Handelman, *Prooftexts* 5, no. 1 (January 1985): 75–103.

17. Butz and company print a scandalous journal of "historical review," funded by neo-nazi and "national front" organizations in America and England, in which they deny that the Holocaust happened, in *or* out of narrative.

18. "The Holocaust as Literary Inspiration," p. 5.

19. Elie Wiesel, *A Beggar in Jerusalem* (New York: Random House, 1970), p. 135.

20. Philippe Lejeune, *Le Pacte autobiographique* (Paris: Editions du Seuil, 1975), p. 26.

21. See Lennard J. Davis, *Factual Fictions: The Origins of the English Novel* (New York: Columbia University Press, 1983), p. 74.

22. Karl J. Weintraub, "Autobiography and Historical Consciousness," *Critical Inquiry* 1, no. 3 (1975): 827.

23. For further discussion of this aspect in the diaries of Herman Kruk and Zelig Kalmanovitsh, see Robert Liberles, "Diaries of the Holocaust," *Orim* 1, no. 2 (Spring 1986): 44–45.

24. David Roskies has made this point before me in *Against the Apocalypse,* pp. 199–212.

25. Anne Frank, *The Diary of a Young Girl,* trans. B. M. Mooyaart-Doubleday (Garden City, N.Y.: Doubleday and Company, Inc., 1952), p. 278.

26. Frances Goodrich and Albert Hackett, *The Diary of Anne Frank* (New York: Random House, 1956), pp. 168–69.

27. Moshe Flinker, *Young Moshe's Diary: The Spiritual Torment of a Young Boy in Nazi Europe* (Jerusalem: Yad Vashem, 1979), p. 121.

28. For an excellent history of these first reports, see John Conway, "The First Report about Auschwitz," in *Simon Wiesenthal Center Annual* 1 (1984): 133–51.

29. "Eye-Witness Report of the Annihilation of the Jews of Poland," in *The Ghetto Speaks* (press release issued by the American Representation of the General Jewish Workers' Union of Poland), no. 9, 1 March 1943, p. 1.

30. Benzion Dinur, "Problems Confronting 'Yad [V]ashem' in its Work of Research," in Benzion Dinur and Shaul Esh, eds., *Yad [V]ashem Studies on the European Catastrophe and Resistance* (Jerusalem: Publishing Department of the Jewish Agency, 1957), p. 19.

31. K. Y. Ball-Kaduri, "Evidence of Witnesses, its Value and Limitations," *Yad [V]ashem Studies on the European Jewish Catastrophe and Resistance* 3 (1959): 80.

32. David Roskies, "The Holocaust According to the Literary Critics," *Prooftexts* 1, no. 2 (May 1981): 211.

33. Yechiel Szeintuch, *Yiddish and Hebrew Literature under the Nazi Rule in Eastern Europe* (Ph.D. diss., The Hebrew University of Jerusalem, 1978), quoted in Roskies, "The Holocaust According to the Literary Critics," p. 211.

34. Emil Fackenheim, *The Jewish Return into History: Reflections in the Age of Auschwitz and a New Jerusalem* (New York: Schocken Books, 1978), p. 58.

35. Kaplan, *The Warsaw Diary*, pps. 41, 53, 189.

36. From the appendix to *The Warsaw Diary of Adam Czerniakow: Prelude to Doom* (New York: Stein and Day, 1979), p. 402.

37. Nachman Blumental, "A Martyr or Hero? Reflections on the Diary of Adam Czerniakow," *Yad Vashem Studies* 7 (1968): 168.

38. C. S. Peirce, *Collected Papers* (Cambridge, Mass.: Harvard University Press, 1931–58), vol. 2, para. 228.

39. Quoted in Sidra Ezrahi, *By Words Alone: The Holocaust in Literature* (Chicago and London: University of Chicago Press, 1980), p. 21 (emphasis added).

40. Jacques Derrida, *Writing and Difference* (London and Henley: Routledge and Kegan Paul, 1981), p. 65.

2. FROM WITNESS TO LEGEND

1. Yaffa Eliach, *Hasidic Tales of the Holocaust* (New York: Oxford University Press, 1982).

2. Sara Nomberg-Przytyk, *Auschwitz: True Tales from a Grotesque Land*, ed. Eli Pfefferkorn and David H. Hirsch, trans. Roslyn Hirsch (Chapel Hill and London: The University of North Carolina Press, 1985).

3. Wieslaw Kielar, *Anus Mundi: Five Years in Auschwitz* (New York: Penguin Books, 1982), pp. 178–79.

4. See Bruno Bettelheim, *The Informed Heart: Autonomy in a Mass Age* (New York: The Free Press of Glencoe, 1960), pp. 264–65, for a version based on Eugene Kogon, *Der SS-Staat* (Stockholm: Bermann-Fischer Verlag, 1947), p. 180. Both of these versions are cited by Pfefferkorn and Hirsch in the editors' afterword, *Auschwitz: True Tales from a Grotesque Land*, p. 176.

5. Filip Müller, *Eyewitness Auschwitz: Three Years in the Gas Chambers* (New York: Stein and Day, 1979), pp. 88–89.

6. "Deposition of Stanislaw Jankowski," in Jadwiga Bezwińska and Danuta Czech, eds., *Amidst a Nightmare of Crime: Manuscripts of Members of Sonderkommando* (Oświęcim: Publications of State Museum, 1973), pp. 55–56; "Reminiscences of Broad," in Jadwiga Bezwińska and Danuta Czech, eds., *KL Auschwitz Seen by the SS: Höss, Broad, Kremer* (Oświęcim: Publications of the State Museum, 1978), p. 179.

7. In addition to the versions cited above by Bettelheim, Broad, Jankowski, Kielar, Kogon, Müller, and Nomberg-Przytyk, see Tadeusz Borowski, "The Death of Schillinger," in *This Way for the Gas, Ladies and Gentlemen* (New York: Penguin Books, 1982), pp. 143–46; Arnošt Lustig, *A Prayer for Katerina Horovitzova* (New York: Harper and Row, 1973); and Sylvia Rothchild, ed., *Voices from the Holocaust* (New York: New American Library, 1981), p. 162.

3. HOLOCAUST DOCUMENTARY FICTION

1. Hana Wirth-Nesher, "The Ethics of Narration in D. M. Thomas's *The White Hotel*," *The Journal of Narrative Technique* 15, no. 1 (Winter 1985): 17.
2. Arnold Wesker, "Art Between Truth and Fiction: Thoughts on William Styron's Novel," *Encounter* (January 1980): 52.
3. Barbara Foley, "Fact, Fiction, Fascism: Testimony and Mimesis in Holocaust Narratives," *Comparative Literature* 34, no. 4 (Fall 1982): 337.
4. "The White Hotel," *Times Literary Supplement*, 26 March 1982.
5. Anatoli Kuznetsov, *Babi Yar: A Documentary Novel* (New York: The Dial Press, 1967), pp. 74–75.
6. D. M. Thomas, *The White Hotel* (New York: The Viking Press, 1981), pp. 246–47.
7. "The White Hotel," *Times Literary Supplement*, 2 April 1982, p. 24.
8. "The Memories," *New York Times Book Review*, 9 April 1967, p. 45. Also quoted in Ezrahi, *By Words Alone*, p. 31.
9. Cf. the descriptions on p. 243 of *The White Hotel* and photographs of massacres in Lijepaja, Latvia, and Sniadowa, Poland, in Gerhard Schoenberner, *The Yellow Star* (New York, London, and Toronto: Bantam Books, 1969), pp. 92–97.
10. See Roland Barthes, *Camera Lucida: Reflections on Photography* (New York: Hill and Wang, 1981), and *Image-Music-Text* (New York: Hill and Wang, 1977), pp. 15–51.

Susan Sontag, *On Photography* (New York: Farrar, Straus, and Giroux, 1973); it is worth noting here that Sontag writes specifically of Holocaust photographs she saw when she was twelve years old that "Nothing I had seen—in photographs or in real life—ever cut me as sharply, deeply, instantaneously," suggesting the sheer "power" of referential evidence in the photograph.

Also see Joel Snyder and Neil Walsh Allen, "Photography, Vision, and Representation," *Critical Inquiry*, Autumn 1975, p. 145; John Berger, *About Looking* (New York: Pantheon Press, 1980); and Kendall L. Walton, "Transparent Pictures: On the Nature of Photographic Realism," *Critical Inquiry* 11, no. 2 (December 1984): 246–77.

11. Alfred Andersch, *Efraim's Book* (New York: Viking Penguin, 1984), p. 143.
12. Pierre Julitte, *Block 26: Sabotage at Buchenwald* (New York: Doubleday, 1971), p. xi. Also quoted in Ezrahi, *By Words Alone*, p. 25, as part of an excellent discussion of "Documentation as Art."
13. Ezrahi suggests we compare Steiner's account, for example, with Yankel Wiernik's diary, *A Year in Treblinka*, and Vasili Grossman's *L'Enfer de Treblinka* (*By Words Alone*, p. 32).
14. Jean-François Steiner, *Treblinka* (New York: New American Library, 1979), p. 304. In the afterword to the original French edition, Steiner's reference is exactly the same ("*L'Enfer de Treblinka*, par un correspondant de guerre de l'armée soviétique qui interrogea les premiers témoins"). *Treblinka* (Paris: Librairie Artheme Fayand, 1966), p. 394.
15. In her study, *The Theme of Nazi Concentration Camps in French Literature* (The Hague and Paris: Mouton and Company, 1973), Cynthia Haft cites Steiner's and Reiner's as instances of dishonest fiction, "part of a trend which we abhor," and notes that after legal proceedings, Reiner reedited his book to include acknowledgments where they were due (p. 191).
16. Leon W. Wells, *The Death Brigade* (New York: Holocaust Library, 1978), p. 133. See, among many other excellent memoirs, Erich Kulka, *Escape from Auschwitz* (South Hadley, Mass.: Bergin and Garvey Publishers, Inc., 1986), and Filip Müller, *Eyewitness Auschwitz: Three Years in the Gas Chambers* (New York: Stein and Day, 1979).

17. Alvin H. Rosenfeld, *A Double Dying: Reflections on Holocaust Literature* (Bloomington and London: Indiana University Press, 1980), p. 66. John Hersey, *The Wall* (New York: Knopf, 1950). Leon Uris, *Mila 18* (New York: Doubleday, 1961).

18. Ronald Weber, *The Literature of Fact* (Athens: Ohio University Press, 1980), p. 163 (emphasis mine).

19. Lennard Davis, *Factual Fictions: The Origins of the English Novel* (New York: Columbia University Press, 1983), pp. 212–13.

4. DOCUMENTARY THEATER, IDEOLOGY, AND THE RHETORIC OF FACT

1. Andreas Huyssen, "The Politics of Identification," *New German Critique* 19 (Winter 1980): 133. This essay is reprinted in Huyssen's *After the Great Divide: Modernism, Mass Culture, Postmodernism* (Bloomington and Indianapolis: Indiana University Press, 1986), pp. 94–114.

Also see Alvin H. Rosenfeld's remarks on Weiss in "Exploiting Atrocity," *A Double Dying: Reflections on Holocaust Literature,* pp. 154–59, and Oliver Clausen, "Weiss/Propagandist and Weiss/Playwright," *New York Times Magazine,* 2 October 1966, p. 132.

2. Jack D. Zipes, "The Aesthetic Dimensions of the German Documentary Drama," *German Life and Letters* 24, no. 4 (1971): 346.

3. Roland Barthes, *Mythologies* (New York: Hill and Wang, 1970), p. 11.

4. Jacques Derrida, "White Mythology," *New Literary History* 6 (1974): 5–74.

5. See Roland Barthes, "Historical Discourse," in *Introduction to Structuralism,* ed. Michael Lane (New York: Basic Books, 1970), p. 151.

6. For a fuller discussion of the origins, aims, and methods of socialist realism, see Katerina Clark, *The Soviet Novel: History as Ritual* (Chicago and London: The University of Chicago Press, 1981), pp. 3–45.

7. Fredric Jameson, "The Ideology of the Text," *Salmagundi* 31 (1975–76): 235.

8. Terry Eagleton, "Ideology, Fiction, Narrative," *Social Text* (1979): 63.

9. One of the working assumptions underlying the very process of documentary narrative thus recalls Louis Althusser's definition of ideology as " . . . the expression of the relation between men and their world, that is, the . . . unity of the real relation and the imaginary relation between them and their real conditions of existence" (*For Marx* [London, 1977], pp. 233–34).

10. Peter Weiss, *Die Ermittlung: Oratorium in 11 Gesängen* (Frankfurt am Main: Suhrkamp Verlag, 1965). Translations here are from *The Investigation,* trans. Jon Swan and Ulu Grosbard (New York: Atheneum, 1966).

11. See Peter Weiss, "The Material and the Models: Notes Towards a Definition of Documentary Theatre," trans. Heinz Bernard, *Theatre Quarterly* 1 (1971): 41. This essay was originally delivered by Weiss as a paper to the Brecht-Dialogue held at the Berliner Ensemble in East Berlin, 12–16 February 1968, and later published in *Theatre Heute,* March 1968.

12. This paradox in Weiss's intentions is also discussed in Rosenfeld, *A Double Dying,* pp. 154–55; in Otto Best, *Peter Weiss,* trans. Ursula Molinaro (New York: Frederick Ungar Publishing Company, 1976), pp. 83–84; and in R. C. Perry, "Historical Authenticity and Dramatic Form: Hochhuth's '*Der Stellvertreter*' and Weiss's '*Die Ermittlung*,' " *Modern Language Review* 64 (1969): 828.

13. In "The Materials and the Models," Weiss simultaneously protests the press's mystification of daily events, calling for explanations, and condemns the obscurantism and opacity that "keep the population in a state of stupefaction and bewilderment" (p. 41). Though, as we see here, by suggesting that his explanation is natural (or "scientific" as it were), Weiss essentially replaces "meaninglessness" with

one large determinate meaning; by thus denying the possibility of multiple meanings in these events, however, Weiss seems to counter one kind of mystification with another, less obvious, mystification.

14. Paul Gray, "A Living World" (interview with Weiss), *Tulane Drama Review* 2 (1966): 106.

15. Compare pp. 53–54 in *The Investigation* with Herman Langbein, *Der Auschwitz Prozess, eine Dokumentation*, 2 vols. (Frankfurt: Europäische Verlagsanstalt, 1965), p. 253.

16. Trans. Christopher Middleton, "My Place," *Encounter* 25, no. 6 (December 1965): 3; it appeared before this as "Meine Ortschaft," in *Rapporte* (Frankfurt am Main: Suhrkamp, 1968), p. 114.

17. Gray, "A Living World," p. 108.

18. Georg Lukács, *The Meaning of Contemporary Realism* (London: Merlin Press, 1963), p. 96.

19. Fredric Jameson, *The Political Unconscious: Narrative as a Socially Symbolic Act* (Ithaca: Cornell University Press, 1981).

20. William C. Dowling, *Jameson, Althusser, Marx: An Introduction to the Political Unconscious* (Ithaca: Cornell University Press, 1984), pp. 48–49.

21. See the minutes of the Wannsee Conference held in Berlin on 20 January 1942: "Under suitable management, related to the final solution, the Jews will be put to work in an appropriate manner in the eastern territories. In huge work columns, separated by sex, the work-able Jews will be led into these areas while building roads; through this a large part will, without doubt, fall out due to natural depreciation . . . " (Quoted in Gerhard Schoenberner, *The Yellow Star* [New York: Bantam Books, 1973], p. 133).

22. Hayden White, "The Historical Text as Literary Artifact," in *The Writing of History*, ed. Robert Canary and Henry Kozicki (Madison: University of Wisconsin Press, 1978), p. 42.

23. Hayden White, "Historicism, History, and the Figurative Imagination," *History and Theory* 14 (1975): 53.

5. NAMES OF THE HOLOCAUST

1. Edward Alexander, "Stealing the Holocaust," *Midstream* (November 1980), p. 49.

2. In Bill Henderson, ed., *The Pushcart Prize: Best of the Small Presses* (Yonkers, N.Y.: Pushcart Book Press, 1973), p. 127.

3. See Richard G. Hovinnisian, *The Armenian Holocaust: A Bibliography Relating to the Deportations, Massacres, and Dispersion of the Armenian People, 1915–23* (Cambridge, Mass.: Armenian Heritage Press, 1978). In this context, it is also worth noting that Abram L. Sachar, as Chancellor of Brandeis University, was invited to write the foreword to this volume.

4. Franz Werfel, *The Forty Days of Musa Dagh* (New York: Viking Press, 1934).

5. For further historical discussion of similarities and the language in which they are both reflected and created, see Yehuda Bauer, "The Place of the Holocaust in Contemporary History," in Jonathan Frankel, ed., *Studies in Contemporary Jewry*, vol. 1 (Bloomington: Indiana University Press, 1984), pp. 215–17.

6. *Tesha B'Av* (the Ninth of Av) is according to Mishnah (Ta'anit 4:6) the commemoration of the punishment of the Israelites in the wilderness, the destructions of the First and Second temples, and the fall of Betar (see Shaye J. D. Cohen, "The Destruction: From Scripture to Midrash," *Prooftexts* 2, no. 1 (January 1982): 20. And now it must be added that even though a separate day (*Yom Hasho'ah*) is set aside in Israel to mark the Holocaust, in more orthodox quarters Tesha B'Av

also recalls the European destruction, thus grouping these destructions collectively and locating them in a single continuum.

7. For an excellent "Excursus on Hermeneutical Aspects of the Term *Sho'ah*," see Uriel Tal, "Holocaust and Genocide," *Yad Vashem Studies* XIII (1979): 46–52. Also see "Excursus on the Term: *Shoah*," *Shoah* 1, no. 4 (1979).

8. Gerd Korman, "The Holocaust in American Historical Writing," *Societas* 2 (Summer 1972): 250–70. Also see Leon A. Jick, "The Holocaust: Its Use and Abuse within the American Public," *Yad Vashem Studies* 14 (1981): 303–18.

For the record, the earliest use of the term "holocaust" in this context that I know comes in a footnote to Dr. A. A. Brill's 1938 introduction to his collected edition of Sigmund Freud's works, to which Dr. Brill has added: "Alas! As these pages are going to the printer we have been startled by the terrible news that the Nazi holocaust has suddenly encircled Vienna and that Professor Freud and his family are virtual prisoners in the hands of civilization's greatest scourge" (Dr. A. A. Brill, ed. and trans., *The Basic Writings of Sigmund Freud* [New York: The Modern Library, 1938], p. 32n).

9. For more in this vein, see Jakob J. Petuchowski, "Dissenting Thoughts About the 'Holocaust,'" *Journal of Reform Judaism* (Fall 1981): 1–9.

10. Yehuda Bauer, *The Holocaust in Historical Perspective* (Seattle: University of Washington Press, 1978), p. 31.

11. For further discussion of the epistemological problems of the Holocaust's uniqueness, see among others Yehuda Bauer, "The Place of the Holocaust in Contemporary History" (cited above) and "Whose Holocaust?" *Midstream* (November 1980), pp. 42–46; Henry L. Feingold, "Determining the Uniqueness of the Holocaust: The Factor of Historical Valence," *Shoah* 2, no. 2 (Spring 1981): 3–11; and Steven T. Katz, "The 'Unique' Intentionality of the Holocaust," in *Post-Holocaust Dialogues: Critical Studies in Modern Jewish Thought* (New York: New York University Press, 1983), pp. 287–317.

12. Alvin H. Rosenfeld, *A Double Dying*, p. 180.

13. Alvin H. Rosenfeld, "On Holocaust and History," *Shoah* 1, no. 1 (1978).

14. In *The Dehumanization of Art and Other Essays on Art, Culture, and Literature* (Princeton: Princeton University Press, 1968), José Ortega y Gasset suggests that where the one "predominant [aim] in poetry had been to exact the real object . . . , to embellish and to throw into relief beloved reality," the opposite might now be true for modern poetry. "[I]nstead of ennobling and enhancing [reality, metaphor] now belittles and disparages poor reality" (pp. 35–36). That is, metaphor no longer celebrates reality but now diminishes it. If this presupposes a certain loathing—or, more gently, a distaste—for contemporary realities, Ortega y Gasset would probably not argue. Instead, he merely observes that "the metaphor alone furnishes an escape," and then adds thoughtfully, "A strange thing, indeed, the existence in man of this mental activity which substitutes one thing for another—from an urge not so much to get at the first as to get rid of the second. The metaphor disposes of an object by having it masquerade as something else. Such a procedure would make no sense if we did not discern beneath it an instinctive avoidance of certain realities" (p. 33).

15. Karsten Harries, "Metaphor and Transcendence," in *On Metaphor*, ed. Sheldon Sachs (Chicago and London: University of Chicago Press, 1978), p. 78.

16. Paul Ricoeur, *The Rule of Metaphor* (Toronto: University of Toronto Press, 1978), p. 198.

17. Raul Hilberg, *The Destruction of European Jewry* (Chicago: Quadrangle Books, 1965), p. 17.

18. See Vladimir Jabotinsky, *The Jewish War Front* (London, 1940), pp. 9, 15, 19, 22 for specific comparisons of the Jewish situtation with that of the Armenians during World War I.

19. This was the term Jacob Lestschinsky used in 1941 to describe events that now stretched to breaking the capacity of traditional terms (cited by Gerd Korman, "The Holocaust in American Historical Writing").

20. Robert Alter, "Deformations of the Holocaust," *Commentary* (February 1981), p. 52.
See section II of chapter 8 for a discussion of this particular analogy in Israel.

21. David Roskies, *Against the Apocalypse: Responses to Catastrophe in Modern Jewish Culture* (Cambridge, Mass., and London: Harvard University Press, 1984), pp. 13–14.

22. In addition to Roskies's early chapters in *Against the Apocalypse*, see Alan Mintz's excellent discussions of the troping process in Lamentations in "The Rhetoric of Lamentations and the Representation of Catastrophe," *Prooftexts: A Journal of Jewish Literary History* 2, no. 1 (January 1982): 1–17, and his elaboration of this article in *Ḥurban: Responses to Catastrophe in Hebrew Literature* (New York: Columbia University Press, 1984), pp. 17–48.

23. Michael Fishbane, "Revelation and Tradition: Aspects of Inner-Biblical Exegesis," *Journal of Biblical Literature* 99, no. 3 (1980): 343–61.

24. In *Versions of Survival: The Holocaust and the Human Spirit* (Albany: State University of New York Press, 1982), Lawrence Langer essentially accuses Viktor Frankl, Bruno Bettelheim, and Terrence Des Pres of dressing the Holocaust in their respective Judeo-Christian moral systems *in order* to mediate—and thereby vitiate—some of the horror. I discuss this problem at more length in "Versions of the Holocaust," *Modern Judaism* 3, no. 3 (October 1983): 339–46.

6. THE HOLOCAUST BECOMES AN ARCHETYPE

1. Yitzhak Katzenelson, *The Song of the Murdered Jewish People*, translated and annotated by Noah H. Rosenbloom (Beit Lohamei Hagettaot, Israel: Hakibbutz Hameuchad Publishing House, 1980), p. 19.

2. Sidra Ezrahi, *By Words Alone: The Holocaust in Literature* (Chicago and London: University of Chicago Press, 1980), p. 55.

3. Tadeusz Borowski, *This Way for the Gas, Ladies and Gentlemen* (New York: Penguin Books, 1976), pps. 105, 152, 153.

4. Elie Wiesel, *Messengers of God: Biblical Portraits and Legends* (New York: Random House, 1976).

5. Jean Améry, *At the Mind's Limits: Contemplations by a Survivor on Auschwitz and Its Realities*, trans. Sidney Rosenfeld and Stella P. Rosenfeld (Bloomington: Indiana University Press, 1980), pp. 94–95.

6. Philip Roth, *The Ghost Writer* (New York: Farrar, Straus and Giroux, 1979), pp. 103–104.

7. Sander Gilman, *Jewish Self-Hatred: Anti-Semitism and the Hidden Language of the Jews* (Baltimore and London: Johns Hopkins University Press, 1986), p. 357.

8. Philip Roth, *Zuckerman Bound: A Trilogy and Epilogue* (New York: Farrar, Straus and Giroux, 1985), p. 759.

9. John Berryman, "The Development of Anne Frank," in *The Freedom of the Poet* (New York: Farrar, Straus and Giroux, 1976), pp. 92, 93.

10. See "Author's Notes" at the end of Berryman's novel, *Recovery* (New York: Farrar, Straus and Giroux, 1973), p. 241.

11. James D. Bloom, *The Stock of Available Reality: R. P. Blackmur and John Berryman* (Lewisburg: Bucknell University Press, 1984), p. 183. Also see references to Berryman's Jewish identification in John Haffenden, *The Life of John Berryman* (London: Routledge & Kegan Paul, 1982), pp. 236, 382.

12. "The Imaginary Jew" first appeared in *The Kenyon Review* VII, no. 4 (Autumn 1945): 529–39. It won first prize in the journal's story contest that year and was later reprinted in both *The Freedom of the Poet* and in *Recovery*. Quotations here are from *The Freedom of the Poet*, p. 359.

7. THE HOLOCAUST CONFESSIONS OF SYLVIA PLATH

1. Collections of "Holocaust poetry" by nonvictims include William Heyen, *Erika: Poems of the Holocaust* (including *The Swastika Poems*) (New York: The Vanguard Press, Inc., 1984); Charles Reznikoff, *Holocaust* (Santa Barbara: Black Sparrow Press, 1977); Irving Feldman, *The Pripet Marshes and Other Poems* (New York: The Viking Press, 1965); and Barbara Helfgott Hyett, *In Evidence: Poems of the Liberation of Nazi Concentration Camps* (Pittsburgh: University of Pittsburgh Press, 1986).

In light of earlier sections, it is also worth noting here that of these works, those by Reznikoff and Hyett are explicitly based on others' eyewitness testimony, which the authors have converted to verse.

2. Alvin H. Rosenfeld, *A Double Dying: Reflections on Holocaust Literature* (Bloomington and London: Indiana University Press), p. 181.

3. Edward Butscher, *Sylvia Plath: Method and Madness* (New York: The Seabury Press, 1976), p. 327.

4. From *Sylvia Plath's Letters Home* (New York: Harper and Row, 1975), quoted in Dannie Abse, "The Dread of Sylvia Plath," *Poesis* 7, no. 1 (1986): 19 (emphasis added).

5. Sylvia Plath, *The Bell Jar* (New York: Bantam Books, 1971), p. 1.

6. From the "Tarot Card," quoted in Butscher, *Sylvia Plath: Method and Madness*, p. 113.

7. A. Alvarez, *The Savage God: A Study of Suicide* (New York: Random House, 1970), p. 17.

8. Arthur Oberg, *Modern American Lyric: Lowell, Berryman, Creely, and Plath* (New Brunswick: Rutgers University Press, 1978), p. 146.

9. Sylvia Plath, "Mary's Song," copyright ©1963 by Ted Hughes. From *The Collected Poems of Sylvia Plath*, edited by Ted Hughes. Reprinted by permission of Harper & Row, Publishers, Inc., and Faber and Faber, London.

10. From the introductory notes to "New Poems," a reading prepared for the BBC Third Program but never broadcast. Quoted in Charles Newman, *The Art of Sylvia Plath: A Symposium* (London: Faber and Faber, 1970), p. 65. Sylvia Plath, "Daddy," copyright © 1963 by Ted Hughes. From *The Collected Poems of Sylvia Plath*, edited by Ted Hughes. Reprinted by permission of Harper & Row, Publishers, Inc., and Faber and Faber, London.

11. *The Bell Jar*, p. 128.

12. In *Sylvia Plath: Method and Madness*, Edward Butscher reports that on meeting poet George Macbeth, Plath remarked, "I see you have a concentration camp in your mind too" (p. 335).

13. A. Alvarez, "Literature of the Holocaust," *Commentary* (November 1964), p. 64.

14. Alvarez, *The Savage God*, p. 38.

15. Dori Laub, "Holocaust Themes: Their Expression in Poetry and in the Psychological Conflicts of Patients in Psychotherapy," in *The Nazi Concentration Camps: Structure and Aims; The Image of the Prisioner; The Jews in the Camps*, Proceedings of the Fourth Yad Vashem International Historical Conference—January 1980, (Jerusalem: Yad Vashem, 1984), p. 576.

16. Hayden White, *Metahistory: The Historical Imagination in Nineteenth Century Europe* (Baltimore and London: Johns Hopkins University Press, 1973), p. 35.

17. E. D. Hirsch, Jr., *The Aims of Interpretation* (Chicago and London: University of Chicago Press, 1976), p. 105.

18. Rosenfeld, *A Double Dying*, p. 99.

19. From Olof Lagercrantz, *Versuch über die Lyrik der Nelly Sachs* (Frankfurt: Suhrkamp Verlag, 1967), p. 48–49. Quoted in Hamida Bosmajian, *Metaphors of Evil: Contemporary German Literature and the Shadow of Nazism* (Iowa City: University of Iowa Press, 1979), p. 197.

20. Edmond Jabès, *The Book of Questions* (Middletown: Wesleyan University Press, 1976), p. 163.

21. Uri Zvi Greenberg, "We Were Not Likened to Dogs among the Gentiles," in Ruth Finer Mintz, ed., *Modern Hebrew Poetry* (Berkeley and Los Angeles: University of California Press, 1966), pp. 124–26.

22. Irving Howe, "The Plath Celebration: A Partial Dissent," in Edward Butscher, ed., *Sylvia Plath: The Woman and the Work* (New York: Dodd, Mead & Company, 1977), p. 235.

23. George Steiner, "In Extremis," in *The Cambridge Mind* (Cambridge: Cambridge University Press, 1976), p. 305.

24. See Edward Alexander, "Stealing the Holocaust," *Midstream* (November 1980), pp. 46–50.

25. Robert Alter, *Defenses of the Imagination: Jewish Writers and Modern Historical Crisis* (Philadelphia: Jewish Publication Society, 1977), p. 8.

26. Ted Cohen, "Metaphor and the Cultivation of Intimacy," in Sheldon Sachs, ed., *On Metaphor* (Chicago and London: The University of Chicago Press, 1978), p. 6.

8. WHEN SOLDIER-POETS REMEMBER THE HOLOCAUST

1. Testimony of Edith P. (T-107), Video Archives for Holocaust Testimony at Yale University.

2. *The Seventh Day: Soldiers Talk About the Six-Day War*, recorded and edited by a group of young Kibbutz members (Middlesex: Penguin Books, 1971), p. 38.

3. Amos Oz, "Hitler kvar met, adoni rosh ha-memshalah" (Hitler is Already Dead, Mr. Prime Minister), reprinted in *Chatziat Gevul: Shirim Mimilhemet Levanon* (Border Crossing: Poems from the Lebanon War) (Tel Aviv: Sifriat Poalim, 1983), p. 71, in Hebrew. This translation as well as others from the Hebrew are mine unless noted otherwise. Also see Yehuda Bauer, "Fruits of Fear," *Jerusalem Post*, 3 June 1982, p. 8; and Ze'ev Mankowitz, "Beirut is not Berlin," *Jerusalem Post*, 4 August 1982, p. 8.

4. *Ve'eyn tikhlah lakeravot velahereg: Shirah politit bemilhemet Levanon* (Fighting and Killing without End: Political Poetry in the Lebanon War), edited with an Afterword by Hannan Hever and Moshe Ron (Tel Aviv: Hakibbutz Hame'uchad, 1984).

5. For further illustration of this perceived tremendum created in the suffering of children during the Holocaust, see David Roskies, *Against the Apocalypse: Responses to Catastrophe in Modern Jewish Culture* (Cambridge, Mass., and London: Harvard University Press, 1984), p. 221.

6. From the program notes of *Ha-patriot* (The Patriot), as quoted and translated by Sidra Ezrahi, "Revisioning the Past: The Changing Legacy of the Holocaust in Hebrew Literature," *Salmagundi* (Fall 1985–Winter 1986): 268. I am indebted to Ezrahi for leading me to this play in Israel in 1983. For further insight into this

play and related poems, see, in addition to Ezrahi's essay, Hannan Hever, "Hebrew Poetry under Occupation," *Tikkun* 2 (1987): 84–87, 122–26.

9. HOLOCAUST VIDEO AND CINEMAGRAPHIC TESTIMONY

1. Lawrence Langer, "Preliminary Reflections on the Videotaped Interviews at the Yale Archive for Holocaust Testimonies," *Facing History and Ourselves News* (Winter 1985): 4–5. Also see his extended argument against a unified literary vision in *Versions of Survival: The Holocaust and the Human Spirit* (Albany: State University of New York Press, 1982).

2. In Bill Nichols, *Ideology and the Image: Social Representation in the Cinema and Other Media* (Bloomington: Indiana University Press, 1981), p. 218. For a particularly rich critique of the formal aspects of film and documentary, see pp. 43–103.

3. We might recall here after Hayden White and others that this sense of creating knowledge in narrative is intrinsic to the verb "to narrate" itself, which derives from the Latin *gnarus* (knowing), which in turn derives from the Sanskrit root *gna* (know). See Hayden White, "The Value of Narrativity in the Representation of the Real," *Critical Inquiry* (Autumn 1980): 5n.

4. Annette Insdorf, *Indelible Shadows: Film and the Holocaust* (New York: Vintage Books, 1983), p. 77.

5. Langer, "Preliminary Reflections on the Videotaped Interviews," p. 4.

6. Lawrence Langer, "Holocaust Testimonies and Their Audience," *Orim: A Jewish Journal at Yale* 1, no. 1 (Spring 1986): 97.

7. Testimony of Edith P. (T-107), Video Archive for Holocaust Testimonies at Yale.

8. Langer, "Preliminary Reflections on the Videotaped Interviews," p. 4.

9. Claude Lanzmann, *Shoah: An Oral History of the Holocaust* (New York: Pantheon Books, 1985), p. 88.

10. Geoffrey Hartman, from *Video Archive for Holocaust Testimonies at Yale Newsletter*, Spring–Summer 1985, p. 1.

11. Geoffrey Hartman, "Preserving the Personal Story: The Role of Video Documentation," *Dimensions: A Journal of Holocaust Studies* 1, no. 1 (Spring 1985): 15.

12. Hartman, "Preserving the Personal Story," p. 17.

13. Testimony of Leon S. (T-45), Video Archive for Holocaust Testimonies at Yale.

14. Testimony of Father John S. (T-216), Video Archive for Holocaust Testimonies at Yale.

15. In Timothy Garton Ash, "The Life of Death," *The New York Review of Books*, 19 December 1985, p. 30.

16. Susan Sontag, *On Photography* (New York: Delta Books, 1973), p. 15.

17. Nora Levin, "Some Reservations about Lanzmann's *Shoah*," *Sh'ma: A Journal of Jewish Responsibility*, 18 April 1986, p. 92.

18. Lanzmann, *Shoah*, p. 116.

19. Langer, "Preliminary Reflections on the Videotaped Interviews," p. 5.

20. Hartman, "Preserving the Personal Story," p. 14.

21. Langer, "Holocaust Testimonies and Their Audience," p. 96.

22. Hartman, "Preserving the Personal Story," p. 17.

10. THE TEXTURE OF MEMORY

1. Other than my own essay from which this chapter is adapted, "Memory and Monument" (in Geoffrey Hartman, ed., *Bitburg in Moral and Political Perspective* [Bloomington: Indiana University Press, 1986]), and a full-length study by the author now underway, critical work on Holocaust monuments in English has been limited to an extensive cataloguing and aesthetic evaluation of these monuments by Sybil Milton, *In Fitting Memory? Holocaust Memorials and Postwar Political Culture* (research in progress), and the following works: Adolf Rieth, *Monuments to the Victims of Tyranny* (New York and London: Frederick A. Praeger, 1968); Harold Marcuse, Frank Schimmelfennig, and Jochen Spielmann, *Steine des Anstosses: Nationalsozialismus und Zweiter Weltkrieg in Denkmalen, 1945–85* (Hamburg: Museum für Hamburgische Geschichte, 1985); Erich Fein, *Die Steine Reden, Gedenkstätten des österreichischen Freiheitskampfes: Mahnmale für die Opfer des Faschismus, Eine Dokumentation* (Vienna: Europe Verlag, 1975); Detlev Garbe, ed., *Die vergessenen KZs? Gedenkstätten für die Opfer des NS-Terrors in der Bundesrepublik* (Bornheim-Merten: Lamuv, 1983); Bernd Eichmann, *Versteinert Verharmlost Vergessen: KZ-Gedenkstätten in der Bundesrepublik Deutschland* (Frankfurt am Main: Fischer Taschenbuch Verlag, 1985); and Herbert Holte, "Vergangenheitsbewältigung und Ausländerfeindlichkeit: Eine Befragung von Jugendlichen im Dokumentenhaus KZ Neuengamme," in *Argument zur museums-pädagogischen Praxis* (Hamburg: Museums-pädagogischer Dienst, 1984).

Related articles include: Michael Berenbaum, "On the Politics of Public Commemoration of the Holocaust," *Shoah* (Fall/Winter 1982): 6–37; Stephen Brockmann, "Bitburg Deconstruction," *The Philosophical Forum* XVII, no. 3 (Spring 1986): 159–75; Yosef Lishinsky, "Yad Vashem as Art," *Ariel: A Review of Arts and Letters in Israel*, no. 55 (1983): 7–25; Annette Wieviorka, "Un lieu de mémoire Le Mémorial du martyr juif inconnu," *Pardes* 2 (1985): 80–98, translated in *Dimensions*, Summer 1987; James D. Wilkinson, "Remembering World War II: The Perspective of the Losers," *The American Scholar* (Summer 1985): 329–43; Efraim Zurof, "Yad Vashem: More Than a Memorial, More Than a Name," *Shoah* 1, no. 3 (Winter 1979): 4–9.

2. Henry Moore, "On Sculpture & Primitive Art," in Robert L. Herbert, ed., *Modern Artists On Art: Ten Unabridged Essays* (Englewood Cliffs, N.J.: Prentice-Hall, Inc., 1964), p. 140.

3. According to Yehuda Bauer, the actual number of Jews killed at Babi Yar between September 29 and October 1, 1941, was probably 33,000 (*History of the Holocaust* [New York, London, Toronto, Sidney: Franklin Watts, 1982], pp. 198–99). The larger figure cited on the plaque at the memorial here refers to all Kiev citizens killed by the Germans between 1941 and 1943.

4. Janusz Wieczorek, Chairman of the Council for the Preservation of Monuments to Struggle and Martyrdom, Address delivered at the opening ceremony of the Jewish Pavilion at the former concentration camp of Oświęcim-Brzezinka, April 17, 1978 (published by the State Museum at Oświęcim).

5. Quoted in Stanislaw Duzak, ed., *Majdanek* [official guidebook of the State Museum] (Lublin: Krajowa Agencja Wydawnicza, 1985).

6. Even the statistics themselves encourage this kind of exchange in Poland. Of six million Jews who died in the Holocaust, three million were Poles; of the six million Poles who died in World War Two, three million were Jews. If three million Poles and three million Polish Jews died in the Holocaust, then the total number of Poles (including Jews) who died is the same as the total number of Jews who died in the Holocaust: six million. For many Poles, this Jewish figure thus emblematizes both Jewish and Polish destruction.

7. In a further twist, it is worth noting that the granite blocks supporting the Warsaw ghetto memorial were originally cut in Sweden by Hitler's own state sculptor, Arno Breker, for a projected monument to the Germans' victory over Polish Jewry.

8. For further discussion of the archetypal sources for these figures, see David Roskies, *Against the Apocalypse: Responses to Catastrophe in Modern Jewish Culture* (Cambridge, Mass., and London: Harvard University Press, 1984), pp. 297–301.

9. For further insight into the commissioning and building of this monument, see the sculptor's own description of the process in Richard Yaffe, *Nathan Rapoport Sculptures and Monuments* (New York: Shengold Publishers, Inc., 1980).

10. For complete accounts of this incident and surrounding controversies, see Günther Schwarberg, *Angriffsziel Cap Arcona* (Hamburg: Stern-Buch im Verlag Gruner, 1983), and Rudi Goguel, *Cap Arcona: Report über den Untergang der Häftlingsflotte in der Lübecker Bucht am 3. Mai 1945* (Frankfurt/Main: Röderberg-Verlag GmbH, 1982).

11. Theodor W. Adorno, "Valery Proust Museum," in *Prisms*, trans. Samuel and Shierry Weber (Cambridge, Mass.: The MIT Press, 1981), p. 175.

12. From "Martyrs' and Heroes' Remembrance (Yad Vashem) Law, 5713–1953," reprinted fully in *Yad Vashem: The Holocaust Martyrs' and Heroes' Remembrance Authority, Jerusalem* (Jerusalem: Yad Vashem Publications, 1986), p. 4. This law is also translated and reprinted in *State of Israel Yearbook* (Jerusalem: Government Printing Press, 1954), pp. 250–51. Parts of this law's articles are reprinted and discussed as well in Benzion Dinur, "Problems confronting 'Yad Vashem' in its Work of Research," *Yad Vashem Studies on the European Jewish Catastrophe and Resistance* 1 (1957): 7–30.

13. For a more complete discussion of Hitler's plans for a "Central Jewish Museum" in Prague, see Linda A. Altshuler and Anna R. Cohn, "The Precious Legacy," in *The Precious Legacy: Judaic Treasures from the Czechoslovak State Collections*, ed. David Altshuler (New York: Summit Books, 1983), pp. 24–38.

CONCLUSION

1. Jacques Derrida, "White Mythology: Metaphor in the Text of Philosophy," *New Literary History* 6 (1974): 11.

2. Friedrich Nietzsche, *Beyond Good and Evil* (New York: Random House, 1966), p. 4.

3. Mark Warren, "Nietzsche and the Concept of Ideology," *Theory and Society* 13, no. 4 (July 1984): 549.

4. Yosef Hayim Yerushalmi, *Zakhor: Jewish History and Jewish Memory* (Seattle and London: University of Washington Press, 1982), pp. 99–100.

Bibliography

The following list comprises primary and secondary sources cited in this study as well as works not explicitly mentioned but that have informed the author's writing nonetheless. The result is an extended bibliography of Holocaust narrative and its critical literature. It is not exhaustive so much as it is comprehensive of the author's approach to and treatment of Holocaust narrative. Given the author's own critical method, the divisions between kinds of narrative (diaries, memoirs, fiction, poetry, drama, and critical literature) are made advisedly here. As such, the following categories are not intended to resolve questions of generic classification but are meant only to assist further research in each of these general areas:

    I. Diaries, Chronicles, and Accounts
       from Ghettos and Camps
   II. Memoirs, Biographies, and Remembrances
  III. Fiction and Imaginative Literature
  IV. Drama
   V. Poetry
  VI. Critical Literature, Anthologies,
      and Bibliographies

I. DIARIES, CHRONICLES, AND ACCOUNTS FROM GHETTOS AND CAMPS

Auerbach, Rokhl. *Varshever tsavoes* (Warsaw Testaments: Encounters, Activities, Fates, 1933–1943). Tel Aviv: Yisroel-bukh, 1974.

Berg, Mary. *Warsaw Ghetto: A Diary.* Trans. Norbert and Sylvia Glass. New York: L. B. Fisher, 1945.

Bezwinska, Jadwiga, ed. *Amidst a Nightmare of Crime: Manuscripts of Members of Sonderkommando.* Trans. Krystyna Michalik. Krakow: State Museum of Oświęcim, 1973.

Czerniakow, Adam. *The Warsaw Diary of Adam Czerniakow: Prelude to Doom.* Ed. Raul Hilberg, Stanislaw Staron, Josef Kermisz, trans. Stanislaw Staron et al. New York: Stein & Day, 1979.

Dobroszycki, Lucjan, ed. *The Chronicle of the Lodz Ghetto.* Trans. Richard Lourie et al. New Haven and London: Yale University Press, 1984.

Epstein, Lazar. "Diary of Dr. Lazar Epstein. MS. 36, Yad Vashem Archives, Jerusalem (in Yiddish).

Flinker, Moshe. *Young Moshe's Diary: The Spiritual Torment of a Jewish Boy in Nazi Europe.* Jerusalem: Yad Vashem, 1971.

Frank, Anne. *The Diary of a Young Girl.* Trans. B. M. Mooyaart-Doubleday. Garden City, N.Y.: Doubleday & Co., 1952.

Gleykh, Sarra. "The Diary of Sarra Gleykh (Mariupol)." Prepared by Ilya Ehrenburg in *The Black Book: Documents of the Nazis' destruction of 1.5 million Soviet Jews.* Ed. Ilya Ehrenburg and Vasily Grossman. New York: Holocaust Library, 1980, pp. 70–76.

Heyman, Éva. *The Diary of Éva Heyman.* Trans. Moshe M. Kohn. Jerusalem: Yad Vashem, 1974.

Hillesum, Etty. *Etty Hillesum: Letters from Westerbork.* Ed. Jan G. Gaarlandt, trans. Arnold J. Pomerans. New York: Pantheon Books, 1986.

————. *An Interrupted Life: The Diaries of Etty Hillesum, 1941–43.* Ed. and trans. J. G. Gaarlandt. New York: Pantheon Books, 1984.

Huberband, Shimon. *Kiddush Hashem: ktavim miymey hasho'ah* (Kiddush Hashem: Writings from the Holocaust). Ed. Nachman Blumental and Joseph Kermish. Tel Aviv: Zakhor, 1969.

Kalmanovitsh, Zelig. "A Diary of the Nazi Ghetto in Vilna." *YIVO Annual* 8 (1953): 9–81.

————. *Yoman begeto Vilna ukhtavim miha'izavon shenimtsa baharisot* (A Diary of the Vilna Ghetto and Posthumous Writings Discovered in the Ruins). Ed. Shalom Luria. Israel: Moreshet and Sifriat Poalim, 1977.

Kaplan, Chaim A. *Megilat yishurin: yoman geto Varshah* (Scroll of Agony: A Diary of the Warsaw Ghetto). Ed. Abraham I. Katsh. Tel Aviv and Jerusalem: Am Oved and Yad Vashem, 1966.

————. *The Warsaw Diary of Chaim A. Kaplan.* Ed. and trans. Abraham I. Katsh. New York: Collier Books, 1973.

Katzenelson, Yitzhak. *Ktavim aharonim* (Posthumous Writings, 1940–1943). Ed. Yitzhak Zuckerman and Shlomo Even-Shoshan. Israel: Hakibbutz Hameuchad, 1956.

————. *Vittel Diary.* Trans. Myer Cohen. Israel: Beit Lohamei Hagettaot and Hakibbutz Hameuchad Publishing House, 1972.

————. *Yidishe geto ksovim fun Varshe, 1940–1943* (Yiddish Ghetto Writings from Warsaw, 1940–1943). Ed. Yechiel Szeintuch. Israel: Beit Lohamei Hagettaot and Hakibbutz Hameuchad Publishing House, 1984.

Kermish, Joseph, Ed. *To Live with Honor and Die with Honor: Selected Documents from the Underground Archives "O.S." ["Oneg Shabbat"].* Jerusalem: Yad Vashem, 1986.

Komoly, Otto. "Budapest Jewry in the Summer of 1944: Otto Komoly's Diaries." Ed. Bela Vago. *Yad Vashem Studies* 8 (1970): 81–105.

Korczak, Janusz. *The Ghetto Years.* Trans. Jerzy Bachrach and Barbara Krzywicka. Israel: Beit Lohamei Hagettaot and Hakibbutz Hameuchad Publishing House, 1980.

Kruk, Herman. "Diary of the Vilna Ghetto." *YIVO Annual* 13 (1958): 9–78.

————. *Togbukh fun vilner geto* (Diary of the Vilna Ghetto). Ed. Mordecai W. Bernstein. New York: YIVO, 1961.

Levin, Abraham. "Extract from the Diary of Abraham Levin." *Yad Vashem Studies* 6 (1967): 315–30.

————. *Mipinkaso shel hamoreh miyehudia* (From the Notebook of the Teacher from Yehudia: Warsaw Ghetto, April 1942–January 1943). Ed. Zvi Szner. Israel: Beit Lohamei Hagettaot and Hakibbutz Hameuchad Publishing House, 1969.

Levy-Hass, Hannah. *Inside Belsen.* Trans. Ronald Taylor. New Jersey: Barnes & Noble Books, 1982.

Lissner, Abraham. "Diary of a Jewish Partisan in Paris." In Yuri Suhl, ed. *They Fought Back: The Story of the Jewish Resistance in Nazi Europe*, pp. 282–97. New York: Schocken Books, 1975.

Marcuse, Gunther. "The Diary of Gunther Marcuse—the Last Days of the Gross-Breesen Training Center." Ed. Joseph Walk. *Yad Vashem Studies* 8 (1970): 159–81.

Mark, Ber, ed. *Tsvishn lebn un toyt* (Between Life and Death). Warsaw: Yidish-bukh, 1955.

Mechanicus, Philip. *Waiting for Death: A Diary.* Trans. Irene R. Gibbons. London: Calder and Boyars, 1968.

Opoczynski, Peretz. *Reshimot* (Sketches from the Warsaw Ghetto). Trans. Avraham Yeivin, ed. Zvi Szner. Israel: Hakibbutz Hameuchad, 1970.

Ringelblum, Emmanuel. "Emmanuel Ringelblum's Notes hitherto Unpublished." Ed. Joseph Kermish. *Yad Vashem Studies* 7 (1968): 173–83.

———. *Ksovim fun geto* (Notes from the Warsaw Ghetto). Vol. 2: Notes and Treatises (1942–1943). Ed. A. Eisenbach et al. Warsaw: Jewish Historical Institute, 1963.
———. *Notes from the Warsaw Ghetto.* Trans. Jacob Sloan. New York: McGraw-Hill, 1958.
Rubinowicz, David. *The Diary of David Rubinowicz.* Trans. Derek Bowman. Edmonds, Wash.: Creative Options, 1982.
Rudashevski, Yitshok. *The Diary of the Vilna Ghetto, June 1941-April 1943.* Trans. Percy Matenko. Israel: Beit Lohamei Hagettaot and Hakibbutz Hameuchad Publishing House, 1973.
Senesh, Hannah. *Hannah Senesh: Her Life and Diary.* Trans. Marta Cohn. New York: Schocken Books, 1973.
Sheinkinder, S. "The Diary of S. Sheinkinder" (Extracts). *Yad Vashem Studies* V (1963): 255–69.
Sutzkever, Abraham. *Fun vilner geto* (From the Vilna Ghetto). Moscow: Emes, 1946.
Wasser, Hersh. "Daily Entries of Hersh Wasser." Ed. Joseph Kermish. *Yad Vashem Studies* 15 (1983): 201–82.
Wells, Leon Weliczker. "The Death Brigade." In *The Death Brigade (The Janowska Road),* pp. 133–224. New York: Holocaust Library, 1978.
Yerushalmi, Eliezer. *Pinkas Shavli—A Diary from a Lithuanian Ghetto (1941–44).* Jerusalem: Yad Vashem Publications, n.d.
Zuckerman, Yitzhak. "From the Warsaw Ghetto." *Commentary,* December 1975, pp. 62–69.
Zweig, Arnold, ed. *Tagebücher aus dem Ghetto* (Diaries of Leon Weliczker, Gusta Dawidsohn-Draengerowa, and Janina Hescheles). Leipzig: Verlag Philipp Reclam, 1959.

II. MEMOIRS, BIOGRAPHIES, AND REMEMBRANCES

Adler, Stanislaw. *In the Warsaw Ghetto, 1940–1943: An Account of a Witness.* Trans. Sara Philip. Jerusalem: Yad Vashem, 1982.
Améry, Jean. *At the Mind's Limits: Contemplations by a Survivor on Auschwitz and Its Realities.* Trans. Sidney Rosenfeld and Stella P. Rosenfeld. Bloomington: Indiana University Press, 1980.
———. *Radical Humanism: Selected Essays.* Ed. and trans. Sidney Rosenfeld and Stella P. Rosenfeld. Bloomington: Indiana University Press, 1984.
Anger, Per. *With Raoul Wallenberg in Budapest.* Trans. David Mel Paul and Margarita Paul. New York: Holocaust Library, 1981.
Anger, Per, and Margoliot, Abraham, eds. *Documents on the Holocaust.* Jerusalem and New York: Yad Vashem and Ktav, 1982.
Arad, Yitzhak. *The Partisan: From the Valley of Death to Mount Zion.* New York: Holocaust Library, 1979.
Baker, Leonard. *Days of Sorrow and Pain: Leo Baeck and the Berlin Jews.* New York: Macmillan, 1978.
Barkai, Meyer. *The Fighting Ghettos.* Philadelphia: J. B. Lippincott Co., 1962.
Bartoszewski, Wladislaw. *The Bloodshed Unites Us.* Warsaw: Interpress, 1970.
Bartoszewski, Wladislaw, and Lewin, Zofia, eds. *The Samaritans.* New York: Twayne, 1970.
Berkowitz, Sarah. *Where Are My Brothers?* New York: Helios Books, 1965.
Bettelheim, Bruno. *The Informed Heart.* Glencoe, Ill.: Free Press, 1960.
Bezwińska, Jadwiga, ed. *KL Auschwitz Seen by the S.S.: Höss, Broad, Kremer.* Trans. Constantine Fitzgibbon and Krystyna Michalik. Oświęcim: Publications of Państwowe Muzeum, 1972.
Bierman, John. *Righteous Gentile.* New York: Viking Press, 1981.

Birnbaum, Halina. *Hope is the Last to Die*. Trans. David Welsh. New York: Twayne, 1971.
Bitton, Livia E. Jackson. *Elli: Coming of Age in the Holocaust*. New York: Times Books, 1980.
Boehm, Eric H., ed. *We Survived*. New Haven: Yale University Press, 1949.
Borzykowski, Tuvia. *Between Tumbling Walls*. Israel: Beit Lohamei Hagettaot, 1972.
Brand, Joel. *Desperate Mission*. New York: Criterion Books, 1958.
Brand, Sandra. *Between Two Worlds*. New York: Shengold Publishers, Inc., 1983.
―――. *I Dared to Live*. New York: Shengold Publishers, Inc., 1978.
Breitowicz, Jacob. *Through Hell to Life*. New York: Shengold Publishers, Inc., 1983.
Buber-Neumann, Margarete. *Under Two Dictators*. Trans. Edward Fitzgerald. New York: Dodd, Mead & Co., 1949.
Cholawski, Shalom. *Soldiers from the Ghetto: The First Uprising Against the Nazis*. New York and San Diego: A. S. Barnes & Co., Inc., 1980.
Cohen, Elie. *The Abyss: A Confession*. Trans. James Brockway. New York: W. W. Norton & Co., 1973.
―――. *Human Behavior in the Concentration Camp*. Trans. M. H. Braaksma. New York: W. W. Norton & Co., 1953.
Delbo, Charlotte. *Le Convoi du 24 janvier*. Paris: Editions de Minuit, 1965.
―――. *None of Us Will Return*. Trans. John Githens. New York: Grove Press, 1969.
―――. "Phantoms, My Companions." *Massachusetts Review* 12 (1971): 10–30.
―――. "Phantoms, My Faithful Ones." *Massachusetts Review* 14 (1973): 310–15.
Donat, Alexander. *The Holocaust Kingdom*. New York: Holt, Rinehart & Winston, 1965.
Dribben, Judith Strick. *A Girl Called Judith Strick*. New York: Cowles, 1970.
Eck, Nathan. "The March of Death from Serbia to Hungary (September 1944) and the Slaughter of Cservenka." *Yad Vashem Studies* 2 (1958): 255–94.
Edelman, Marek. *The Ghetto Fighters*. New York: American Representation of the Jewish Workers' Union of Poland, 1946.
Edelstein, Dov Beril. *Worlds Torn Asunder*. Hoboken, N.J.: Ktav Publishing House, Inc., 1985.
Ehrenburg, Ilya, and Vasily Grossman, eds. *The Black Book: Documents on the Destruction of 1.5 Million Soviet Jews*. Trans. John Glad and James S. Levine. New York: Holocaust Library, 1981.
Eisenberg, Azriel, ed. *The Lost Generation: Children in the Holocaust*. New York: Pilgrim Press, 1982.
―――. *Witness to the Holocaust: Personal and Eyewitness Accounts of the Holocaust, Resistance and Rebirth*. New York: Pilgrim Press, 1981.
Eisner, Jack. *The Survivor*. New York: William Morrow, 1980.
Eliach, Yaffa, ed. *Hasidic Tales of the Holocaust*. New York: Oxford University Press, 1982.
Feld, Marilla. *I Chose to Live*. New York: Manor Books, 1979.
Fenelon, Fania. *Playing for Time*. Trans. Judith Landry. New York: Atheneum, 1977.
Ferderber-Salz, Bertha. *And the Sun Kept Shining*. New York: Holocaust Library, 1980.
Frankl, Viktor E. *Man's Search for Meaning: An Introduction to Logotherapy*. Trans. Ilse Lasch. New York: Washington Square Press, 1963.
Friedländer, Saul. *Kurt Gerstein: The Ambiguity of Good*. Trans. Charles Fullman. New York: Alfred A. Knopf, 1969.
―――. *When Memory Comes*. Trans. Helen R. Lane. New York: Farrar, Straus & Giroux, 1979.
Friedman, Ina R. *Escape or Die*. Reading, Mass.: Addison-Wesley, 1982.
Friedman, Philip. *Martyrs and Fighters*. London: Routledge & Kegan Paul, 1954.
―――. *Their Brothers' Keepers*. New York: Crown, 1957.

Gabor, Georgia M. *My Destiny*. Alhambra, Calif.: Borden Publishing Company, 1982.
Garlinski, Jozef. *Fighting Auschwitz: The Resistance Movement in the Concentration Camp.* Greenwich, Conn.: Fawcett, 1975.
Gefen, Aba. *Unholy Alliance*. Israel: Yuval Tal Ltd., 1973.
Geve, Thomas. *Youth in Chains*. Jerusalem: Rubin Maas, 1982.
Gilboa, Yehoshua. *Confess! Confess!* Trans. Dov Ben Aba. Boston: Little, Brown & Co., 1968.
Goldberg, Izaak. *The Miracles versus Tyranny*. New York: Philosophical Library, 1978.
Goldman, Pierre. *Souvenirs obscurs d'un Juif polonais né en France*. Paris: Editions du Seuil, 1975.
Goldstein, Bernard. *The Stars Bear Witness*. Trans. Leonard Shatzkin. New York: Viking Press, 1949.
Goldstein, Charles. *The Bunker*. Trans. Esther Malkin. Philadelphia: Jewish Publication Society, 1970.
Graebe, Herman F. "Testimony of Herman F. Graebe, Given in Israel." *Yad Vashem Studies Annual* 14 (1981): pp. 283–314.
Gray, Martin. *For Those I Loved*. Trans. Anthony White. Boston: Little, Brown & Co., 1972.
Gruber, Rifka, ed. *Village of My Brothers*. New York: Shengold Publishers, Inc., 1978.
Gruber, Samuel. *I Chose Life*. Ed. Gertrude Hirschler. New York: Shengold Publishers, Inc., 1978.
Haas, Albert. *The Doctor and the Damned*. New York: St. Martin's Press, 1984.
Haas, Gerda. *These Do I Remember: Fragments from the Holocaust*. Freeport, Maine: Cumberland Press, 1983.
Hahn, Lili. *White Flags of Surrender*. Washington, D.C.: Robert B. Lucey, 1974.
Hallie, Philip. *Lest Innocent Blood Be Shed*. New York: Harper & Row, 1980.
Hart, Kitty. *I Am Alive*. New York: Abelard-Schuman, 1962.
———. *Return to Auschwitz*. New York: Atheneum, 1982.
Heimler, Eugene. *Night of the Mist*. Trans. André Ungar. New York: Vanguard Press, 1959.
Hellman, Peter. *Avenue of the Righteous*. New York: Atheneum, 1980.
Hersh, Gizelle, and Mann, Peggy. *"Gizelle, Save the Children!"* New York: Everett House, 1980.
Hilberg, Raul, ed. *Documents of Destruction: Germany and Jewry 1935–1945*. Chicago: Quadrangle Books, 1971.
Hirshaut, Julien. *Jewish Martyrs of Pawiak*. New York: Holocaust Library, 1983.
Iranek-Osmecki, Kazimierz. *He Who Saves One Life*. New York: Crown, 1971.
Joffroy, Pierre. *A Spy for God: The Ordeal of Kurt Gerstein*. New York: Grosset & Dunlap, 1975.
Kahn, Leo. *No Time to Mourn*. Vancouver: Laurelton, 1979.
Karski, Jan [Jan Kulczynski]. *Story of a Secret State*. Boston: Houghton Mifflin, 1944.
Katz, Josef. *One Who Came Back: Diary of a Jewish Survivor*. Trans. Hilda Reach. New York: Herzl Press and Bergen-Belsen Memorial Press, 1973.
Kessel, Sim. *Hanged at Auschwitz*. New York: Stein & Day, 1972.
Kielar, Wieslaw. *Anus Mundi: Five Years in Auschwitz*. Trans. Susanne Flatauer. New York: Penguin Books, 1982.
Klein, Gerda Weissman. *All But My Life*. New York: Hill & Wang, 1957.
Klein, Jean. *Not Now, Not Ever*. Pittsburgh: Seven Seas Books, 1967.
Klonitski, Ariel. *Diary of Adam's Father*. Israel: Beit Lohamei Hagettaot, n.d.
Koehn, Ilse. *Mischling: Second Degree*. New York: William Morrow, 1977.
Kogon, Eugen. *The Theory and Practice of Hell*. Trans. Heinz Norden. New York: Farrar, Straus & Co., 1950.
Kohner, Hanna and Walter. *Hanna and Walter: A Love Story*. New York: Random House, 1984.

Korman, Gerd, ed. *Hunter and Hunted: Human History of the Holocaust.* New York: Viking Press, 1973.

Krall, Hanna. *Shielding the Flame: An Intimate Conversation with Dr. Marek Edelman, the Last Surviving Leader of the Warsaw Ghetto Uprising.* Trans. Joanna Stasinska and Lawrence Weschler. New York: Holt, Rinehart & Winston, 1986.

Kraus, Ota, and Kulka, Erich. *The Death Factory: Documents on Auschwitz.* Trans. Stephen Jolly. Oxford: Pergamon Press, 1968.

Kulka, Erich. *Escape from Auschwitz.* South Hadley, Mass.: Bergin & Garvey Publishers, Inc., 1986.

Kuper, Jack. *Child of the Holocaust.* Garden City: Doubleday & Co., 1968.

Kwinta, Chava. *I'm Still Living.* Toronto: Simon & Pierre, 1974.

Langbein, Hermann. *Der Auschwitz Prozess, eine Dokumentation.* 2 vols. Frankfurt: Europäische Verlagsanstalt, 1965.

Lanzmann, Claude. *Shoah: An Oral History of the Holocaust.* New York: Pantheon Books, 1985.

Leitner, Isabella. *Fragments of Isabella.* New York: Thomas Y. Crowell, 1978.

Lengyel, Olga. *Five Chimneys: The Story of Auschwitz.* Trans. Paul B. Weiss. Chicago: Ziff-Davis, 1947.

Lester, Eleanore. *Wallenberg: The Man in the Iron Web.* Englewood Cliffs, N.J.: Prentice-Hall, 1982.

Levi, Primo. *Moments of Reprieve.* Trans. Ruth Feldman. New York: Summit Books, 1986.

———. *The Periodic Table.* Trans. Raymond Rosenthal. New York: Schocken Books, 1984.

———. *The Reawakening.* Trans. Stuart Woolf. Boston: Little, Brown & Co., 1965.

———. *Survival in Auschwitz.* Trans. Stuart Woolf. New York: Collier Books, 1969.

Lewinska, Pelagia. *Twenty Months at Auschwitz.* Trans. Albert Teichner. New York: Lyle Stuart, 1968.

Lind, Jakov. *Counting My Steps: An Autobiography.* Toronto: Macmillan, 1969.

———. *Numbers: A Further Autobiography.* London: Jonathan Cape, 1972.

Lingens-Reiner, Ella. *Prisoners of Fear.* London: Viktor Gollancz, 1948.

Lubetkin, Zivia. *In the Days of Destruction and Revolt.* Trans. Ishai Tubbin. Israel: Beit Lohamei Hagettaot and Hakibbutz Hameuchad Publishing House, 1981.

Mark, Ber. *Uprising in the Warsaw Ghetto.* Trans. Gershon Freidlin. New York: Schocken Books, 1975.

Maurel, Micheline. *An Ordinary Camp.* Trans. Margaret S. Summers. New York: Simon & Schuster, 1958.

Meed, Vladka. *On Both Sides of the Wall.* Israel: Beit Lohamei Hagettaot and Hakibbutz Hameuchad Publishing House, 1973.

Meras, I. *Stalemate.* New York: Lyle Stuart, 1980.

Mermelstein, Mel. *By Bread Alone: The Story of A-4685.* Huntington Beach, Calif.: Auschwitz Study Foundation, Inc., 1979.

Michel, Jean, with Nuoera, Louis. *Dora.* Trans. Jennifer Kidd. New York: Holt, Rinehart & Winston, 1980.

Michelson, Frida. *I Survived Rumbuli.* New York: Schocken Books, 1981.

Minco, Marga. *Bitter Herbs.* New York: Oxford University Press, 1960.

Minney, R. J. *I Shall Fear No Evil: The Story of Dr. Alina Brewda.* London: Kimber, 1966.

Müller, Filip. *Eyewitness Auschwitz: Three Years in the Gas Chambers.* New York: Stein & Day, 1979.

Naumann, Bernd. *Auschwitz.* Trans. Jean Steinberg. New York: Praeger, 1966.

Neshamit, Sarah. *The Children of Mapu Street.* Trans. David S. Segal. Israel: Beit Lohamei Hagettaot and Hakibbutz Hameuchad Publishing House, 1979.

Nomberg-Przytyk, Sara. *Auschwitz: True Tales from a Grotesque Land.* Trans. Roslyn

Hirsch, ed. Eli Pfefferkorn and David Hirsch. Chapel Hill and London: The University of North Carolina Press, 1985.

Novak, Jan. *Courier from Warsaw*. Detroit: Wayne State University Press, 1982.

Novitch, Miriam, ed. *Sobibor: Martyrdom and Revolt*. New York: Holocaust Library, 1980.

Nyiszli, Miklos. *Auschwitz: A Doctor's Eyewitness Account*. Trans. Tibere Kremer and Richard Seaver. Greenwich, Conn.: Fawcett Crest, 1960.

Oberski, Jona. *Childhood*. Trans. Ralph Manheim. New York: Doubleday & Co., 1983.

Ornstein, Anna. "Anna Ornstein's Hagaddah: The Tatoo." *Response* 35 (Summer 1978): 61–64.

Pawlowicz, Sala. *I Will Survive*. New York: W. W. Norton & Co., 1962.

Perl, Gisella. *I Was a Doctor in Auschwitz*. New York: New York Times Company, Arno Press, 1979.

Pisar, Samuel. *Of Blood and Hope*. Boston: Little, Brown & Co., 1980.

Rabinowitz, Dorothy, ed. *New Lives: Survivors of the Holocaust Living in America*. New York: Alfred A. Knopf, 1976.

Rashke, Richard. *Escape from Sobibor: The Heroic Story of the Jews Who Escaped from a Nazi Death Camp*. Boston: Houghton Mifflin, 1982.

Rochman, Leyb. *The Pit and the Trap: A Chronicle of Survival*. Ed. Sheila Friedling, trans. Moshe Kohn. New York: Holocaust Library, 1983.

Roiter, Howard, ed. *Voices from the Holocaust*. New York: William Frederick Press, 1975.

Romano, Elio. *A Generation of Wrath*. London: Severn House, 1984.

Rosen, Donia. *The Forest My Friend*. Trans. Mordecai S. Chertoff. New York: Bergen-Belsen Memorial Press, 1971.

Rothchild, Sylvia, ed. *Voices from the Holocaust*. New York: New American Library, 1981.

Rousset, David. *The Other Kingdom*. Trans. Ramon Guthrie. New York: Reynal and Hitchcock, 1947.

Rubenstein, Donna. *I am the Only Survivor of Krasnotsav*. New York: Shengold Publishers, Inc., 1983.

Rubenstein, Erna F. *The Survivor in Us All: A Memoir of the Holocaust*. Hamden, Conn.: Archon Books, 1984.

Salomon, Charlotte. *Charlotte*. New York: Harcourt, Brace & World, 1963.

Sandberg, Moshe. *My Long Year in the Hungarian Labor Service and in the Nazi Camps*. Jerusalem: Yad Vashem Publications, 1968.

Schnabel, Ernst. *Anne Frank: A Portrait in Courage*. Trans. Richard and Clara Winston. New York: Harcourt, Brace, Harbrace Paperback Library, 1958.

Schochet, Simon. *Feldafing*. Vancouver: November House, 1983.

Schoenfeld, Joachim. *Holocaust Memoirs*. New York: Ktav Publishing House, 1984.

Sereny, Gitta. *Into that Darkness: An Examination of Conscience*. New York: McGraw-Hill, 1974.

Shapell, Nathan. *Witness to Truth*. New York: McKay, 1974.

Shoskes, Henry. *No Traveler Returns: The Story of Hitler's Greatest Crime*. Garden City, N.Y.: Doubleday, Doran & Co., 1945.

Shulman, Abraham. *The Case of Hotel Polski*. New York: Holocaust Library, 1981.

Sim, Kevin. *Women at War: Five Heroines Who Defied the Nazis and Survived*. New York: William Morrow, 1982.

Spanjaard, Barry. *Don't Fence Me In! An American Teenager in the Holocaust*. Los Angeles: B & B Publishing, 1981.

Spiegelman, Art. *Maus: A Survivor's Tale*. New York: Pantheon Books, 1986.

Starhopf, Adam. *There is Always Time to Die*. New York: Holocaust Library, 1981.

Stiffel, Frank. *The Tale of the Ring: A Kaddish: A Personal Memoir of the Holocaust.* New York: Pushcart Press, 1984.
Strauss, Walter, ed. *Signs of Life: Jews from Württemberg; Reports for the Period after 1933 in Letters and Descriptions.* New York: Ktav Publishing House, 1982.
Suhl, Yuri, ed. and trans. *They Fought Back: The Story of the Jewish Resistance in Nazi Europe.* New York: Schocken Books, 1967.
Symonowicz, Wanda, ed. *Beyond Human Endurance: The Ravensbrück Women Tell Their Stories.* Trans. Doris Ronowicz. Warsaw: Interpress, 1970.
Szmaglewska, Seweryna. *Smoke over Birkenau.* Trans. Jadwiga Rynas. New York: Henry Holt, 1947.
Tec, Nechama. *Dry Tears: The Story of a Lost Childhood.* New York: Oxford University Press, 1984.
Temchin, Michael. *Witch Doctor: Memoirs of a Partisan.* New York: Holocaust Library, 1983.
Tillion, Germaine. *Ravensbrück.* Trans. Gerald Satterwhite. New York: Doubleday, Anchor Books, 1975.
Trepman, Paul. *Among Beasts and Men.* New York: A. S. Barnes & Co., 1978.
Trunk, Isaiah, ed. *Jewish Responses to Nazi Persecution.* New York: Stein & Day, 1980.
Unsdorfer, S. B. *The Yellow Star.* New York: Thomas Yoseloff, 1961.
Vrba Rudolf, and Bestic, Alan. *Escape from Auschwitz: I Cannot Forgive.* New York: Grove Press, 1964.
Wdowinski, David. *And We Are Not Saved.* New York: Philosophical Library, 1985.
Wechsberg, Joseph, ed. *The Murderers Among Us: The Wiesenthal Memoirs.* New York: McGraw-Hill, 1967.
Weinstein, Frida Scheps. *A Hidden Childhood: A Jewish Girl's Sanctuary in a French Convent, 1942–1945.* Trans. Barbara Loeb Kennedy. New York: Hill & Wang, 1985.
Weinstock, Earl, and Wilner, Herbert. *The Seven Years.* New York: E. P. Dutton, 1959.
Wells, Leon. *The Janowksa Road.* New York: Macmillan, 1963.
Werbell, Frederich E., and Clarke, Thurston. *Lost Hero: The Mystery of Raoul Wallenberg.* New York: McGraw-Hill, 1982.
Wiechert, Ernst. *Forest of the Dead.* Trans. Ursula Stechow. New York: Greenberg, 1947.
Wiernik, Jankiel. "A Year in Treblinka." In Alexander Donat, ed. *The Death Camp Treblinka: A Documentary,* pp. 147–88. New York: Holocaust Library, 1979.
Wiesel, Elie. *Night.* Trans. Stella Rodway. New York: Hill & Wang, 1960.
———. *. . . Un di velt hot geshvign* (And the World Was Silent). Buenos Aires: Tsentral-Farband fun poylishe yidn in Argentine, 1956.
Wolfe, Jacqueline. *"Take Care of Josette."* New York: Franklin Watts, 1981.
Zeimian, Joseph. *The Cigarette Sellers of Three Crosses Square.* London: Valentine-Mitchell, 1970.
Zylberberg, Michael. *A Warsaw Diary 1939–1945.* London: Valentine-Mitchell, 1969.
Zyskind, Sara. *Stolen Years.* Minneapolis: Lerner, 1981.
Zywulska, Krystana. *I Came Back.* Trans. Krystyna Cenkalska. London: Dennis Dobson, 1951.

III. FICTION AND IMAGINATIVE LITERATURE

Adams, Nathan M. *The Fifth Horseman.* New York: Random House, 1967.
Aichinger, Ilse. *Herod's Children.* Trans. Cornelia Schaeffer. New York: Atheneum, 1963.
Amichai, Yehuda. *Not of This Time, Not of This Place.* Trans. Shlomo Katz. New York: Harper & Row, 1968.

Andersch, Alfred. *Efraim's Book*. Trans. Ralph Manheim. New York: Doubleday & Co., 1970.
Anissimov, Myriam. *Comment va Rachel?* Paris: Editions Denoël, 1975.
———. *Rue de nuit*. Paris: Julliard, 1977.
Apitz, Bruno. *Naked Among Wolves*. Trans. Edith Anderson. Berlin: Seven Seas Publishers, 1960.
Appelfeld, Aharon. *The Age of Wonders*. Trans. Dalya Bilu. Boston: David R. Godine, Publisher, Inc., 1981.
———. *Badenheim, 1939*. Trans. Dalya Bilu. Boston: David R. Godine, Publisher, Inc., 1980.
———. *The Retreat*. Trans. Dalya Bilu. New York: E. P. Dutton, 1984.
———. *Tzili: The Story of a Life*. Trans. Dalya Bilu. New York: E. P. Dutton, 1983.
Arieti, Silvano. *The Parnas*. New York: Basic Books, 1980.
Arnold, Elliot. *A Night of Watching*. New York: Charles Scribner's Sons, 1967.
Asch, Sholem. *Tales of My People*. Trans. Meyer Levin. New York: Putnam, 1948.
Barcovitch, Reuben. *Hasen*. New York: Alfred A. Knopf, 1978.
Bartov, Hanoch. *The Brigade*. Trans. David Segal. Philadelphia: Jewish Publication Society, 1967.
Bassani, Georgio. *The Garden of the Finzi-Continis*. Trans. William Weaver. New York: Harcourt Brace Jovanovich, 1977.
———. *The Heron*. Trans. William Weaver. New York: Harcourt, Brace & World, 1970.
———. "A Plaque on Via Mazzinio." In *Five Stories of Ferrara*. Trans. William Weaver. New York: Harcourt Brace Jovanovich, 1971.
Beauvais, Robert. *The Half Jew*. Trans. Harold J. Salemson. New York: Taplinger, 1980.
Becker, Jurek. *Jacob the Liar*. Trans. Melvin Kornfeld. New York: Harcourt Brace Jovanovich, 1975.
Bellow, Saul. *Mr. Sammler's Planet*. New York: Viking Press, 1970.
Ben-Amotz, Dan. *To Remember, To Forget*. Trans. Eva Shapiro. Philadelphia: Jewish Publication Society, 1968.
Berger, Naomi. *Echoes of Yesterday*. New York: Playboy Books, 1981.
Berger, Zdena. *Tell Me Another Morning*. New York: Harper & Row, 1961.
Berri, Claude. *The Two of Us*. Trans. Helen Weaver. New York: William Morrow, 1968.
Berryman, John. "The Imaginary Jew." *The Kenyon Review* 7 (1945): 529–39.
Black, Campbell. *Death's Head*. Philadelphia: J. B. Lippincott Co., 1972.
Bloch-Michel, Jean. *The Witness*. Trans. Eithne Wilkins. New York, 1949.
Blunden, Godfrey. *The Time of the Assassins: A Novel*. Philadelphia: J. B. Lippincott Co., 1959.
Böll, Heinrich. *The Train Was on Time. / And Where Were You, Adam?* Trans. Leila Vennewitz. New York: McGraw-Hill, 1970.
Bor, Josef. *The Terezin Requiem*. Trans. Edith Pargeter. New York: Alfred A. Knopf, 1963.
Borges, Jorge Luis. "Deutsches Requiem" and "The Secret Miracle." In *Labyrinths, Selected Stories and Other Writings*. Ed. Donald A. Yates and James E. Irby. New York: New Directions, 1964.
Borowski, Tadeusz. *This Way for the Gas, Ladies and Gentlemen*. Trans. Barbara Vedder. New York: Viking Press, 1967.
Boyarsky, Abraham. *Schreiber*. New York: Beaufort Books, 1981.
Bryks, Rachmil. *A Cat in the Ghetto*. Trans. S. Morris Engel. New York: Bloch Publishing Company, 1959.
———. *Kiddush Hashem*. Trans. S. Morris Engel. New York: Behrman House, 1977.

Buczkowski, Leopold. *Black Torrent*. Trans. David Welsh. Cambridge, Mass.: MIT Press, 1969.
Chaneles, Sol. *Three Children of the Holocaust*. New York: Avon Books, 1974.
Child, Philip. *Day of Wrath*. Toronto: Ryerson, 1945.
Cohen, Arthur A. *In the Days of Simon Stern*. New York: Random House, 1973.
Comfort, Alex. *On This Side of Nothing*. New York: Viking Press, 1949.
Condon, Richard. *An Infinity of Mirrors*. New York: Random House, 1964.
Crawford, Oliver. *The Execution*. New York: St. Martin's Press, 1978.
Davis, Christopher. *The Shamir of Dachau*. New York: New American Library, 1966.
Dayan, Yael. *Death Had Two Sons*. New York: McGraw-Hill, 1968.
del Castillo, Michel. *Child of Our Time*. Trans. Peter Green. New York: Alfred A. Knopf, 1959.
Doubrovsky, Serge. *La dispersion*. Paris: Mercure de France, 1969.
Durrenmatt, Friedrich. *The Quarry*. Greenwich, Conn.: New York Graphic Society, 1962.
Elman, Richard. *Lilo's Diary*. New York: Charles Scribner's Sons, 1968.
———. *The Reckoning: The Daily Ledgers of Newman Yagodah, Advokat and Factor*. New York: Charles Scribner's Sons, 1969.
———. *The 28th Day of Elul*. New York: Charles Scribner's Sons, 1967.
Elon, Amos. *Timetable*. Garden City, N.Y.: Doubleday & Co., 1980.
Epstein, Leslie. *King of the Jews*. New York: Coward, McCann & Geoghegan, 1979.
Ettinger, Elžbieta. *Kindergarten*. Boston: Houghton Mifflin, 1970.
Falstein, Louis. *Face of a Hero*. New York: Harcourt, Brace, 1950.
Faust, Irvin. *Roar Lion Roar and Other Stories*. New York: Random House, 1965.
Federman, Raymond. *The Twofold Vibration*. Bloomington: Indiana University Press, 1982.
———. *The Voice in the Closet*. Madison, Wis.: Coda Press, 1979.
Feld, Yehudo. *In di tsaytn fun Homen dem tsveytn* (In the Times of Haman the Second). From the Ringelblum Archive. Warsaw: Yidish-bukh, 1954.
Feuchtwanger, Lion. *The Devil in France: My Encounter with Him in the Summer of 1940*. Trans. Elisabeth Abbott. New York: Viking Press, 1941.
Field, Hermann, and Mierzenski, Stanislaw. *Angry Harvest*. New York: Thomas Y. Crowell, 1958.
Fink, Ida. *A Scrap of Time and Other Stories*. Trans. Madeline Levine and Francine Prose. New York: Pantheon Books, 1987.
Fish, Robert L. *Pursuit*. Garden City, N.Y.: Doubleday & Co., 1978.
Freeden, Gerbert H. *Grist to God's Mill*. London: Godfrey & Stephens, 1947.
Fuks, Ladislaw. *Mr. Theodore Mundstock*. Trans. Iris Unwin. New York: Orion Press, 1968.
Gary, Romain. *The Dance of Ghengis Cohn*. Trans. author and Camilla Sykes. New York: World Publishing Company, 1968.
Gascar, Pierre. *Beasts and Men and the Seed*. Trans. Jean Stewart and Merloyd Lawrence. New York: Meridian Books, 1960.
Gheorghiu, Constantin Virgil. *The Twenty-Fifth Hour*. Trans. Rita Eldon. Chicago: Regnery, 1950.
Ginzburg, Natalia. *Family Sayings*. Trans. D. M. Low. New York: E. P. Dutton, 1967.
———. *A Light for Fools*. Trans. Angus Davidson. New York: E. P. Dutton, 1967.
Goes, Albrecht. *The Burnt Offering*. Trans. Michael Hamburger. New York: Pantheon Books, 1956.
Goldring-Goding, Henry. *Out of Hell*. Boston: Chapman & Grimes, 1955.
Goldsmith, John. *Exodus 43*. New York: Coward, McCann & Geoghegan, 1982.
Gouri, Haim. *The Chocolate Deal*. Trans. Seymour Simckes. New York: Holt, Rinehart & Winston, 1968.

Grade, Chaim. *The Seven Little Lanes.* Trans. Curt Leviant. New York: Bergen-Belsen Memorial Press, 1972.
Green, Gerald. *Holocaust.* New York: Bantam Books, 1978.
———. *The Legion of Noble Christians.* New York: Trident Press, 1965.
Grossman, Ladislav. *The Shop on Main Street.* Trans. Iris Urwin. New York: Doubleday & Co., 1970.
Grynberg, Henryk. *Child of the Shadows.* Trans. Celina Wieniewoka. Hartford, Conn.: Hartmore House, 1969.
Habe, Hans. *The Mission.* Trans. Michael Bullock. New York: Coward-McCann, 1966.
Hersey, John. *The Wall.* New York: Alfred A. Knopf, 1950.
Hilsenrath, Edgar. *The Nazi and the Barber.* Trans. Andrew White. New York: Doubleday & Co., 1971.
———. *Night.* Trans. Michael Roloff. New York: Doubleday & Co., 1966.
Hoffman, William. *The Trumpet Unblown.* New York: Doubleday & Co., 1955.
Jabès, Edmond. *The Book of Questions,* vol. I. Trans. Rosmarie Waldrop. Middletown, Conn.: Wesleyan University Press, 1976.
———. *The Book of Questions: The Book of Yukel / Return to the Book,* vols. II and III. Trans. Rosmarie Waldrop. Middletown, Conn.: Wesleyan University Press, 1977.
Julitte, Pierre. *Block 26: Sabotage at Buchenwald.* Trans. Francis Price. New York: Doubleday & Co. 1971.
Kanfer, Stefan. *The Eighth Sin.* New York: Random House, 1978.
———. *Fear Itself.* New York: Putnam, 1981.
Kaniuk, Yoram. *Adam Resurrected.* Trans. Seymour Simckes. New York: Atheneum, 1971.
Karmel, Ilona. *An Estate of Memory.* Boston: Houghton Mifflin Co., 1969.
———. *Stephania.* Boston: Houghton Mifflin Co., 1953.
Karmel-Wolfe, Henia. *The Baders of Jacob Street.* New York: J. B. Lippincott Co., 1970.
———. *Marek and Lisa.* New York: Dodd, Mead & Co., 1984.
Ka-Tzetnik 135633 (Yehiel Dinur). *Atrocity.* New York: Lyle Stuart, 1963.
———. *House of Dolls.* Trans. Moshe M. Kohn. New York: Simon & Schuster, 1955.
———. *Star Eternal.* Trans. Nina DeNur. New York: Arbor House, 1971.
———. *Sunrise over Hell.* Trans. Nina DeNur. London: W. H. Allen, 1977.
Keneally, Thomas. *Schindler's List.* New York: Simon & Schuster, 1982.
Klein, A. M. *The Second Scroll.* Canada: McClelland & Stewart, 1966.
Klein, Edward. *The Parachutists.* New York: Doubleday & Co., 1981.
Koestler, Arthur. *Scum of the Earth.* London: Jonathan Cape, 1941.
Kolitz, Zvi. *The Tiger Beneath the Skin: Stories and Parables of the Years of Death.* New York: Creative Age, 1947.
Kosinski, Jerzy. *The Painted Bird.* New York: Pocket Books, 1965.
Kotowska, Monika. *The Bridge to the Other Side.* Garden City, N.Y.: Doubleday & Co., 1970.
Kuznetsov, Anatoli. *Babi Yar: A Document in the Form of a Novel.* Trans. David Floyd. London: Jonathan Cape, 1970.
Langfus, Anna. *The Lost Shore.* Trans. Peter Wiles. New York: Pantheon Books, 1963.
———. *Saute, Barbara.* Paris: Gallimard, 1965.
———. *The Whole Land Brimstone.* Trans. Peter Wiles. New York: Pantheon Books, 1962.
Laqueur, Walter. *The Missing Years.* Boston: Little, Brown & Co., 1980.
Levi, Carlo. *The Watch.* New York: Farrar, Straus & Yoring, 1951.

Levi, Primo. *If Not Now, When?* Trans. William Weaver. New York: Summit Books, 1985.
Levin, Meyer. *Eva: A Novel of the Holocaust.* New York: Simon & Schuster, 1959.
———. *The Harvest.* New York: Simon & Schuster, 1978.
———. *My Father's House.* New York: Viking Press, 1947.
———. *The Stronghold.* New York: Simon & Schuster, 1965.
Lewisohn, Ludwig. *Breathe Upon These.* Indianapolis: Bobbs-Merrill, 1944.
Lind, Jakov. *Landscape in Concrete.* Trans. Ralph Manheim. New York: Grove Press, 1966.
———. *Soul of Wood and Other Stories.* Trans. Ralph Manheim. New York: Grove Press, 1964.
Lustig, Arnošt. *Darkness Casts No Shadow.* Trans. Jeanne Němcová. Washington, D.C.: Inscape Publishers, 1978.
———. *Diamonds of the Night.* Trans. Jeanne Němcová. Washington, D.C.: Inscape Publishers, 1978.
———. *Dita Sax.* Trans. George Theiner. London: Hutchinson, 1966.
———. *Night and Hope.* Trans. George Theiner. New York: E. P. Dutton, 1962.
———. *A Prayer for Katerina Horovitzova.* Trans. Jeanne Němcová. New York: Harper & Row, 1973.
Malamud, Bernard. "The German Refugee." *Idiots First.* New York: Delta Books, 1963.
Malaparte, Curzio. *Kaputt.* Trans. Cesare Foligno. New York: E. P. Dutton, 1946.
Margolian, Abraham. *A Piece of Blue Heaven.* Fredericton, N.B.: New Elizabethan, 1956.
Mazzetti, Lorenza. *The Sky Falls.* Trans. Marguerite Waldman. New York: McKay, 1963.
Miller, Arthur. *Focus.* New York: Reynal and Hitchcock, 1945.
Modiano, Patrick. *Les boulevards de ceinture.* Paris: Gallimard, 1972.
———. *La place de l'étoile.* Paris: Gallimard, 1968.
———. *La ronde de nuit.* Paris: Gallimard, 1969.
Morante, Elsa. *History, A Novel.* Trans. William Weaver. New York: Alfred A. Knopf, 1977.
Morgenstern, Soma. *The Third Pillar.* Trans. Ludwig Lewisohn. New York: Farrar, Straus, 1955.
Neumann, Robert. *By the Waters of Babylon.* New York: Simon & Schuster, 1940.
Obletz, Rose Meyerson. *The Long Road Home.* New York: Exposition, 1958.
Olivier, Stefan. *Rise Up in Anger.* New York: Putnam, 1963.
Orlev, Uri. *The Lead Soldiers.* Trans. Hillel Halkin. New York: Taplinger, 1980.
Ozick, Cynthia. "Rosa." *The New Yorker,* 21 March 1983, pp. 38–71.
———. "The Shawl." *The New Yorker,* 26 May 1980, pp. 33–34.
Pawel, Ernst. *The Island in Time.* Garden City, N.Y.: Doubleday & Co., 1951.
Plath, Sylvia. *The Bell Jar.* New York: Harper & Row, 1975.
Prager, Moshe. *Sparks of Glory.* Trans. Mordecai Schreiber. New York: Shengold Publishers, Inc., 1974.
Presser, Jacob. *Breaking Point.* Trans. Barrows Mussey. New York and Cleveland: World, 1958.
Raczymow, Henri. *Contes d'exil et d'oubli.* Paris: Gallimard, 1979.
———. *Un cri sans voix.* Paris: Gallimard, 1985.
———. *Rivières d'exil.* Paris: Gallimard, 1982.
———. *La saisie.* Paris: Gallimard, 1973.
Raphael, Frederic. *Lindmann: A Novel.* New York: Holt, Rinehart & Winston, 1964.
Rawicz, Piotr. *Blood from the Sky.* Trans. Peter Wiles. New York: Harcourt, Brace & World, 1964.

Remarque, Erich Maria. *The Night in Lisbon*. Trans. Ralph Manheim. New York: Harcourt, Brace & World, 1964.
———. *Spark of Life*. Trans. James Stern. New York: Appleton-Century-Crofts, 1952.
Richter, Hans Werner. *They Fell from God's Hand*. Trans. Geoffrey Saintsbury. New York: E. P. Dutton, 1956.
Romanowicz, Zofia. *Passage Through the Red Sea*. Trans. Virgilia Peterson. New York: Harcourt, Brace & World, 1962.
Rosen, Norma. *Touching Evil*. New York: Harcourt, Brace & World, 1969.
Rostov, Mara. *Eroica*. New York: Putnam, 1977.
Roth, Philip. *The Ghost Writer*. New York: Farrar, Straus & Giroux, 1979.
———. *Zuckerman Bound: A Trilogy and Epilogue*. New York: Farrar, Straus & Giroux, 1985.
Rudnicki, Adolf. *Ascent to Heaven*. Trans. H. C. Stevens. New York, Toronto, and London: Roy McLeod & Dennis Dobson Publishers, 1951.
Rybakov, Anatoli. *Heavy Sand*. Trans. Harold Shukman. New York: Viking Press, 1981.
St. John, Robert. *The Man Who Played God*. Garden City, N.Y.: Doubleday & Co., 1962.
Samelson, William. *All Life in Wait*. Englewood Cliffs, N.J.: Prentice-Hall, 1969.
Samuels, Gertrude. *Mottele*. New York: Harper & Row, 1976.
Sayre, Joel. *The House Without a Roof*. New York: Farrar, Straus, 1948.
Schaeffer, Susan Fromberg. *Anya*. New York: Macmillan, 1974.
Schwarz-Bart, André. *The Last of the Just*. Trans. Stephen Becker. New York: Atheneum, 1961.
Segal, Lore. *Other People's Houses*. New York: New American Library, 1973.
Seiden, O. J. *The Survivors of Babi Yar*. Athens, Ohio: Stonehenge Books/Ohio University Press, 1980.
Semprun, Jorge. *The Long Voyage*. Trans. Richard Seaver. New York: Grove Press, 1964.
———. *What a Beautiful Sunday!* Trans. Alan Sheridan. New York: Harcourt Brace Jovanovich, 1982.
Silberstang, Edwin. *Nightmare of the Dark*. New York: Alfred A. Knopf, 1967.
Singer, Isaac Bashevis. *Enemies; A Love Story*. Trans. Aliza Shevrin and Elizabeth Shub. New York: Farrar, Straus & Giroux, 1972.
Solomon, Michael. *The "Struma" Incident: A Novel of the Holocaust*. Trans. Carol Dunlop-Herbert. Toronto: McClelland & Stewart, 1979.
Sperber, Manès. *The Abyss*. Trans. Constantine Fitzgibbon. Garden City, N.Y.: Doubleday & Co., 1952.
———. *Journey without End*. Trans. Constantine Fitzgibbon. Garden City, N.Y.: Doubleday & Co., 1954.
———. . . . . *Than a Tear in the Sea*. Trans. Constantine Fitzgibbon. New York and Tel Aviv: Bergen-Belsen Memorial Press, 1967.
Spiraux, Alain. *Time Out*. Trans. Frances Keene. New York: Times Books, 1978.
Steiner, George. *The Portage to San Cristobal of A.H.* New York: Simon & Schuster, 1982.
Steiner, Jean-François. *Treblinka*. Trans. Helen Weaver. New York: Simon & Schuster, 1967.
Stern, Daniel. *Who Shall Live, Who Shall Die?* New York: Crown, 1963.
Stolzfuss, Ben. *The Eye of the Needle*. New York: Viking Press, 1967.
Styron, William. *Sophie's Choice*. New York: Random House, 1979.
Suhl, Yuri. *On the Other Side of the Gate*. New York: Avon, 1976.
———. *Uncle Misha's Partisans*. New York: Four Winds Press, 1973.
Tannenbaum, Silvia. *Yesterday's Streets*. New York: Random House, 1981.

Taube, Herman, and Taube, Suzanne. *Remember.* Trans. Helena Frank. Baltimore: Nicholas A. Grossman, 1951.

Thomas, D. M. *The White Hotel.* New York: Viking Press, 1981.

Tomkiewicz, Mina. *Of Bombs and Mice.* Trans. Stefan Grazel. New York: Thomas Yoseloff, 1970.

Tournier, Michel. *The Ogre.* Trans. Barbara Bray. New York: Doubleday & Co., 1972.

Traub, Barbara Fishman. *The Matrushka Doll.* New York: Richard Marek, 1979.

Uhlman, Fred. *Reunion.* New York: Farrar, Straus & Giroux, 1977.

Uris, Leon. *Mila 18.* Garden City, N.Y.: Doubleday & Co., 1962.

————. *QB VII.* Garden City, N.Y.: Doubleday & Co., 1970.

Von Rezzori, Gregor. *Memoirs of an Anti-Semite: A Novel in Five Stories.* New York: Penguin Books, 1982.

Wallant, Edward Lewis. *The Pawnbroker.* New York: Harcourt, Brace & World, 1961.

Weil, Grete. *My Sister, My Antigone.* New York: Avon Books, 1984.

Weinberg, Marcel. *Spots of the Time.* New York: Macmillan, 1972.

Werfel, Franz. *The Forty Days of Musa Dagh.* Trans. Geoffrey Dunlop. New York: Viking Press, 1934.

Wiesel, Elie. *The Accident.* Trans. Anne Borchardt. New York: Hill & Wang, 1962.

————. *A Beggar in Jerusalem.* Trans. Lily Edelman and the Author. New York: Random House, 1970.

————. *Dawn.* Trans. Anne Borchardt. New York: Hill & Wang, 1961.

————. *The Gates of the Forest.* Trans. Frances Frenaye. New York: Holt, Rinehart & Winston, 1966.

————. *Legends of Our Time.* New York: Holt, Rinehart & Winston, 1968.

————. *The Oath.* Trans. Marion Wiesel. New York: Random House, 1973.

————. *One Generation After.* New York: Random House, 1970.

————. *The Town Beyond the Wall.* Trans. Stephen Becker. New York: Atheneum, 1964.

Wiesenthal, Simon. *Max and Helen.* New York: William Morrow, 1982.

————. *The Sunflower.* Trans. H. A. Piehler. London: W. H. Allen, 1970.

Wiseman, Thomas. *Journey of a Man.* Garden City, N.Y.: Doubleday & Co., 1967.

————. *The Quick and the Dead.* New York: Viking Press, 1968.

Wood, Bari. *The Tribe.* New York: New American Library, 1981.

Wouk, Herman. *War and Remembrance.* Boston: Little, Brown & Co., 1978.

————. *The Winds of War.* Boston: Little, Brown & Co., 1971.

Yaffe, James. *The Voyage of the "Franz Joseph."* New York: Putnam, 1970.

Zweig, Arnold. *The Axe of Wandbek.* Trans. Eric Sutton. New York: Viking Press, 1947.

IV. DRAMA

Amichai, Yehuda. *Bells and Trains. Midstream* 12 (October 1966): 55–66.

Amir, Anda. *This Kind, Too.* Trans. Shoshana Perla. New York: World Zionist Organization, 1972.

Borchert, Wolfgang. *The Outsider.* In *Postwar German Theatre: An Anthology of Plays,* ed. and trans. Michael Benedikt and George E. Wellwarth, pp. 52–113. New York: E. P. Dutton, 1967.

Dagan, Gabriel. *The Reunion. Midstream* 19 (April 1973): 3–32.

Eliach, Yaffa, and Assaf, Uri. *The Last Jew.* Trans. Yaffa Eliach. Israel: Alef-Alef Theatre Publications, 1977.

Frisch, Max. *Andorra.* Trans. Michael Bullock. New York: Hill & Wang, 1964.

Fuchs, Elinor, ed. *Plays of the Holocaust: An International Anthology.* New York: Theatre Communications Group, 1987.

Goldberg, Leah. *The Lady of the Castle*. Trans. T. Carmi. Tel Aviv: Institute for the Translation of Hebrew Literature, 1974.

Goodrich, Frances, and Hackett, Albert. *The Diary of Anne Frank*. New York: Random House, 1956.

Heimler, Eugene. *The Storm (The Tragedy of Sinai)*. Trans. Anthony Rudolf. London: The Menard Press, 1976.

Hochhuth, Rolf. *The Deputy*. Trans. Richard and Clara Winston. New York: Grove Press, 1964.

Lampell, Millard. *The Wall: A Play in Two Acts Based on the Novel by John Hersey*. New York: Alfred A. Knopf, 1961.

Lind, Jakov. *Ergo: A Comedy*. New York: Hill & Wang, 1968.

Megged, Aharon. *The Burning Bush*. Trans. Shoshana Perla. New York: World Zionist Organization, 1972.

Miller, Arthur. *Incident at Vichy*. New York: Viking, 1965.

Pilchik, Ely E. *Strength: A Play in Three Acts*. New York: Bloch Publishing Co., 1964.

Sachs, Nelly. *Eli: A Mystery Play of the Sufferings of Israel*. Trans. Christopher Holme. In *O the Chimneys!* New York: Farrar, Straus & Giroux, 1967.

Sartre, Jean-Paul. *The Condemned of Altona*. Trans. Sylvia and George Leeson. New York: Alfred A. Knopf, 1961.

Shaw, Robert. *The Man in the Glass Booth*. New York: Harcourt, Brace and World, 1967.

Sherman, Martin. *Bent*. New York: Avon Books, 1980.

Skloot, Robert, ed. *The Theatre of the Holocaust: Four Plays*. Madison: University of Wisconsin Press, 1983.

Sylvanus, Erwin. *Dr. Korczak and the Children*. In *Postwar German Theatre: An Anthology of Plays*, ed. and trans. Michael Benedikt and George E. Wellwarth, pp. 115–57. New York: E. P. Dutton, 1967.

Tomer, Ben-Zion. *Children of the Shadows*. Trans. Hillel Halkin. New York: World Zionist Organziation, n.d.

Walser, Martin. *The Rabbit Race*. Adapted by Ronald Duncan, trans. Richard Grunberger. London: J. Calder, 1963.

Weiss, Peter. *The Investigation*. Trans. Jon Swan and Ulu Grosbard. New York: Atheneum, 1966.

Werfel, Franz V., and Behrman, S. N. *Jacobowsky and the Colonel*. New York: Random House, 1944.

Wiesel, Elie. *The Trial of God*. Trans. Marion Wiesel. New York: Random House, 1979.

———. *Zalman; or, The Madness of God*. Trans. Nathan Edelman, adapted by Marion Wiesel. New York: Random House, 1974.

Wincelberg, Shimon. "The Windows of Heaven (A Condensation of a Full-Length Play." *Midstream* 8 (December 1962): 44–64.

Zuckmayer, Carl. *The Devil's General*. In *Masters of Modern Drama*. Ed. Haskell M. Bloch and Robert G. Shedd. New York: Random House, 1962.

V. POETRY

Berryman, John. "from *The Black Book*." In *Short Poems*. New York: Farrar, Straus & Giroux, 1967.

Bryks, Rachmil. *Ghetto Factory 76*. Trans. Theodor Primack and Eugen Kullman. New York: Bloch Publishing Co., 1967.

Celan, Paul. *Last Poems*. Trans. Katharine Washburn and Margret Buillemin. San Francisco: North Point Press, 1986.

———. *Selected Poems*. Trans. Michael Hamburger and Christopher Middleton. Middlesex: Penguin Books, 1972.

———. *Speech-Grille and Selected Poems.* Trans. Joachim Neugroschel. New York: E. P. Dutton, 1971.

Fast, Howard. *Never to Forget.* New York: Jewish People's Fraternal Book League, 1946.

Feldman, Irving. *The Pripet Marshes and Other Poems.* New York: Viking Press, 1965.

Ficowski, Jerzy. *A Reading of Ashes.* Trans. Keith Bosley and Krystyna Wandycz. London: The Menard Press, 1981.

Gebirtig, M. *S'brent, 1939–1942* (Fire). Krakow: Regional Jewish Historical Commission, 1946.

Gershon, Karen. *Selected Poems.* New York: Harcourt, Brace & World, 1966.

Gillon, Adam. "Here as in Jerusalem: Selected Poems of the Ghetto." *Polish Review* 10 (1965): 22–45.

Glatstein, Jacob. *Poems.* Trans. Etta Blum. Tel Aviv: I. L. Peretz Publishing House, 1970.

———. *The Selected Poems of Jacob Glatstein.* Trans. Ruth Whitman. New York: October House, 1972.

Glik, Hirsh. *Lider un poemes* (Lyric and Narrative Poems). Ed. Nachman Mayzel. New York: YIKUF, 1953.

Greenberg, Uri Zvi. From *Streets of the River.* Trans. Robert Friend et al. In *Anthology of Modern Hebrew Poetry,* vol. 2, ed. S. Y. Penneli and A. Ukhmani, pp. 259–80. Jerusalem: Israel Universities Press, 1966.

Gross, Natan; Yaoz-Kest, Itamar; Klinov, Rinah, eds. *Hasho'ah beshirah ha'ivrit: Mivhar* (The Holocaust in Hebrew Poetry: An Anthology). Israel: Hakibbutz Hameuchad Publishing House, 1974.

Hamburger, Michael. "In a Cold Season." In *Ownerless Earth: New Selected Poems.* New York: E. P. Dutton, 1973.

Harshav, Benjamin and Barbara. *American Yiddish Poetry: A Bilingual Anthology.* Berkeley and London: University of California Press, 1986.

Hecht, Anthony. *The Hard Hours.* New York: Atheneum, 1967.

———. *Millions of Strange Shadows.* New York: Atheneum, 1978.

Herzberger, Magda. *The Waltz of the Shadows.* New York: Philosophical Library, 1983.

Heyen, William. *Erika: Poems of the Holocaust (including The Swastika Poems).* New York: Vanguard Press, 1984.

———. *The Swastika Poems.* New York: Vanguard Press, 1977.

Hill, Geoffrey. *Somewhere is Such a Kingdom: Poems 1952–1971.* Boston: Houghton Mifflin, 1975.

Hyett, Barbara Helfgott. *In Evidence: Poems of the Liberation of Nazi Concentration Camps.* Pittsburgh: University of Pittsburgh Press, 1986.

Jackson, Ada. *Behold the Jew.* New York: Macmillan, 1944.

Jacobs, A. C. *The Proper Blessing.* London: The Menard Press, 1976.

Jarrell, Randall. "A Camp in the Prussian Forests." In *Losses.* New York: Harcourt, Brace & World, 1948.

Kaczerginski, Shmerke, comp. *Lider fun di getos un lagern* (Songs of the Ghettos and Concentration Camps). Ed. H. Leivick. New York: CYCO, 1948.

Katzenelson, Yitzhak. *The Song of the Murdered Jewish People.* Trans. Noah H. Rosenbloom, rev. Y. Tobin. Israel: Beit Lohamei Hagettaot and Hakibbutz Hameuchad Publishing House, 1980.

———. *Yidishe geto ksovim fun Varshe, 1940–1943* (Yiddish Ghetto Writings from Warsaw, 1940–1943). Ed. Yechiel Szeintuch. Israel: Beit Lohamei Hagettaot and Hakibbutz Hameuchad Publishing House, 1984.

Klein, A. M. *The Collected Poems of A. M. Klein.* Ed. Miriam Waddington. Toronto: McGraw-Hill Ryerson, 1974.

Kolmar, Gertrud. *Dark Soliloquy: The Selected Poems of Gertrud Kolmar*. Trans. Henry A. Smith. New York: Seabury Press, 1975.

Kovner, Abba. *A Canopy in the Desert*. Trans. Shirley Kaufman, with Ruth Adler and Nurit Orchan. Pittsburgh: University of Pittsburgh Press, 1973.

——. *Selected Poems of Abba Kovner and Nelly Sachs*. Trans. Shirley Kaufman and Nurit Orchan. Middlesex: Penguin Books, 1971.

Lask, Israel Meir, ed. *Songs of the Ghettoes*. Tel Aviv: Eked, 1976.

Leftwich, Joseph, ed. and trans. "Songs of the Death Camps—A Selection with Commentary." *Commentary* 12 (1951): 269–74.

Leivick, H. *In Treblinka bin ikh nit geven* (In Treblinka I Never Was). New York: CYCO, 1945.

Levertov, Denise. "During the Eichmann Trial." In *Jacob's Ladder*. New York: New Directions, 1958.

Levi, Primo. *Shema: Collected Poems of Primo Levi*. Trans. Ruth Feldman and Brian Swann. London: The Menard Press, 1976.

Manger, Itzik. *Shtern in shtoyb* (Star in the Dust). New York, 1967.

Meyers, Bert. *The Dark Birds*. Garden City, N.Y.: Doubleday & Co., 1969.

Mezey, Robert. "Theresienstadt Poems." In *Naked Poetry: Recent American Poetry in Open Forms*. Ed. Stephen Berg and Robert Mezey. Indianapolis: Bobbs-Merrill, 1969.

Miłocz, Czeslaw. *Selected Poems*. New York: Seabury Press, 1973.

Molodowsky, Kadia, ed. *Lider fun khurbn* (Poems of the Holocaust, 1940–1945). Tel Aviv: I. L. Peretz, 1962.

Moss, Stanley. "A Valentine's Day Sketch of Negro Slaves, Jews in Concentration Camps, and Unhappy Lovers." In *The Wrong Angel: Poems*. New York: Macmillan, 1966.

Orten, Jiři [Ohrenstein, Jiři]. *Elegie*. Trans. Lyn Coffin, with Eva Eckert. Czechoslovakia: Czechoslovak Society of Art and Sciences, Inc., 1980.

Pagis, Dan. *Points of Departure*. Trans. Stephen Mitchell. Philadelphia: Jewish Publication Society, 1981.

Pilinszky, Janos. *Selected Poems*. Trans. Ted Hughes and Janos Csokits. New York: Persea Books, 1976.

Plath, Sylvia. *Ariel*. New York: Harper & Row, 1965.

Radnoti, Miklos. *Clouded Sky*. Trans. Steven Polgar, Stephen Berg, and S. J. Marks. New York: Harper & Row, 1972.

——. *Forced March*. Trans. Clive Wilmer and George Gömöri. Manchester: Carcanet New Press Limited, 1979.

Reznikoff, Charles. *Holocaust*. Los Angeles: Black Sparrow Press, 1975.

Rosensaft, Menachem Z. *Fragments: Past and Future*. New York: Shengold Publishers, Inc., 1968.

Róśewicz, Tadeusz. *"The Survivor" and Other Poems*. Trans. Magnus J. Krynski and Robert McGuire. Princeton: Princeton University Press, 1976.

Rothenberg, Jerome. *Vienna Blood & Other Poems*. New York: New Directions Books, 1980.

Sachs, Nelly. *O the Chimneys!* Trans. Michael Hamburger, Ruth and Matthew Mead, and Michael Roloff. New York: Farrar, Straus & Giroux, 1967.

——. *The Seeker and Other Poems*. Trans. Ruth and Matthew Mead and Michael Hamburger. New York: Farrar, Straus & Giroux, 1970.

Schmuller, Aaron, ed. and trans. *Treblinka Grass*. New York: Shulsinger Brothers, 1957.

——, ed. *While Man Exists: Poems and Translations*. New York: Pantheon Books, 1970.

Shayevitsh, S. B. *Lekh-lekho* (Go You Forth). Ed. Nachman Blumental. Lodz: Central Jewish Historical Commission, 1946.

Siegel, Danny. *Nine Entered Paradise Alive.* New York: Town House Press, 1980.
Sklarew, Myra. *From the Backyard of the Diaspora.* Washington, D.C.: Dryad Press, 1976.
Snodgrass, W. D. *The Fuhrer Bunker.* Brockport, N.Y.: BOA Editions, 1977.
Sutzkever, Abraham. *Burnt Pearls: Ghetto Poems.* Trans. Seymour Mayne. Oakville, Ont.: Mosaic Press/Valley Editions, 1981.
————. *Di ershte nakht in geto* (The First Night in the Ghetto: Poems, Variants, and Fragments Written during the Holocaust, 1941–1944). Tel Aviv: Di goldene keyt, 1979.
————. *Di Festung* (The Fortress). New York: YKUF, 1945.
————. *Green Aquarium.* Trans. Ruth Wisse. *Prooftexts* 2, no. 1 (January 1982): 95–121.
————. *Lider fun Yam Hamavet* (Poems from the Dead Sea). Tel Aviv: Farlag Bergen-Belsen, 1968.
————. *Poetishe Verk.* Tel Aviv, 1963.
Taube, Herman. *A Chain of Images.* New York: Shulsinger Brothers, 1979.
Volakova, Hana, ed. *I Never Saw Another Butterfly.* Trans. Jeanne Němcová. New York: McGraw-Hill, 1964.
Voznesensky, Andrei. From "The Ditch: A Spiritual Trial." *The New York Times,* 20 October 1986, p. A10.
Wiesel, Elie. *Ani Maamin: A Song Lost and Found Again.* Trans. Marion Wiesel. New York: Random House, 1973.
Wolfskehl, Karl. *1933—A Poem Sequence.* Trans. Carol North Valhope and Ernst Morwitz. New York: Schocken Books, 1947.
Yevtushenko, Yevgeni. "Babi Yar." In *Selected Poems.* Trans. Robin Milner Gullard and Peter Levi. Baltimore: Penguin Books, 1964.
Zeitlin, Aaron. *Lider fun khurbn un lider fun gloybn* (Poems of the Holocaust and Poems of Faith). 2 vols. New York: Bergen-Belsen Memorial Press, 1967.
————. "Selected Poems." Trans. Robert Friend. In *A Treasury of Yiddish Poetry,* ed. Irving Howe and Eliezer Greenberg, pp. 318–25. New York: Holt, Rinehart & Winston, 1969.

VI. CRITICAL LITERATURE, ANTHOLOGIES, AND BIBLIOGRAPHIES

Aaron, Frieda. *Of Songs and Smokestacks: Yiddish and Polish Poetry in the Ghettos and Concentration Camps.* Albany: State University of New York Press, 1989.
Abramowitz, Molly. *Elie Wiesel: A Bibliography.* Metuchen, N.J.: Scarecrow Press, 1974.
Abse, Dannie. "The Dread of Sylvia Plath." *Poesis* 7 (1986): 8–22.
Adorno, T. W. "Engagement." In *Noten zur Literatur* III, pp. 109–35. Frankfurt: Suhrkamp Verlag, 1963.
————. "Erziehung nach Auschwitz." In *Stichworte: kritische Modelle II.* Frankfurt am Main: Suhrkamp Verlag, 1970.
————. "Valery Proust Museum." In *Prisms,* trans. Samuel and Shierry Weber, pp. 173–85. Cambridge, Mass.: The MIT Press, 1981.
Alexander, Edward. *The Resonance of Dust: Essays on Holocaust Literature and Jewish Fate.* Columbus: Ohio State University Press, 1979.
Alter, Robert. *After the Tradition: Essays on Modern Jewish Writing.* New York: E.P. Dutton & Co., Inc., 1969.
————. *Defenses of the Imagination: Jewish Writers and Modern Historical Crisis.* Philadelphia: Jewish Publication Society, 1977.
————. "Deformations of the Holocaust." *Commentary,* February 1981, pp. 43–54.
————. "A Poet of the Holocaust." *Commentary,* November 1973, pp. 57–63.

———. "Vistas of Annihilation." *Commentary*, January 1985, pp. 39–44.
Altshuler, Linda A., and Cohn, Anna R. "The Precious Legacy." In *The Precious Legacy: Judaic Treasures from the Czechoslovak State Collections*, ed. David Altshuler, pp. 24–38. New York: Summit Books, 1983.
Alvarez, A. "The Literature of the Holocaust." *Commentary*, November 1964, pp. 65–69.
———. *The Savage God: A Study of Suicide*. New York: Random House, 1970.
Angress, Ruth K. "Discussing Holocaust Literature." *Simon Wiesenthal Center Annual* 2 (1985): 179–92.
Ash, Timothy Garton. "The Life of Death." *The New York Review of Books*, 19 December 1985, pp. 26–39.
Ball-Kaduri, K. Y. "Evidence of Witnesses, Its Value and Limitations." *Yad [V]ashem Studies on the European Jewish Catastrophe and Resistance* 3 (1959): 79–90.
Barthes, Roland. *Camera Lucida: Reflections on Photography*. Trans. Richard Howard. New York: Hill & Wang, 1981.
———. "Historical Discourse." In *Introduction to Structuralism*, ed. Michael Lane, pp. 145–55. New York: Basic Books, 1970.
———. *Image-Music-Text*. Trans. Stephen Heath. New York: Hill & Wang, 1977.
———. *Mythologies*. Trans. Annette Lavers. New York: Hill & Wang, 1970.
Bauer, Yehuda. "Fruits of Fear." *Jerusalem Post*, 3 June 1982, p. 8.
———. *History of the Holocaust*. New York and London: Franklin Watts, 1982.
———. *The Holocaust in Historical Perspective*. Seattle: University of Washington Press, 1978.
———. "The Place of the Holocaust in Contemporary History." In *Studies in Contemporary Jewry*, vol. 1, ed. Jonathan Frankel, pp. 201–24. Bloomington: Indiana University Press, 1984.
———. "Whose Holocaust?" *Midstream*, November 1980, pp. 42–46.
Baumgart, Reinhard. "In die Moral entwischt? Der Weg des politischen Stückeschreibers Peter Weiss." *Text und Kritik* 37 (January 1973): 8–18.
———. "Unmenschlichkeit beschreiben." In *Literatur für Zeitgenossen: Essays*, pp. 12–36. Frankfurt am Main: Suhrkamp Verlag, 1966.
Bentley, Eric, ed. *The Storm over "The Deputy."* New York: Grove Press, 1965.
Berenbaum, Michael. "On the Politics of Public Commemoration of the Holocaust." *Shoah* (Fall/Winter 1982): 6–9, 37.
———. *The Vision of the Void: Theological Reflections on the Works of Elie Wiesel*. Middletown, Conn.: Wesleyan University Press, 1979.
Berger, Alan L. *Crisis and Covenant: The Holocaust in American Jewish Fiction*. Albany: State University of New York Press, 1985.
Berger, John. *About Looking*. New York: Pantheon Books, 1980.
Berryman, John. "The Development of Anne Frank." In *The Freedom of the Poet*, pp. 91–106. New York: Farrar, Straus & Giroux, 1976.
Best, Otto F. *Peter Weiss*. Trans. Ursula Molinaro. New York: Frederick Ungar Publishing Co., 1976.
Betsky, Sarah Zweig, ed. *Onions and Cucumbers and Plums: 46 Yiddish Poems in English*. Detroit: Wayne State University Press, 1958.
Bilik, Dorothy Seidman. *Immigrant-Survivors: Post-Holocaust Consciousness in Recent Jewish American Literature*. Middletown, Conn.: Wesleyan University Press, 1981.
Blanchot, Maurice. *The Writing of the Disaster*. Trans. Ann Smock. Lincoln and London: University of Nebraska Press, 1986.
Blatter, Janet. "Art from the Whirlwind." In *Art of the Holocaust*, ed. Janet Blatter and Sybil Milton. London: Pan Books, 1982.
Bloom, James D. *The Stock of Available Reality: R. P. Blackmur and John Berryman*. Lewisburg, Pa.: Bucknell University Press, 1984.

Blumental, Nachman. "A Martyr or Hero? Reflections on the Diary of Adam Czerniakow." *Yad Vashem Studies* 7 (1968): 165–71.

Boas, Henriette. "Jewish Figures in Post-War Dutch Literature." *Jewish Journal of Sociology* 5 (June 1963): 55–83.

Boder, David P. *I Did Not Interview the Dead.* Urbana: University of Illinois Press, 1949.

Bosmajian, Hamida. "German Literature about the Holocaust—A Literature of Limitations." *Modern Language Studies* 16 (Winter 1986): 51–61.

———. *Metaphors of Evil: Contemporary German Literature and the Shadow of Nazism.* Iowa City: University of Iowa Press, 1979.

Boyers, Robert. "Political Holocaust Fiction." In *Atrocity and Amnesia: The Political Novel Since 1945.* New York and Oxford: Oxford University Press, 1985.

Brockman, Stephen. "Bitburg Deconstruction." *The Philosophical Forum* 17 (Spring 1986): 159–75.

Bronses, David. "The Dead among the Living: Nelly Sachs' 'Eli.' " *Judaism* 16 (Winter 1967): 120–28.

Brown, Robert McAfee. *Elie Wiesel: Messenger to All Humanity.* Notre Dame, Ind.: Notre Dame University Press, 1983.

Butscher, Edward. *Sylvia Plath: Method and Madness.* New York: Seabury Press, 1976.

———, ed. *Sylvia Plath: The Woman and Her Work.* New York: Dodd, Mead, and Company, 1977.

Cameron, Esther. " 'Over the Thorn': The Post-Holocaust Poetry of Paul Celan." *Tikkun* 2 (1986): 38–43.

Cargas, Harry James. *Harry James Cargas in Conversation with Elie Wiesel.* New York: Paulist Press, 1976.

———. *The Holocaust: An Annotated Bibliography,* 2d ed. Chicago: American Library Association, 1985.

———, ed. *Responses to Elie Wiesel: Critical Essays by Major Jewish and Christian Scholars.* New York: Persea Books, 1978.

Cassirer, Ernst. *An Essay on Man.* New Haven: Yale University Press, 1944.

Cernyak-Spatz, Susan E. *German Holocaust Literature.* New York, Berne and Frankfurt: Peter Lang, 1985.

Clark, Katerina. *The Soviet Novel: History as Ritual.* Chicago and London: The University of Chicago Press, 1981.

Cohen, Shaye J. D. "The Destruction: From Scripture to Midrash." *Prooftexts* 2, no. 1 (January 1982): 18–39.

Cohen, Ted. "Metaphor and the Cultivation of Intimacy." In *On Metaphor*, ed. Sheldon Sachs, pp. 1–10. Chicago and London: The University of Chicago Press, 1977.

Conway, John. "The First Report about Auschwitz." *Simon Wiesenthal Center Annual* 1 (1984): 133–51.

Daiches, David. "After Such Knowledge . . . " *Commentary*, December 1965, pp. 105–10.

Davis, Lennard J. *Factual Fictions: The Origins of the English Novel.* New York: Columbia University Press, 1983.

Dawidowicz, Lucy. *The Holocaust and the Historians.* Cambridge, Mass., and London: Harvard University Press, 1981.

Derrida, Jacques. "White Mythology." *New Literary History* 6 (1974): 5–74.

———. *Writing and Difference.* Trans. Alan Bass. London and Henley: Routledge & Kegan Paul, 1981.

Des Pres, Terrence. "The Dreaming Back." *Centerpoint* 4 (Fall 1980): 13–18.

———. *The Survivor: An Anatomy of Life in the Death Camps.* New York: Oxford University Press, 1976.

Dinur, Benzion. "Problems Confronting 'Yad [V]ashem' in Its Work of Research." *Yad [V]ashem Studies on the European Catastrophe and Resistance* 1 (1957): 7–30.

Dowling, William C. *Jameson, Althusser, Marx: An Introduction to the Political Unconscious.* Ithaca: Cornell University Press, 1984.

Eichmann, Bernd. *Versteinert Verharmlost Vergessen: KZ-Gedenkstätten in der Bundesrepublik Deutschland.* Frankfurt am Main: Fischer Taschenbuch Verlag, 1985.

Eilbott, Ben. "Representative Works of Holocaust Literature." *Tradition* 7 (1965): 102–106.

Eliach, Yaffa. "The Holocaust in Hebrew Drama." *Jewish Book Annual* 36 (1978): 37–49.

Ezrahi, Sidra Dekoven. "Agnon Before and After." *Prooftexts* 2, no. 1 (1982): 78–94.

———. "Aharon Appelfeld: The Search for a Language." In Frankel, ed., *Studies in Contemporary Jewry*, vol. 1, pp. 366–80.

———. *By Words Alone: The Holocaust in Literature.* Chicago and London: University of Chicago Press, 1980.

———. "Holocaust Literature in European Languages." *Encyclopaedia Judaica.* 1973 Yearbook, pp. 106–19.

———. "The Holocaust Writer and the Lamentation Tradition: Responses to Catastrophe in Jewish Literature." In Alvin H. Rosenfeld and Irving Greenberg, eds., *Confronting the Holocaust: The Impact of Elie Wiesel.* Bloomington: Indiana University Press, 1978, pp. 133–49.

———. "Revisioning the Past: The Changing Legacy of the Holocaust in Hebrew Literature." *Salmagundi* (Fall 1985–Winter 1986): 245–70.

Fackenheim, Emil. *The Jewish Return into History: Reflections in the Age of Auschwitz and a New Jerusalem.* New York: Schocken Books, 1978.

———. "Midrashic Existence after the Holocaust: Reflections Occasioned by the Work of Elie Wiesel." In Rosenfeld and Greenberg, eds., *Confronting the Holocaust*, pp. 99–116.

Fein, Erich. *Die Steine Reden, Gedenkstätten des österreichischen Freiheitskampfes: Mahnmale für die Opfer des Faschismus, Eine Dokumentation.* Vienna: Europe Verlag, 1975.

Feingold, Henry L. "Determining the Uniqueness of the Holocaust: The Factor of Historical Valence." *Shoah* 2 (Spring 1981): 3–11.

Felstiner, John. "The Biography of a Poem: Reconsideration: Paul Celan." *The New Republic*, 2 April 1984, pp. 27–31.

———. "Translating Celan's Last Poem." *American Poetry Review* (July–August 1982): 21–27.

———. "Translating Paul Celan's 'Du sei wie du.'" *Prooftexts* 3 (1983): 91–108.

———. "Translating Paul Celan's 'Jerusalem' Poems." *Religion and Literature* 16 (Winter 1984): 37–47.

Fine, Ellen S. "The Act of Listening." *Midstream*, August/September 1981, pp. 54–57.

———. "The Journey Homeward: The Theme of the Town in the Works of Elie Wiesel." In *Responses to Elie Wiesel*, ed. Harry James Cargas, pp. 231–58. New York: Persea Books, 1978.

———. *Legacy of Night: The Literary Universe of Elie Wiesel.* Albany: State University of New York Press, 1982.

———. "Literature as Resistance: Survival in the Camps." *Holocaust and Genocide Studies* 1 (1986): 79–89.

Fishbane, Michael. "Revelation and Tradition: Aspects of Inner-Biblical Exegesis." *Journal of Biblical Literature* 99 (1980): 343–61.

Fishkin, Shelley Fisher. *From Fact to Fiction: Journalism and Imaginative Writing in America.* Baltimore and London: Johns Hopkins University Press, 1986.

Fletcher, Angus, ed. *The Literature of Fact.* New York: Columbia University Press, 1976.

Foley, Barbara. "Fact, Fiction, Fascism: Testimony and Mimesis in Holocaust Narratives." *Comparative Literature* 34 (Fall 1982): 330–60.

———. *Telling the Truth: Theory and Practice of Documentary Literature.* Ithaca and London: Cornell University Press, 1986.

Foucault, Michel. *The Archaeology of Knowledge.* Trans. A. M. Sheridan Smith. New York: Pantheon Books, 1972.

Frankel, Theodore. "The Unredeemed: Postwar German Writing." *Midstream* 3 (Spring 1957): 78–83.

Freeden, Herbert. "Jewish Theater under the Swastika." *Leo Baeck Institute Yearbook* I. London: E. and W. Library, 1956.

Fresco, Nadine. "Remembering the Unknown." Trans. Alan Sheridan. *International Review of Psycho-Analysis* 11 (1984): 417–27.

Friedlander, Albert H. "Biblical Dimensions in the Work of Elie Wiesel." *European Judaism* 12 (Spring 1978): 17–23.

———. "Paul Celan." *European Judaism* 5 (Winter 1970–71): 19–22.

———, ed. *Out of the Whirlwind: A Reader of Holocaust Literature.* New York: Schocken Books, 1976.

Friedländer, Saul. "The Historical Significance of the Holocaust." *Jerusalem Quarterly* 1 (Fall 1976): 36–59.

———. *Reflections of Nazism: An Essay on Kitsch and Death.* New York and London: Harper & Row, 1984.

———. "Some German Struggles with Memory." In *Bitburg in Moral and Political Perspective,* ed. Geoffrey Hartman, pp. 27–42. Bloomington: Indiana University Press, 1986.

Friedman, Philip. "The Bibliography of the Warsaw Ghetto (on the 10th Anniversary of the Uprising in the Warsaw Ghetto)." *Jewish Book Annual* 11 (1952–1953): 121–28.

Garbe, Detlev, ed. *Die vergessenen KZs? Gedenkstätten für die Opfer des NS-Terrors in der Bundesrepublik.* Bornheim-Merten: Lamuv, 1983.

Gilbert, Martin. *The Holocaust: A History of the Jews of Europe during the Second World War.* New York: Holt, Rinehart & Winston, 1985.

Gilman, Sander. *Jewish Self-Hatred: Anti-Semitism and the Hidden Language of the Jews.* Baltimore and London: Johns Hopkins University Press, 1986.

Glatstein, Jacob; Knox, Israel; and Margoshes, Samuel, eds. *Anthology of Holocaust Literature.* Philadelphia: Jewish Publication Society, 1968.

Glenn, Jerry. *Paul Celan.* New York: Twayne, 1973.

Goguel, Rudi. *Cap Arcona: Report über den Untergang der Häflingsflotte in der Lübecker Bucht am 3. Mai 1945.* Frankfurt am Main: Roderberg-Verlag GmbH, 1982.

Golinkin, David. "Yom Hashoah: A Program of Observance." *Conservative Judaism* 37 no. 4 (Summer 1984): 52–64.

Gömöri, George, and Newman, Charles, eds. *The New Writing of East Europe.* Chicago: Quadrangle, 1968.

Gossman, Lionel. "History and Literature: Reproduction or Signification." In *The Writing of History: Literary Form and Historical Understanding,* ed. Robert H. Canary and Henry Kozicki, pp. 3–39. Madison: University of Wisconsin Press, 1978.

Gray, Paul. "A Living World: An Interview with Peter Weiss." *Tulane Drama Review* 2 (1966): 106–14.

Grunberger, Richard. "The Literature of Remorse." London: The Jewish Book Council, 1964.

Gutman, Israel. "Remarks on the Literature of the Holocaust." In *In the Dispersion:*

Surveys and Monographs, no. 7, pp. 119–34. Jerusalem: World Zionist Organization, 1967.

Hadda, Janet. *Yankev Glatshteyn*. Boston: Twayne, 1980.

Haffenden, John. *The Life of John Berryman*. London: Routledge & Kegan Paul, 1982.

Haft, Cynthia. *The Theme of Nazi Concentration Camps in French Literature*. The Hague: Mouton & Co., 1973.

Halperin, Irving. *Messengers from the Dead: Literature of the Holocaust*. Philadelphia: Westminster Press, 1970.

Hamburger, Michael. *From Prophecy to Exorcism*. London: Longman's, Green & Co., 1965.

Handelman, Susan. "Controversy: Fragments of the Rock: Contemporary Literary Theory and the Study of Rabbinic Texts—A Response to David Stern." *Prooftexts* 5 (January 1985): 75–103.

Handler, Andrew, ed. *The Holocaust in Hungary: An Anthology of Jewish Responses*. University: University of Alabama Press, 1982.

Harries, Karsten. "Metaphor and Transcendence." In *On Metaphor*, ed. Sheldon Sachs, pp. 71–88. Chicago and London: University of Chicago Press, 1978.

Hartman, Geoffrey H. *Criticism in the Wilderness: The Study of Literature Today*. New Haven and London: Yale University Press, 1980.

———. "Preserving the Personal Story: The Role of Video Documentation." *Dimensions: A Journal of Holocaust Studies* 1 (Spring 1985): 14–18.

———. "The War Against Memory." *Orim: A Jewish Journal at Yale* 1 (Spring 1986): 27–33.

———, ed. *Bitburg in Moral and Political Perspective*. Bloomington: Indiana University Press, 1986.

Hever, Hannan. "Hebrew Poetry under Occupation." *Tikkun* 2 (1987): 84–86, 122–26.

Hever, Hannan, and Ron, Moshe, eds. *Ve'eyn tikhlah lakeravot velahereg: Shirah politit bemilhemet levanon* (Fighting and Killing without End: Political Poetry in the Lebanon War). Tel Aviv: Hakibbutz Hameuchad Publishing House, 1983.

Hilberg, Raul. *The Destruction of European Jewry*. Chicago: Quadrangle Books, 1965.

Hirsch, David. "Abraham Sutskever's Vilna Poems." *Modern Language Studies* 16 (1986): 37–48.

Hirsch, E. D. *The Aims of Interpretation*. Chicago and London: University of Chicago Press, 1976.

Hoffman, Frederick. *The Mortal No: Death and the Modern Imagination*. Princeton: Princeton University Press, 1964.

Holte, Herbert. "Vergangenheitsbewältigung und Ausländerfeindlichkeit: Eine Befragung von Jugendlichen im Dokumentenhaus KZ Neuengamme." In *Argument zur museums-pädagogischen Praxis*. Hamburg: Museumpädagogischer Dienst, 1984.

Howe, Irving. "Auschwitz and High Mandarin" and "The Plath Celebration: A Partial Dissent." In *The Critical Point: On Literature and Culture*, pp. 181–90, 158–69. New York: Horizon Press, 1973.

———. "Primo Levi: An Appreciation." Introduction to Primo Levi, *If Not Now, When?* trans. William Weaver. New York: Viking Penguin, Inc., 1985.

———. *Voices from the Yiddish: Essays, Memoirs, Diaries*. Ann Arbor: University of Michigan Press, 1972.

———. "Writing and the Holocaust." *The New Republic*, 27 October 1986, pp. 27–36.

Howe, Irving, and Greenberg, Eliezer, eds. *A Treasury of Yiddish Poetry*. New York: Schocken Books, 1969.

Hupka, Herbert. "Out of the Darknes." *Wiener Library Bulletin* 3 (January–April 1954): 9.

Huyssen, Andreas. "The Politics of Identification." In *After the Great Divide: Modernism, Mass Culture, Postmodernism*. Bloomington and Indianapolis: Indiana University Press, 1986.

Iltis, Rudolf. "Jews and Jewish Subjects in Contemporary Czech Literature." *The Jewish Quarterly* (Summer 1965): 11–14.

Insdorf, Annette. *Indelible Shadows: Film and the Holocaust*. New York: Vintage Books, 1983.

Jameson, Fredric. "The Ideology of the Text." *Salmagundi* 31 (1975–76): 204–46.

———. *The Political Unconscious: Narrative as a Socially Symbolic Act*. Ithaca: Cornell University Press, 1981.

Jick, Leon A. "The Holocaust: Its Use and Abuse within the American Public." *Yad Vashem Studies* 14 (1981): 303–18.

Juhasz, William. "In Lieu of the Fathers: On One Aspect of Today's Hungarian Literature." *The Hungarian Quarterly* 5 (April–June 1965): 27–42.

Kahn, Lothar. *Mirrors of the Jewish Mind: A Gallery of Portraits of European Jewish Writers of Our Time*. New York: Thomas Yoseloff, 1968.

Katz, Shlomo. "An Open Letter to James Baldwin." *Midstream*, April 1971, pp. 3–5.

Katz, Shlomo, and Baldwin, James. "Of Angela Davis and 'the Jewish Housewife Headed for Dachau': An Exchange." *Midstream*, June 1971, pp. 3–7.

Katz, Steven T. "The 'Unique' Intentionality of the Holocaust." In *Post-Holocaust Dialogues: Critical Studies in Modern Jewish Thought*, pp. 287–317. New York: New York University Press, 1983.

Knopp, Josephine Zadovsky. *The Trial of Judaism in Contemporary Jewish Writing*. Urbana: University of Illinois Press, 1975.

Knopp, Josephine Zadovsky, and Lustig, Arnošt. "Holocaust Literature II: Novels and Short Stories." In *Encountering the Holocaust: An Interdisciplinary Survey*, ed. Bryon L. Sherwin and Susan G. Ament, pp. 267–315. Chicago: Impact Press, 1979.

Kohn, Murray J. "Holocaust Motives in Hebrew Poetry." *The Jewish Quarterly* 20 (Winter 1973): 20–23.

Korman, Gerd. "The Holocaust in American Historical Writing." *Societas* 2 (Summer 1972): 251–70.

Lagercrantz, Olof. *Versuch über die Lyrik der Nelly Sachs*. Frankfurt am Main: Suhrkamp Verlag, 1967.

Lang, Berel. "Writing-the-Holocaust: Jabès and the Measure of History." In *The Sin of the Book: Edmond Jabès*, ed. Eric Gould, pp. 191–206. Lincoln and London: University of Nebraska Press, 1985.

Langer, Lawrence. *The Age of Atrocity: Death in Modern Literature*. Boston: Beacon Press, 1978.

———. "Cultural Resistance to Genocide." *Witness* 1 (Spring 1987): 82–96.

———. *The Holocaust and the Literary Imagination*. New Haven: Yale University Press, 1975.

———. "Holocaust Testimonies and Their Audience." *Orim: A Jewish Journal at Yale* 1 (Spring 1986): 96–110.

———. "Preliminary Reflections on the Videotaped Interviews at the Yale Archive for Holocaust Testimonies." *Facing History and Ourselves News* (Winter 1985): 4–5.

———. *Versions of Survival: The Holocaust and the Human Spirit*. Albany: State University of New York Press, 1982.

Laub, Dori. "Holocaust Themes: Their Expression in Poetry and in the Psychological Conflicts of Patients in Psychotherapy." In *The Nazi Concentration Camps:*

Structure and Aims; the Image of the Prisoners; the Jews in the Camps. Proceedings of the Fourth Yad Vashem International Historical Conference—January 1980, pp. 573–87. Jerusalem: Yad Vashem, 1984.

Leftwich, Joseph. *Abraham Sutzkever: Partisan Poet.* New York: Thomas Yoseloff, 1971.

———. *The Way We Think: A Collection of Essays from the Yiddish.* 2 vols. New York: Thomas Yoseloff, 1969.

Lejeune, Philippe. *Le Pacte autobiographique.* Paris: Editions du Seuil, 1975.

Levin, Nora. "Some Reservations about Lanzmann's *Shoah.*" *Sh'ma: A Journal of Jewish Responsibility,* 18 April 1986, pp. 89–93.

Liberles, Robert. "Diaries of the Holocaust." *Orim: A Jewish Journal at Yale* 1 (Spring 1986): 35–47.

Lind, Jakov. "John Brown and His Little Indians." *Times Literary Supplement,* 25 May 1973, pp. 589, 590.

Lishinsky, Yosef. "Yad Vashem as Art." *Ariel: A Review of Arts and Letters in Israel* 55 (1983): 7–25.

Littell, Marcia Sachs, ed. *Liturgies on the Holocaust: An Interfaith Anthology.* Lewiston, N.Y.: The Edwin Mellen Press, 1986.

Lukács, Georg. *The Meaning of Contemporary Realism.* Trans. John and Necke Mander. London: Merlin Press, 1963.

Mankewitz, Ze'ev. "Beirut is not Berlin." *Jerusalem Post,* 4 August 1982, p. 8.

Marcuse, Harold; Schimmelfennig, Frank; and Spielmann, Jochen, eds. *Steine des Anstosses: Nationalsozialismus und Zweiter Weltkrieg in Denkmalen, 1945–85.* Hamburg: Museum für Hamburgische Geschichte, 1985.

Mark, Ber, ed. *Tsvishn lebn un toyt* (Between Life and Death). Warsaw: Yiddish-bukh, 1955.

Mason, Ann L. "Gunter Grass and the Artist in History." *Contemporary Literature* 14 (Summer 1973): 347–62.

———. "Nazism and Postwar German Literary Style." *Contemporary Literature* 17 (Winter 1976): 63–83.

Maurer, Jadwiga. "The Jew in Contemporary Polish Writing." *Wiener Library Bulletin* 21 (1967): 26–30.

Miller, J. Hillis. "Narrative and History." *English Literary History* 41 (1974): 455–73.

Miłocz, Czeslaw. *The Witness of Poetry.* Cambridge, Mass.: Harvard University Press, 1983.

Milton, Sybil. *In Fitting Memory? Holocaust Memorials and Postwar Political Culture.* Research in progress.

Mintz, Alan. *Ḥurban: Responses to Catastrophe in Hebrew Literature.* New York: Columbia University Press, 1984.

———. "The Rhetoric of Lamentations and the Representation of Catastrophe." *Prooftexts* 2 (January 1982): 1–17.

Mintz, Ruth Finer, ed. *Modern Hebrew Poetry.* Berkeley: University of California Press, 1966.

Moore, Henry. "On Sculpture & Primitive Art." In *Modern Artists on Art: Ten Unabridged Essays,* ed. Robert L. Herbert, pp. 138–49. Englewood Cliffs, N.J.: Prentice-Hall, 1964.

Murdoch, Brian. "Transformation of the Holocaust: Auschwitz in Modern Lyric Poetry." *Comparative Literature Studies* 2 (1974): 123–50.

Neher, André. *The Exile of the Word: From the Silence of the Bible to the Silence of Auschwitz.* Trans. David Maisel. Philadelphia: Jewish Publication Society, 1981.

Newman, Charles, ed. *The Art of Sylvia Plath: A Symposium.* London: Faber & Faber, 1970.

Nichols, Bill. *Ideology and the Image: Social Representation in the Cinema and Other Media.* Bloomington: Indiana University Press, 1981.

Nietzsche, Friedrich. *Beyond Good and Evil.* New York: Random House, 1966.
Norich, Anita. "Yiddish Poetry: From Vilna to Tel Aviv, Lublin to New York." *University of Hartford Studies in Literature* 18 (1986): 27–35.
Nowerstern, Avram, ed. *Avram Sutskever: bemla'ot lo shivim* (Abraham Sutzkever: On His Seventieth Birthday). Jerusalem: Hebrew University Press, 1984.
Oberg, Arthur. *Modern American Lyric: Lowell, Berryman, Creely, and Plath.* New Brunswick: Rutgers University Press, 1978.
Olney, James. *Metaphors of the Self.* Princeton: Princeton University Press, 1972.
Ortega y Gasset, José. *The Dehumanization of Art and Other Essays on Art, Culture, and Literature.* Princeton: Princeton University Press, 1968.
Oz, Amos. "Hitler kvar met, adoni rosh hamemshalah" (Hitler is Already Dead, Mr. Prime Minister). In *Chatzi'at Gevul: Shirim Mimilhemet Levanon* (Border Crossing: Poems from the Lebanon War), ed. Yehudith Karpi, pp. 71–73. Tel Aviv: Sifri'at Po'alim, 1983.
Ozick, Cynthia. "A Liberal's Auschwitz." In *The Pushcart Prize: Best of the Small Presses,* ed. Bill Henderson. Yonkers: Pushcart Book Press, 1976.
Peirce, C. S. *Elements of Logic,* vol. 2. In *Collected Papers of Charles Saunders Peirce,* ed. Charles Hartshorne and Paul Weiss. Cambridge, Mass.: Harvard University Press, 1932.
Perry, R. C. "Historical Authenticity and Dramatic Form: Hochhuth's '*Der Stellvertreter*' and Weiss's '*Die Ermittlung.*'" *Modern Language Review* 64 (1969): 828–39.
Petuchowski, Jakob J. "Dissenting Thoughts About the 'Holocaust.'" *Journal of Reform Judaism* (Fall 1981): 1–9.
Pfefferkorn, Eli. "Fractured Reality and Conventional Forms in Holocaust Literature." *Modern Language Studies* 16 (Winter 1986): 88–99.
Pups, Ruta, ed. *Dos lid fun geto: zamlung* (The Song of the Ghetto: Anthology). Warsaw: Yidish-bukh, 1962.
Ramras-Rauch, Gila, and Michman-Melkman, Joseph, eds. *Facing the Holocaust: Selected Israeli Fiction.* Philadelphia: Jewish Publication Society, 1985.
Ricoeur, Paul. *The Rule of Metaphor: Multi-disciplinary Studies of the Creation of Meaning in Language.* Trans. Robert Czerny, with Kathleen McLaughlin and John Costello. Toronto, Buffalo, and London: University of Toronto Press, 1977.
———. *Time and Narrative,* vol. 1. Trans. Kathleen McLaughlin and David Pellauer. Chicago and London: The University of Chicago Press, 1984.
Rieth, Adolf. *Monuments to the Victims of Tyranny.* New York and London: Praeger, 1968.
Robbins, Jill. "The Writing of the Holocaust: Claude Lanzmann's *Shoah.*" *Prooftexts* 7, no. 3 (September 1987): 249–58.
Roditi, Edouard. "Post-Holocaust Prophets." *European Judaism* 5 (September 1971): 51–54.
Rosen, Norma. "The Holocaust and the American Jewish Novelist." *Midstream,* October 1974, pp. 54–62.
———. "The Second Life of Holocaust Imagery." *Witness* 1 (Spring 1987): 10–15.
Rosenbloom, Noah H. "The Threnodist of the Holocaust." *Judaism* 26 (Spring 1977): 232–47.
Rosenfeld, Alvin H. "Arthur Cohen's Messiah." *Midstream,* 19 August–September 1973, pp. 72–75.
———. *A Double Dying: Reflections on Holocaust Literature.* Bloomington and London: Indiana University Press, 1980.
———. *Imagining Hitler.* Bloomington: Indiana University Press, 1985.
———. "Jakov Lind and the Trial of Jewishness." *Midstream,* 20 February 1974, pp. 71–74.
———. "On Holocaust and History." *Shoah* 1 (1978): 19–20.

———. "Paul Celan." *Midstream*, 17 November 1971, pp. 75–80.

———. "Primo Levi." *Witness* 1 (Spring 1987): 35–42.

———. "Steiner's Hitler." *Salmagundi* 52–53 (Spring/Summer 1981): 160–74.

Rosenfeld, Alvin, and Greenberg, Irving, eds. *Confronting the Holocaust: The Impact of Elie Wiesel.* Bloomington and London: Indiana University Press, 1979.

Rosenfeld, Stella P. "Jakov Lind: Writer at the Crossroads." *Modern Austrian Literature* 4 (Winter 1971): 42–47.

Roskies, David. *Against the Apocalypse: Responses to Catastrophe in Modern Jewish Culture.* Cambridge, Mass., and London: Harvard University Press, 1984.

———. "The Holocaust According to the Literary Critics." *Prooftexts* 1 (May 1981): 209–16.

———. *The Literature of Destruction: Jewish Responses to Catastrophe.* Philadelphia: Jewish Publication Society of America, 1988.

———. "Yiddish Writing in the Nazi Ghettos and the Art of the Incommensurate." *Modern Language Studies* 16 (Winter 1986): 29–36.

———, ed. *Night Words: A Midrash on the Holocaust.* Washington, D.C.: B'nai B'rith Hillel Foundations, 1971.

Ryan, Judith. *The Uncompleted Past: Postwar German Novels and the Third Reich.* Detroit: Wayne State University Press, 1983.

Sable, Martin H. *Holocaust Studies: a Directory and Bibliography of Bibliographies.* Greenwood, Fla.: The Penkevill Publishing Company, 1987.

Sanders, Ivan. "Sequels and Revisions: The Hungarian Jewish Experience in Recent Hungarian Literature." *Soviet Jewish Affairs* 14 (1984): 31–45.

Sapir, Edward. *Culture, Language and Personality: Selected Essays.* Berkeley and Los Angeles: University of California Press, 1962.

Schiff, Ellen. *From Stereotype to Metaphor: The Jew in Contemporary Drama.* Albany: State University of New York Press, 1982.

Schneider, Marilyn. *Vengeance of the Victim: History and Symbol in Giorgio Bassani's Fiction.* Minneapolis: University of Minnesota Press, 1986.

Scholes, Robert. *Structural Fabulation.* Notre Dame: University of Notre Dame Press, 1975.

Schoenberner, Gerhard. *The Yellow Star.* New York: Bantam Books, 1973.

Schoenfeld, Joachim, ed. *Holocaust Memoirs: Jews in the Lvov Ghetto, the Janowska Concentration Camp, and as Deportees in Siberia.* New York: Ktav Publishing House, 1985.

Schulman, Elias. *The Holocaust in Yiddish Literature.* New York: Workmen's Circle, 1983.

Schwarberg, Günther. *Angriffsziel Cap Arcona.* Hamburg: Stern-Buch im Verlag Gruner, 1983.

The Seventh Day: Soldiers Talk About the Six-Day War. Edited by a group of young Kibbutz members. Middlesex: Penguin Books, 1971.

Shaked, Gershon. "Facing the Nightmare: Israeli Literature on the Holocaust." In *The Nazi Concentration Camps: Structure and Aims; the Image of the Prisoners; the Jews in the Camps.* Proceedings of the Fourth Yad Vashem International Historical Conference—January 1980, pp. 683–96. Jerusalem: Yad Vashem, 1984.

———. *Gal hadash basiporet ha'ivrit* (A New Trend in Hebrew Fiction). Tel Aviv: Sifri'at hapo'alim, 1971.

———. "Opening Remarks: Discussion." In *The Nazi Concentration Camps.* Proceedings of the Fourth Yad Vashem International Historical Conference. Jerusalem: Yad Vashem, 1984.

Shammas, Anton. "Diary." In *Every Sixth Israeli: Relations between the Jewish Majority and the Arab Minority in Israel,* ed. Alouph Hareven, pp. 29–44. Jerusalem: The Van Leer Foundation, 1983.

Sherwin, Byron L. "Wiesel's Midrash: The Writings of Elie Wiesel and Their Relationship to Jewish Tradition." In Rosenfeld and Greenberg, eds., *Confronting the Holocaust*, pp. 117–32. Bloomington and London: Indiana University Press, 1978.

Sherwin, Byron L., and Ament, Susan G., eds. *Encountering the Holocaust: An Interdisciplinary Survey*. Chicago: Impact Press, 1979.

Snyder, Joel, and Allen, Neil Walsh. "Photography, Vision, and Representation." *Critical Inquiry* 2 (Autumn 1975): 143–69.

Sontag, Susan. *On Photography*. New York: Farrar, Straus & Giroux, 1973.

Steiner, George. *Language and Silence: Essays on Language, Literature, and the Inhuman*. New York: Atheneum, 1967.

———. "The Long Life of Metaphor: An Approach to 'the Shoah.' " *Encounter*, February 1987, pp. 55–61.

Stiehler, Heinrich. "Die Zeit der 'Todesfuge': Zu den Anfängen Paul Celans." *Akzente* 19 (February 1972): 11–39.

Syrkin, Marie. "Diaries of the Holocaust." *Midstream*, May 1966, pp. 3–20.

———. "Nelly Sachs—Poet of the Holocaust." *Midstream*, March 1967, pp. 13–23.

Syrkin, Marie, and Kunzer, Ruth. "Holocaust Literature I: Diaries and Memoirs." In Sherwin and Ament, eds., *Encountering the Holocaust*, pp. 223–66. Chicago: Impact Press, 1979.

Szeintuch, Yechiel. *Yiddish and Hebrew Literature under the Nazi Rule in Eastern Europe* (in Hebrew). Ph.D. diss., The Hebrew University, Jerusalem, 1978.

Szonyi, David M., ed. *The Holocaust: An Annotated Bibliography and Resource Guide*. New York: Ktav Publishing House, Inc., 1985.

Tal, Uriel. "Holocaust and Genocide." *Yad Vashem Studies* 13 (1979): 46–52.

Veyne, Paul. *Writing History: Essay on Epistemology*. Trans. Mina Moore-Rinvolucri. Middletown, Conn.: Wesleyan University Press, 1984.

Walton, Kendall L. "Transparent Pictures: On the Nature of Photographic Realism." *Critical Inquiry* 11 (December 1984): 246–77.

Warren, Mark. "Nietzsche and the Concept of Ideology." *Theory and Society* 13 (July 1984): 541–65.

Weber, Ronald. *The Literature of Fact*. Athens: Ohio University Press, 1980.

Weimar, Karl S. "Paul Celan's 'Todesfuge': Translation and Interpretation." *PMLA* 89 (January 1974): 85–89.

Weintraub, Karl J. "Autobiography and Historical Consciousness." *Critical Inquiry* 1 (June 1975): 821–48.

Weiss, Peter. "The Materials and the Models: Notes Towards a Definition of Documentary Theatre." Trans. Heinz Bernard. *Theatre Quarterly* 1 (1971): 41–43.

———. "My Place." Trans. Christopher Middleton. *Encounter* 25 (December 1965): 3–7.

Wesker, Arnold. "Art Between Truth & Fiction: Thoughts on William Styron's Novel." *Encounter*, January 1980, pp. 48–57.

White, Hayden. *The Content of the Form: Narrative Discourse and Historical Representation*. Baltimore and London: The Johns Hopkins University Press, 1987.

———. *Metahistory: The Historical Imagination in Nineteenth-Century Europe*. Baltimore and London: The Johns Hopkins University Press, 1973.

———. *Tropics of Discourse: Essays in Cultural Criticism*. Baltimore and London: Johns Hopkins University Press, 1978.

Wiechert, Ernst. *The Poet and His Time*. Trans. Irene Tauber. Hinsdale, Ill.: Regnery, 1948.

Wienold, Götz. "Paul Celan's Hölderlin-Widerruf." *Poetica* 2 (1968): 216–28.

Wiesel, Elie. "The Holocaust as Literary Inspiration." In *Dimensions of the Holocaust*. Evanston, Ill.: Northwestern University, 1977.

———. *A Jew Today*. Trans. Marion Wiesel. New York: Random House, 1978.

———. *Legends of Our Time*. Trans. Steven Donadio. New York: Holt, Rinehart & Winston, 1968.

———. *Messengers of God: Biblical Portraits and Legends*. New York: Random House, 1976.

———. *One Generation After*. Trans. Lily Edelman and the Author. New York: Random House, 1970.

Wievorka, Annette. "Un lieu de mémoire Le Mémorial du martyr juif inconnu." *Pardes* 2 (1985): 80–98.

Wilkinson, James D. "Remembering World War II: The Perspective of the Losers." *The American Scholar* (Summer 1985): 329–43.

Wirth-Nesher, Hana. "The Ethics of Narration in D. M. Thomas's *The White Hotel*." *The Journal of Narrative Technique* 15 (Winter 1985): 15–28.

Wisse, Ruth R. "The Ghetto Poems of Abraham Sutzkever." *Jewish Book Annual* 36 (1978): 26–36.

Yaffe, Richard. *Nathan Rapoport: Sculptures and Monuments*. New York: Shengold Publishers, Inc., 1980.

Yaoz, Hannah. *Sipporet hashoah b'ivrit: Kesipporet historit vetranshistorit* (The Holocaust in Hebrew Literature—As Historical and Transhistorical Fiction). Tel Aviv: Eked, 1980.

Yerushalmi, Yosef Hayim. *Zakhor: Jewish History and Jewish Memory*. Seattle and London: University of Washington Press, 1982.

Young, James E. "Anti-war Poetry in Israel: When Soldier-Poets Remember the Holocaust." *Partisan Review* (October 1987): 594–602.

———. "Holocaust Literary Criticism." *Midstream*, June/July 1984, pp. 39–41.

———. " 'I may be a bit of a Jew': The Holocaust Confessions of Sylvia Plath." *Philological Quarterly* (Summer 1987): 125–46.

———. "Interpreting Literary Testimony: A Preface to Rereading Holocaust Diaries and Memoirs." *New Literary History* 18 (Winter 1987): 403–23.

———. "Memory and Monument." In *Bitburg in Moral and Political Perspective*, ed. Geoffrey Hartman, pp. 103–13. Bloomington: Indiana University Press, 1986.

———. "Versions of the Holocaust." *Modern Judaism* 3 (October 1983): 339–46.

Yudkin, Leon. "The Israeli Writer and the Holocaust." *European Judaism* 7 (Summer 1973): 41–46.

Zak, Avrom, ed. *Khurbn: antologye* (Anthology of Holocaust Literature). Buenos Aires: Musterverk fun der yidisher literatur, 1970.

Ziolkowski, Theodore. "Anatomies of Holocaustics." *Sewanee Review* 90 (Fall 1982): 592–604.

Zipes, Jack D. "The Aesthetic Dimensions of the German Documentary Drama." *German Life and Letters* 24 (1971): 346–58.

Zurof, Efraim. "Yad Vashem: More Than a Memorial, More Than a Name." *Shoah* 1 (Winter 1979): 4–9.

Index